EASY PIANO

TOP CHRISTIAN HITS OF '08-'09

ISBN 978-1-4234-6708-3

7777 W. Bluemound Rd. P.O. Box 13819 Milwaukee, WI 53213

Visit Hal Leonard Online at
www.halleonard.com

ALL BECAUSE OF JESUS

Words and Music by
STEVE FEE

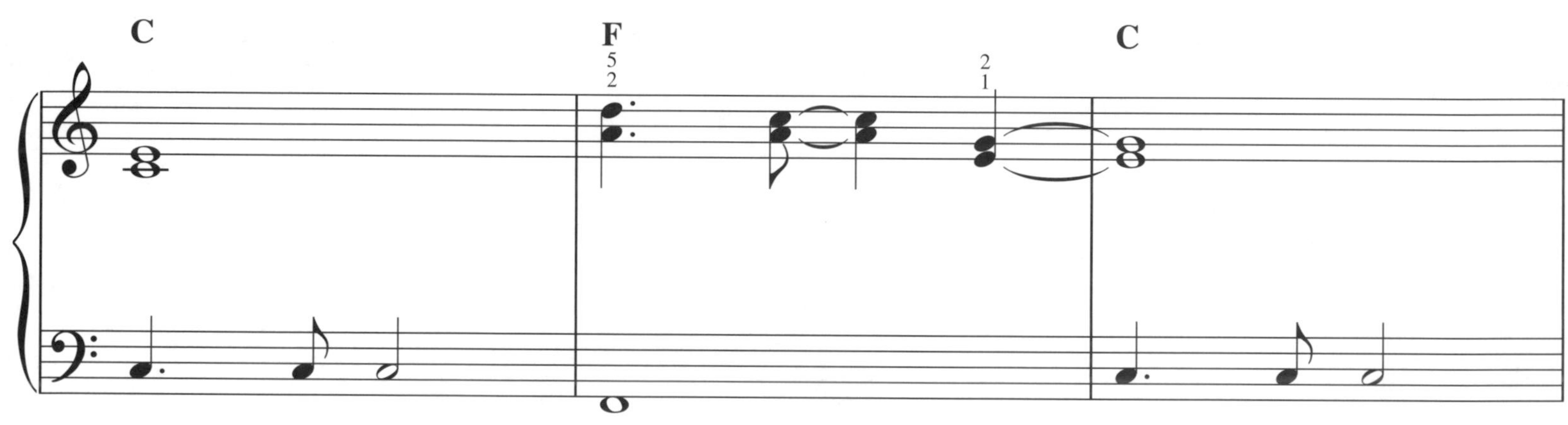

Am7
Gsus
G
5
Giv - er of

F
5
3
C
1
5
F
ev - 'ry breath_ I
breathe, au - thor of
all e - ter - ni -

C
F
Am7
5
1
ty, giv - er of
ev - 'ry per - fect
thing, to You be the

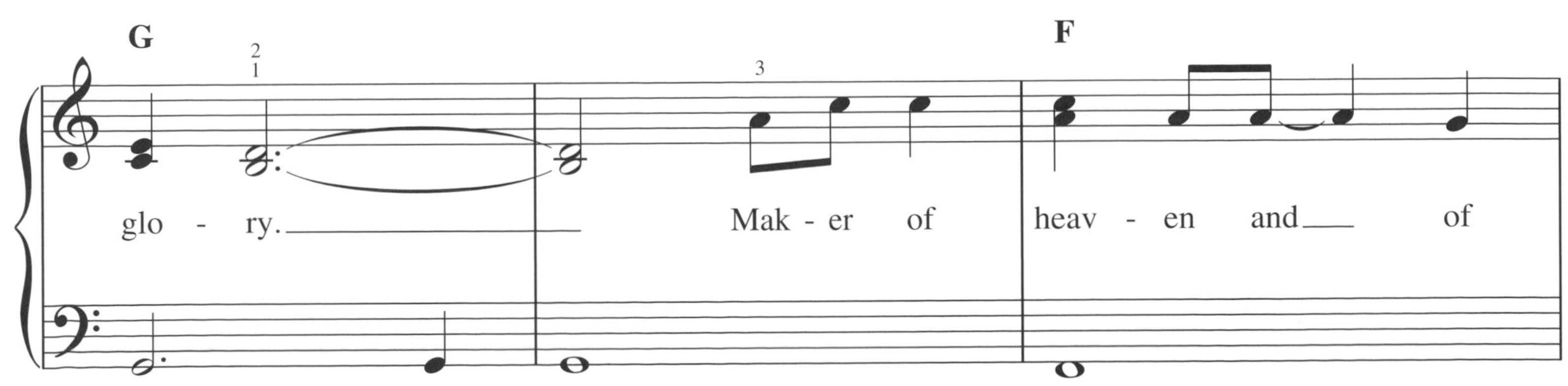
G
2
1
3
F
glo - ry.
Mak - er of
heav - en and of

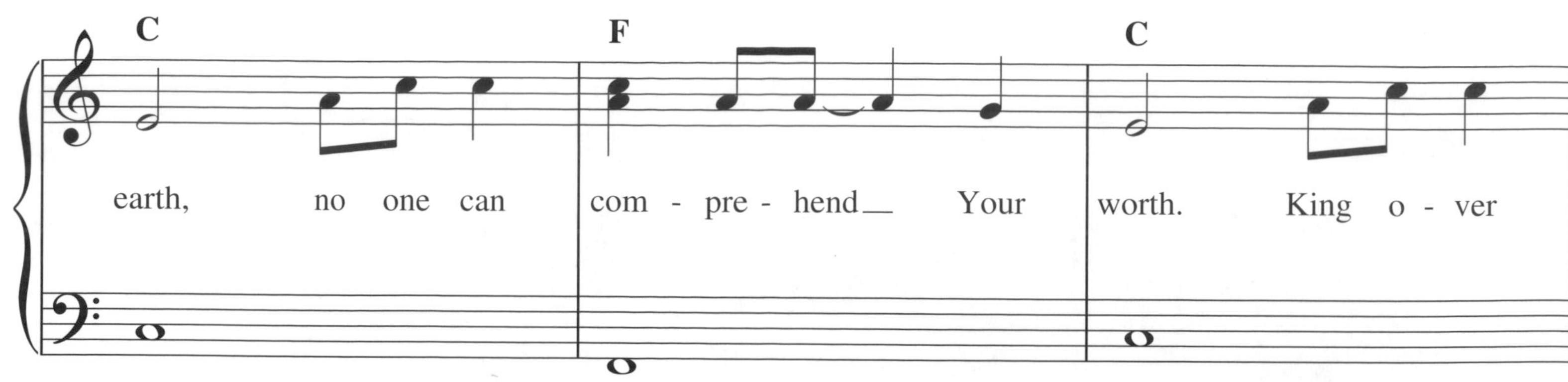
C
F
C
earth, no one can com - pre - hend Your worth. King o - ver

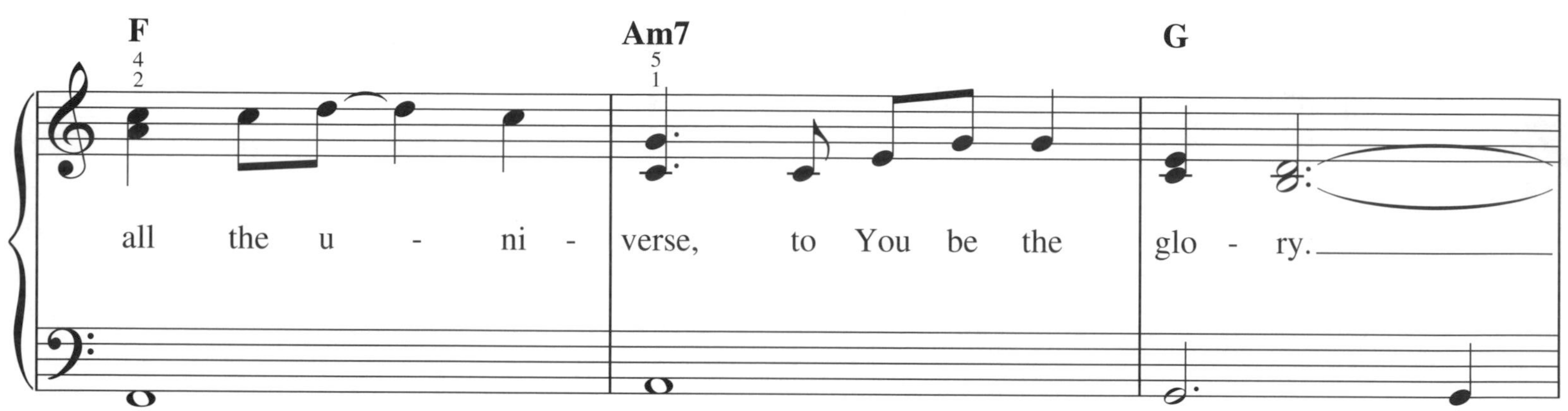
F
Am7
G
all the u - ni - verse, to You be the glo - ry.

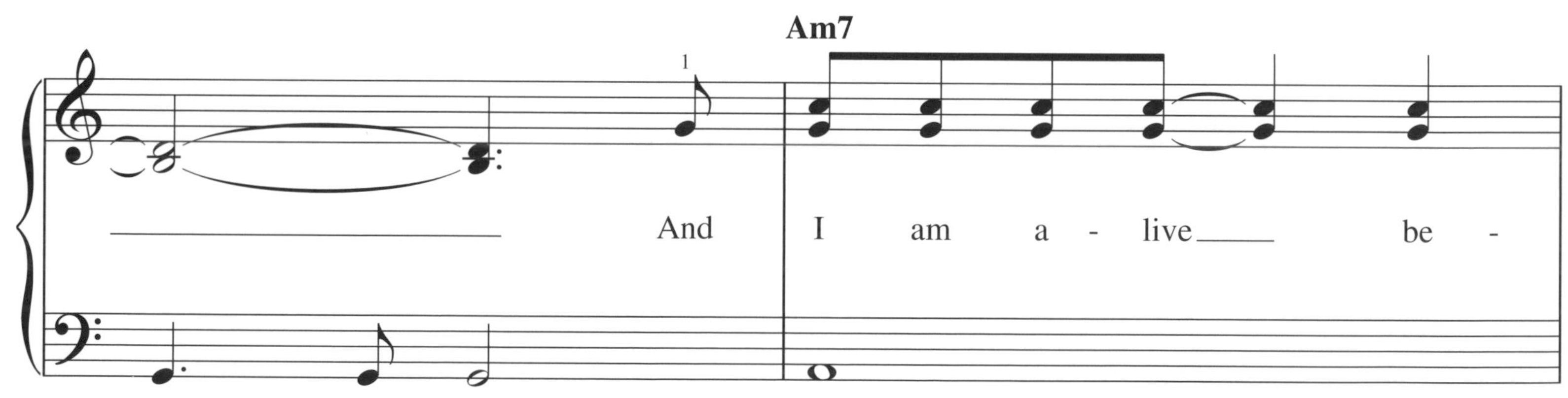
Am7
And I am a - live be -

Em
F
cause I'm a - live in You.

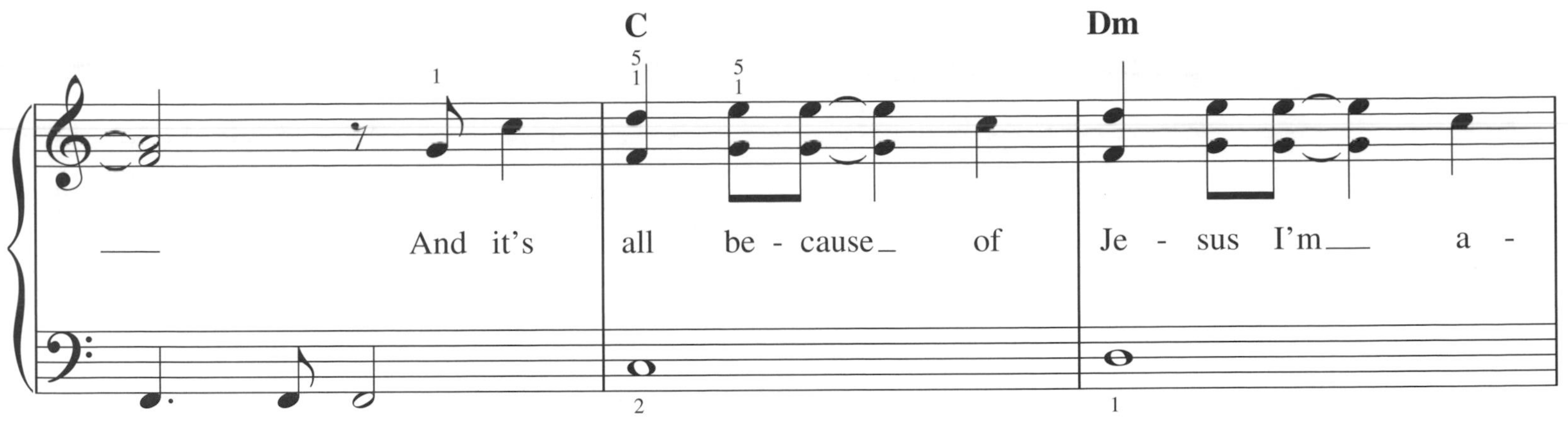
C
Dm
1
5
1
5
1
And it's all be - cause of Je - sus I'm a -
2
1

F
C
2
1
live. And it's all be - cause the
5

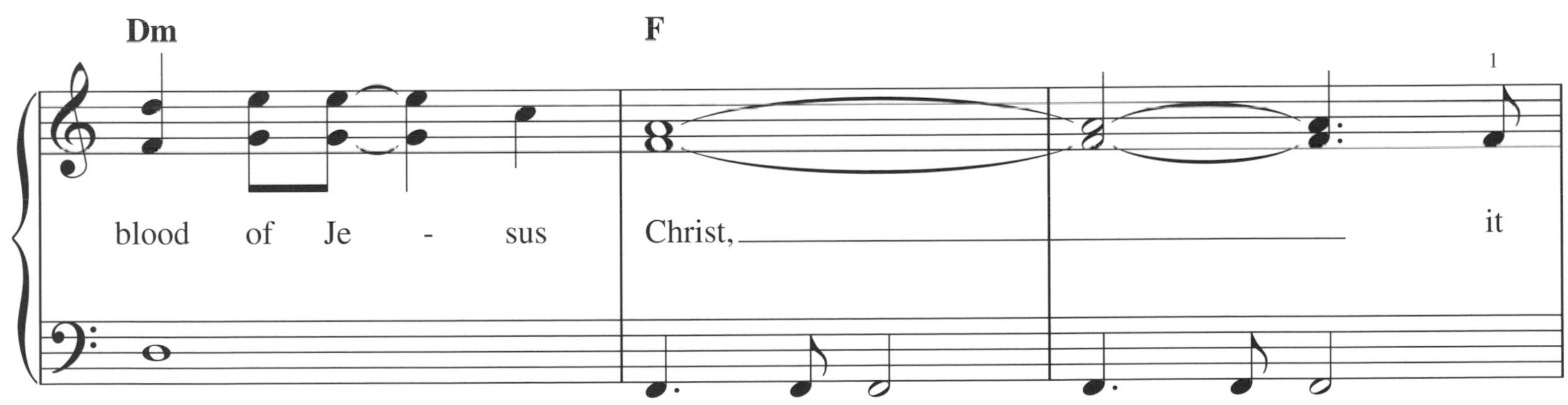
Dm
F
1
blood of Je - sus Christ, it

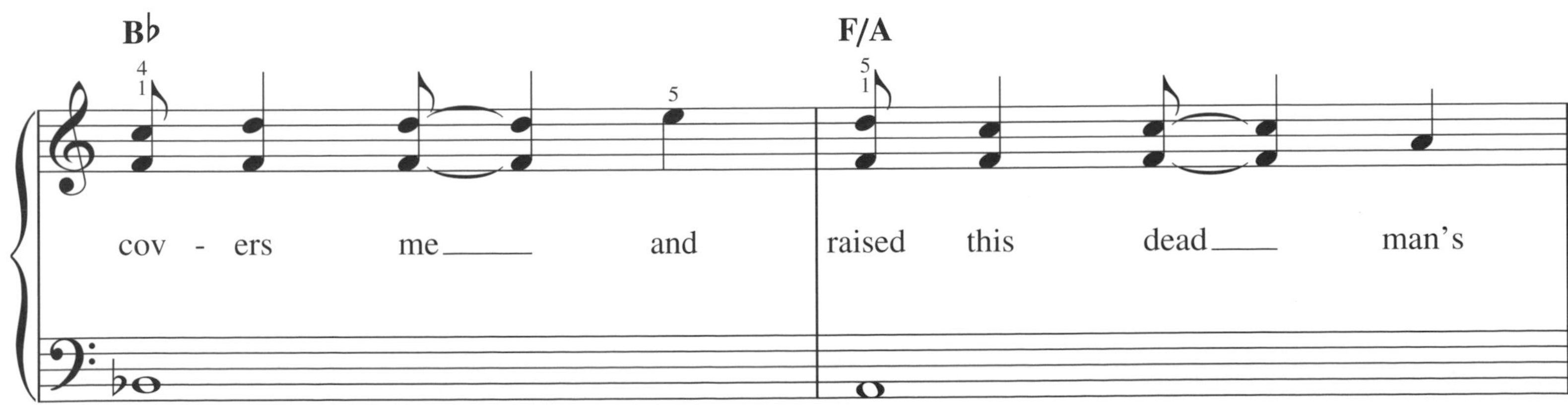
B♭
F/A
4
1
5
5
1
cov - ers me and raised this dead man's

C
Bb
To Coda
life.
It's
all
be - cause
of

F/A
F
C
Je - sus I'm a - live.
I'm a -

F
C
F
live,
I'm a -
live.

Am7
Gsus
G
D.S. al Coda
Giv - er of

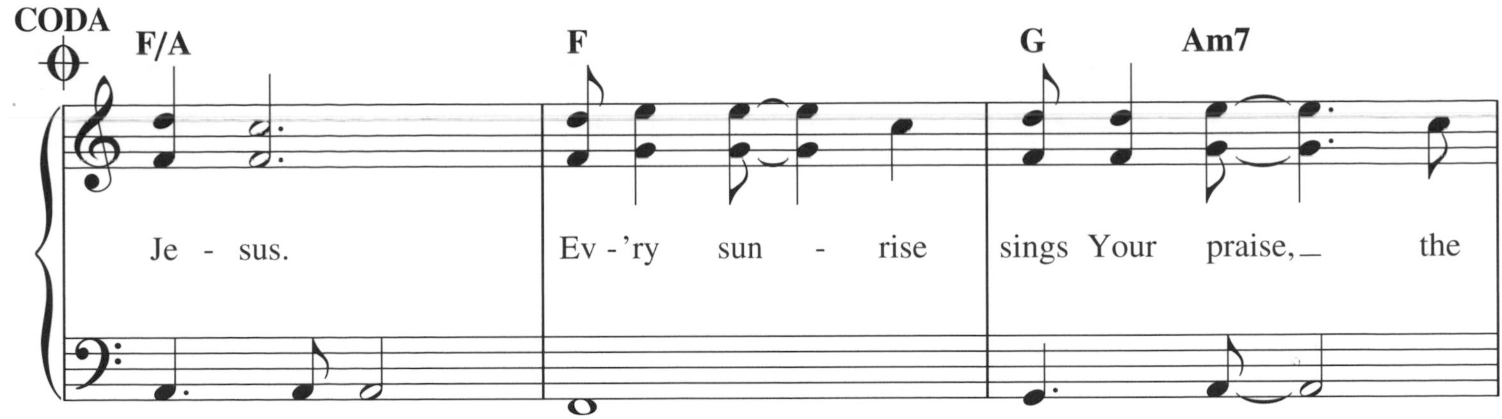
CODA
F/A
F
G
Am7
Je - sus.
Ev - 'ry sun - rise
sings Your praise, the

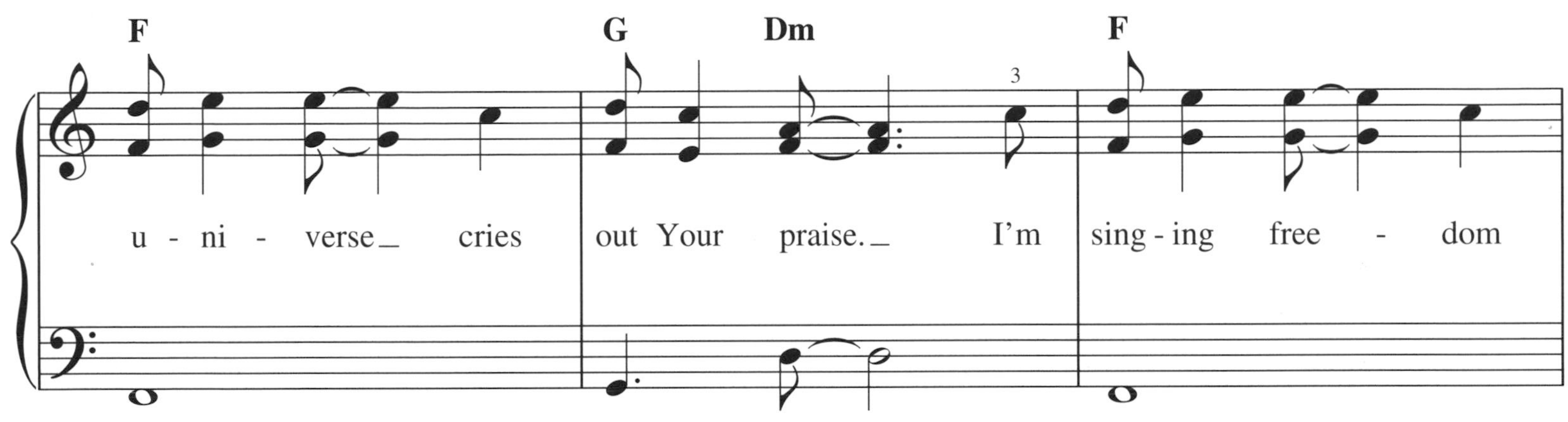
F
G
Dm
F
u - ni - verse cries
out Your praise. I'm
sing - ing free - dom

G
Am7
B♭sus2
G
all my days,
now that I'm a -
live.

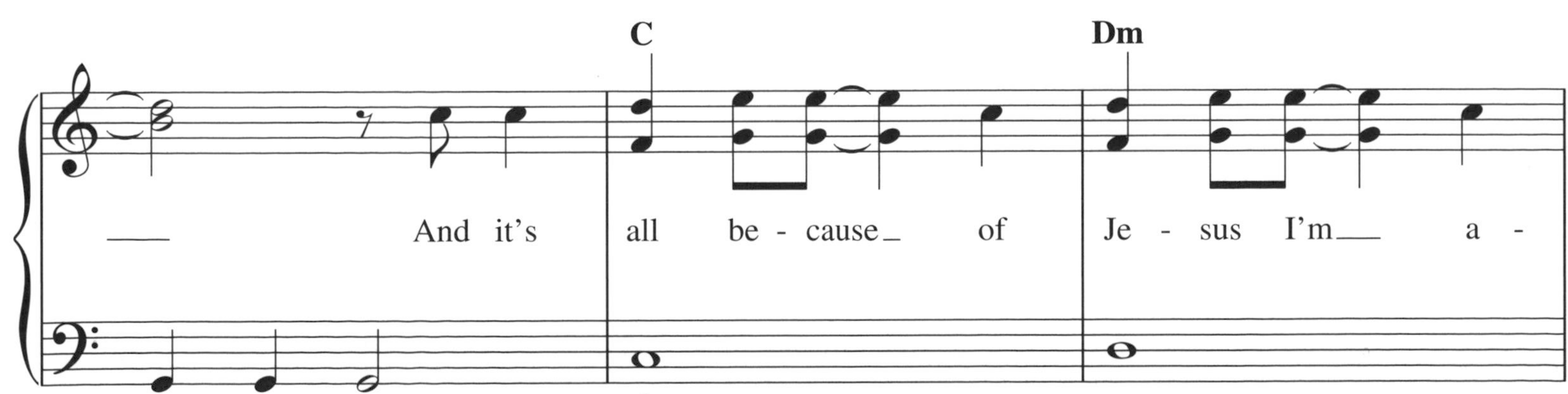
C
Dm
And it's
all be - cause of
Je - sus I'm a -

F
C
live. It's all be - cause the

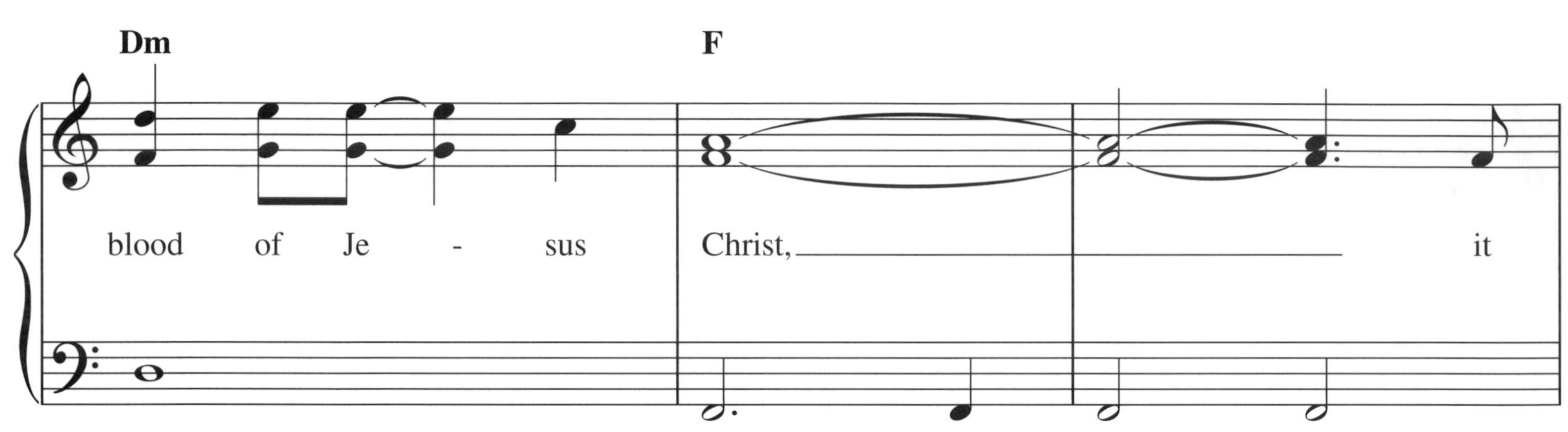
Dm
F
blood of Je - sus Christ, it

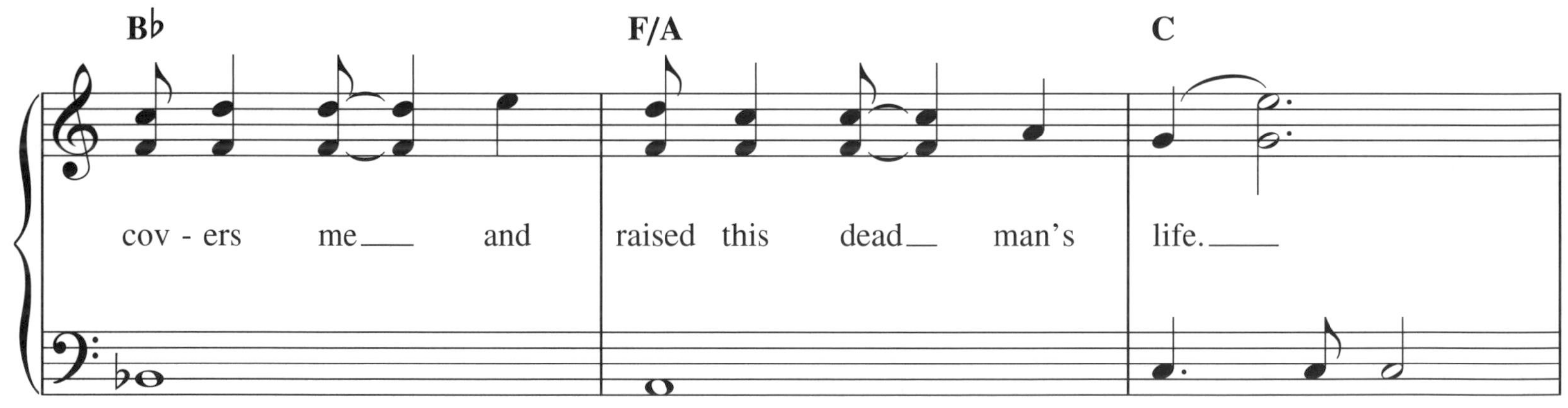
B♭
F/A
C
cov - ers me and raised this dead man's life.

Csus
C
B♭
F/A
4
It's all be - cause of Je - sus. And it's

C
Dm
F
all be - cause of Je - sus I'm a - live.
2

C
Dm
It's all be - cause the blood of Je - sus

F
B♭
Christ, it cov - ers me and

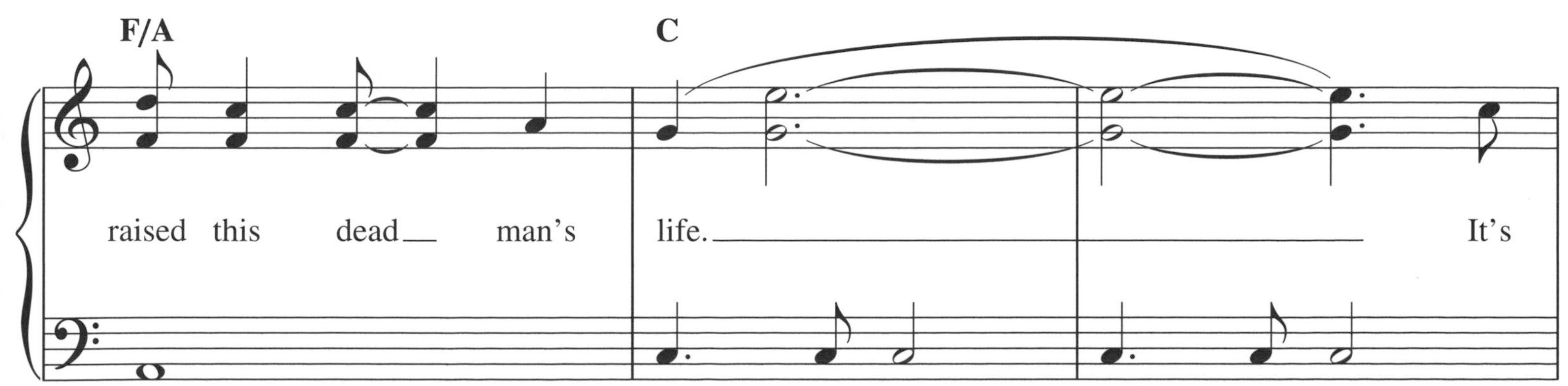
F/A
C
raised this dead man's life. It's

B♭
1.
F/A
2.
F/A
all be - cause_ of
Je - sus. It's
Je - sus I'm a -

F
C
F
live.
I'm a -
live,

C
F
Am7
I'm a -
live.

Gsus
G
C

BY YOUR SIDE

Words and Music by JASON INGRAM,
PHILLIP LARUE and MICHAEL DONEHEY

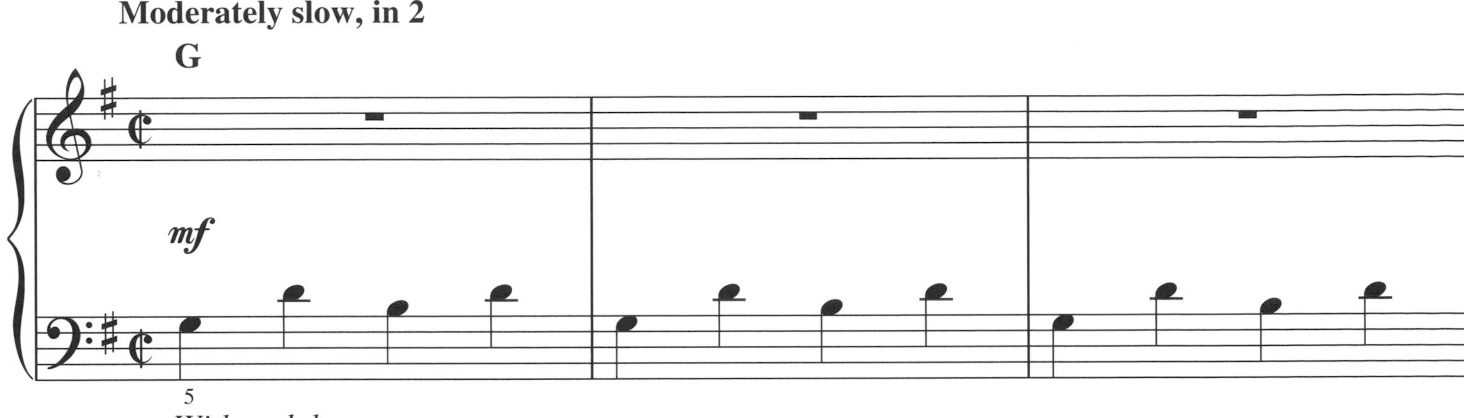

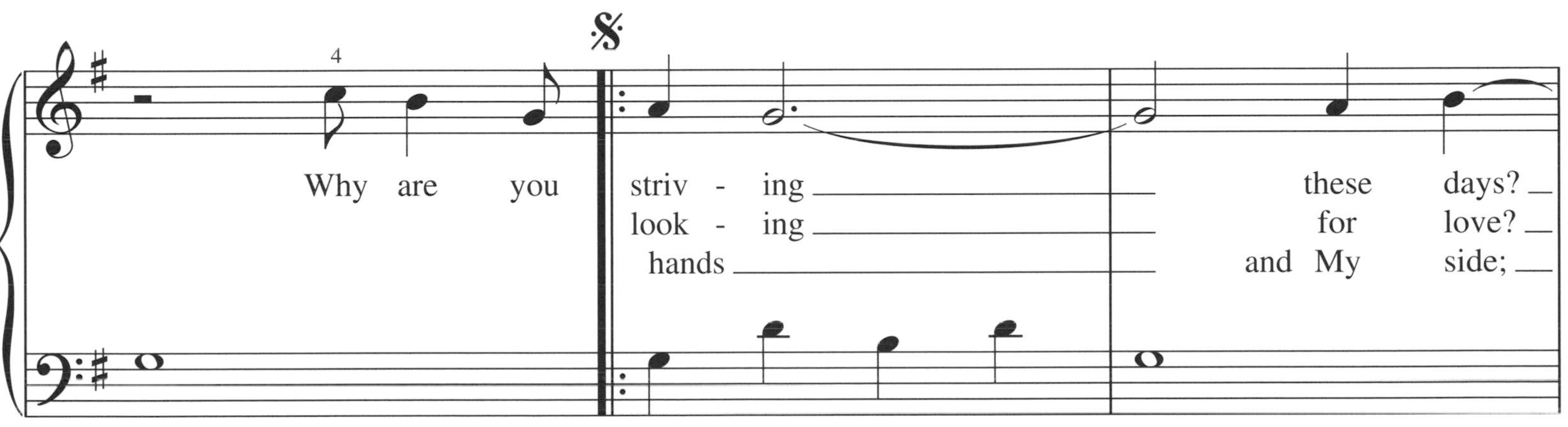

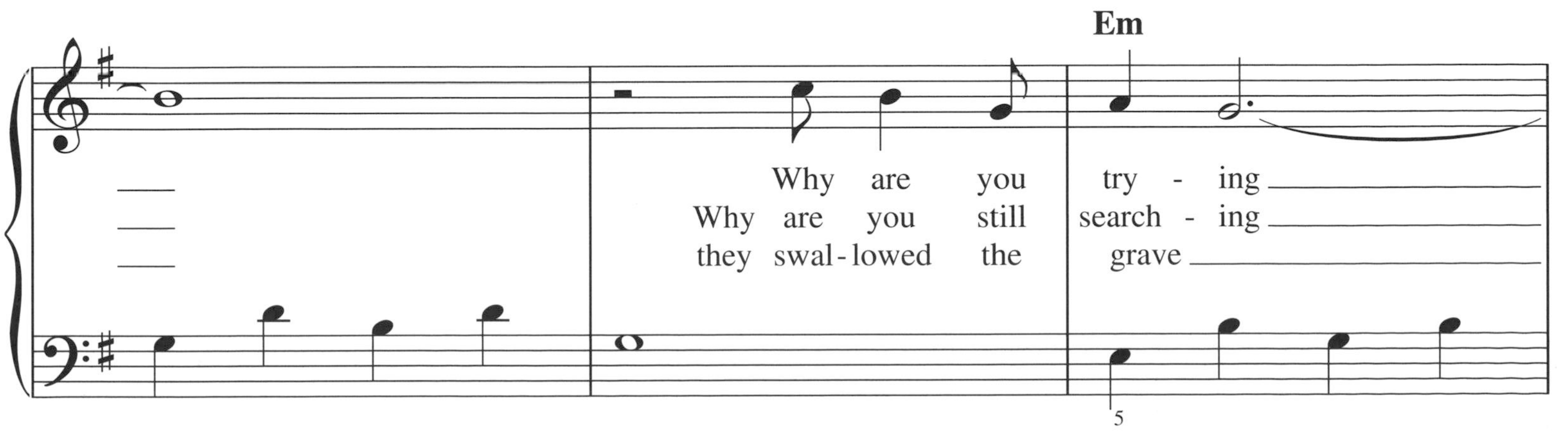

to earn grace?
as if I'm not e - nough?
on that night

D
Why are you cry - ing?
To where will you go, child?
when I drank the world's sin,

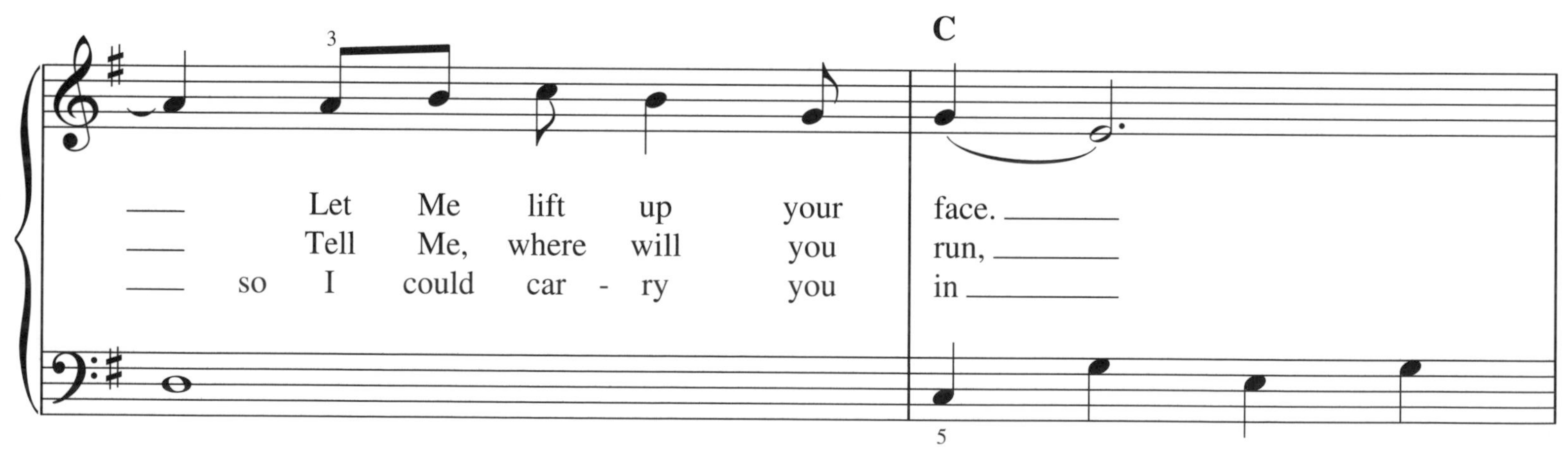
C
Let Me lift up your face.
Tell Me, where will you run,
so I could car - ry you in

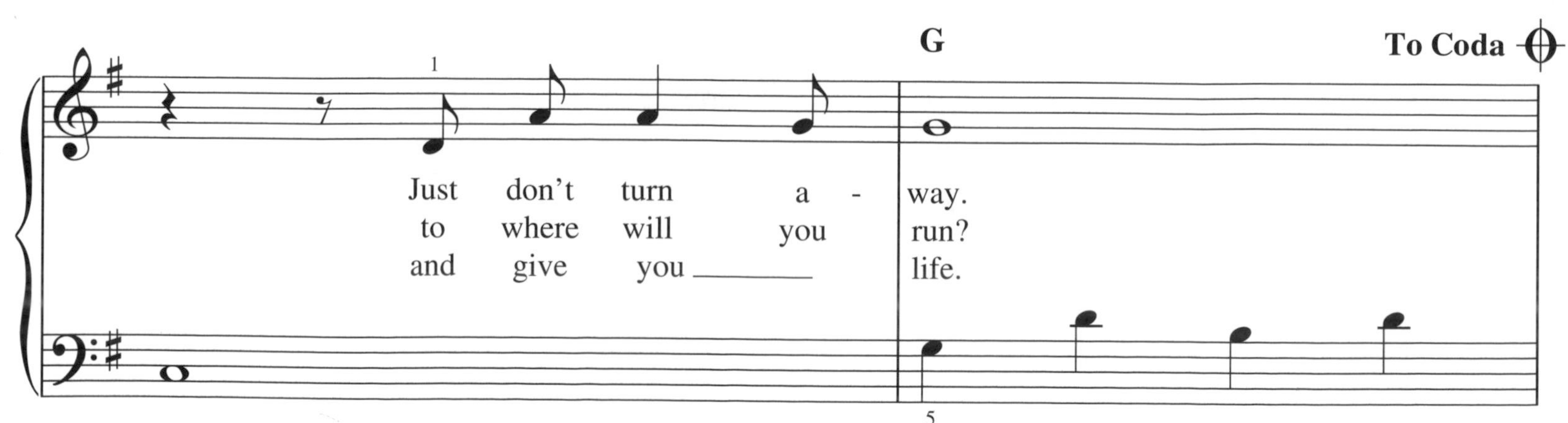
G
To Coda
Just don't turn a - way.
to where will you run?
and give you life.

1.
4
Why are you

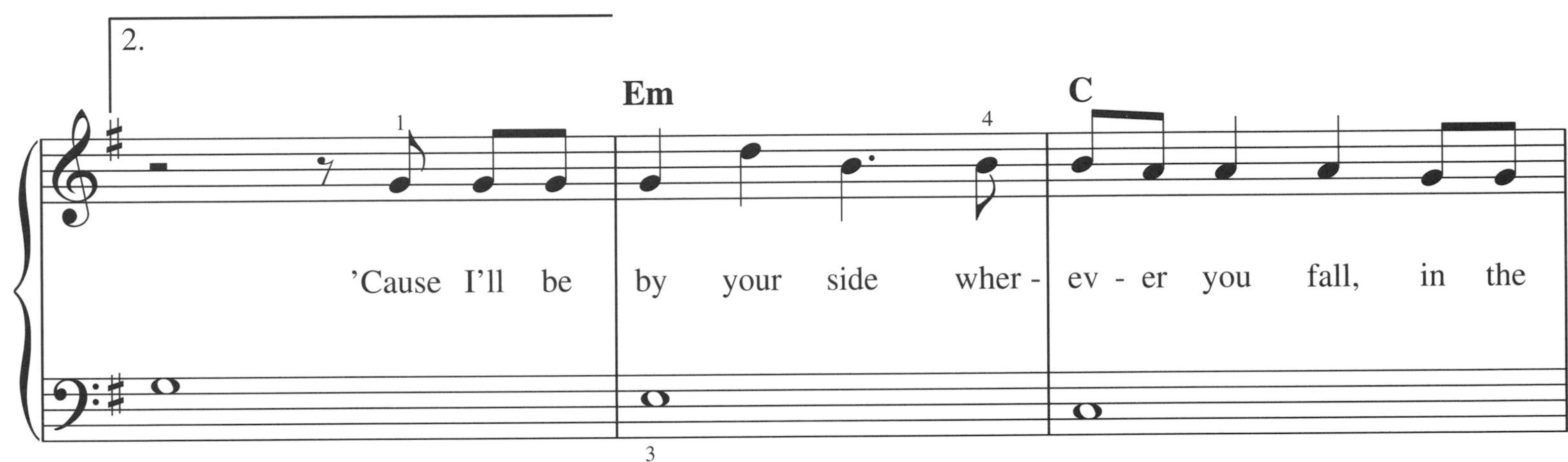
2.
Em
C
1
4
'Cause I'll be by your side wher - ev - er you fall, in the
3

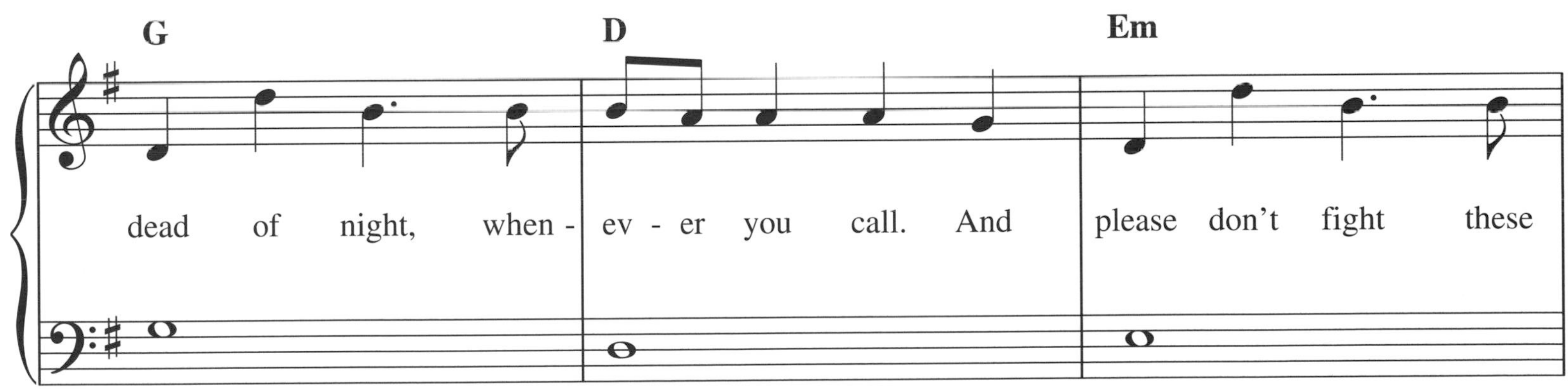
G
D
Em
dead of night, when - ev - er you call. And please don't fight these

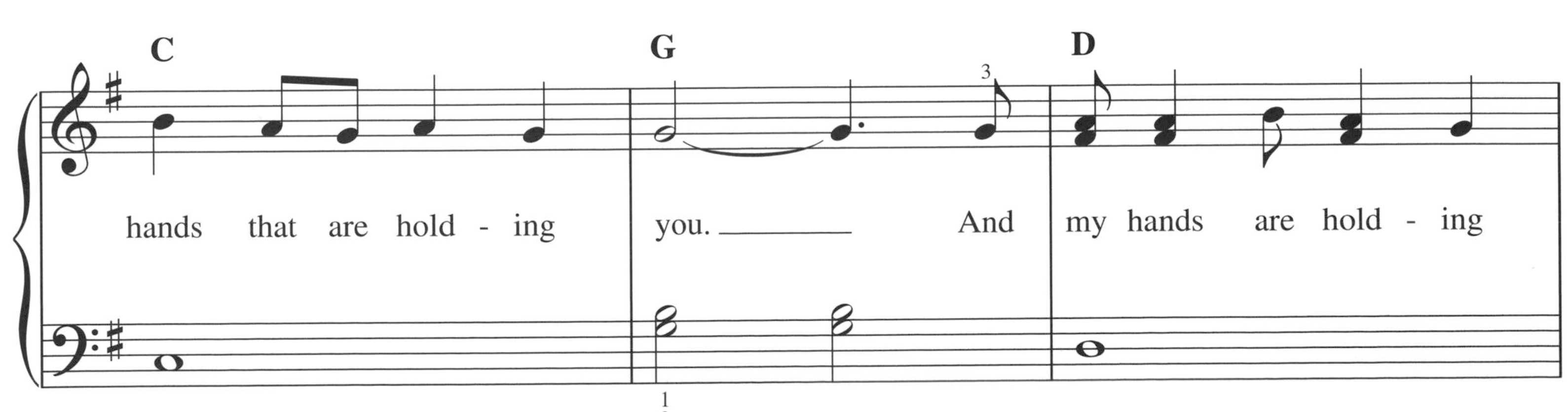
C
G
D
3
hands that are hold - ing you. And my hands are hold - ing
1
2

G
D.S. al Coda
4
you.
Look at these
5

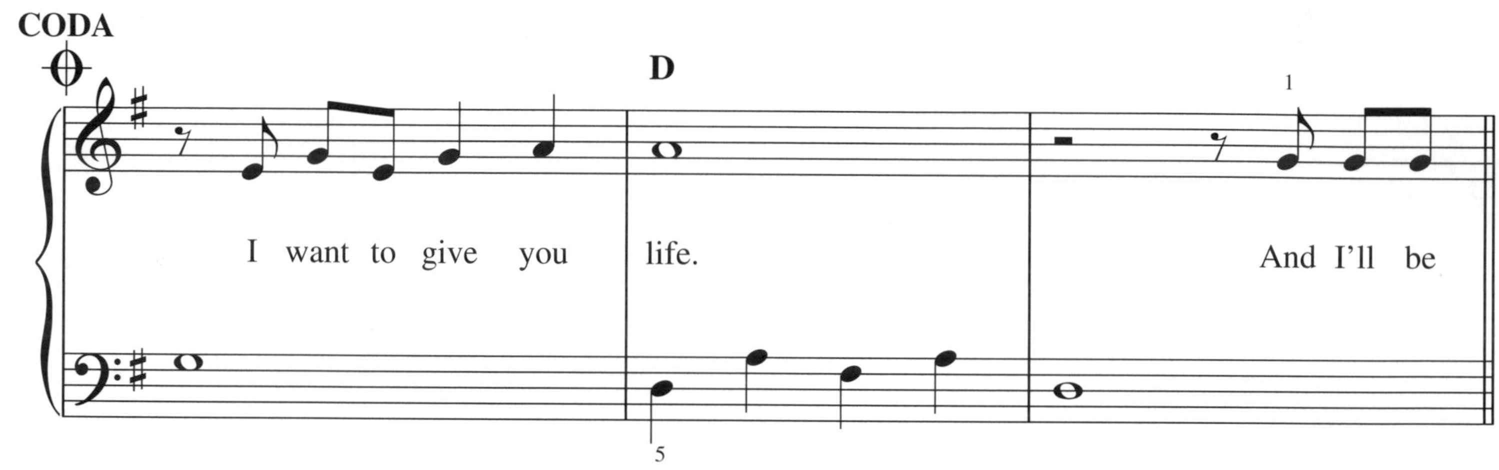
CODA
D
1
I want to give you
life.
And I'll be
5

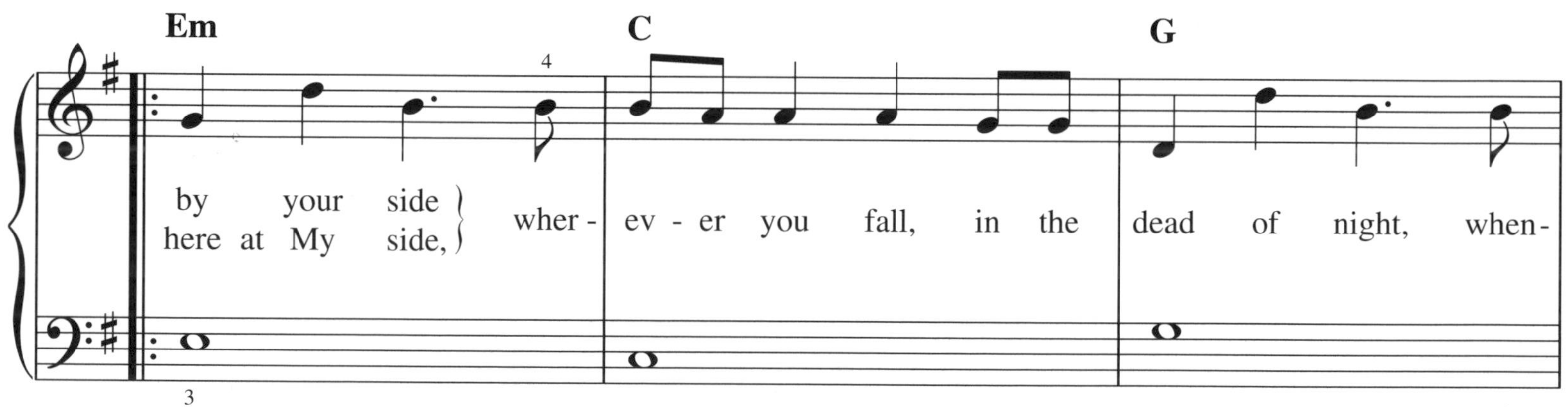
Em
C
G
4
by your side
here at My side,
wher -
ev - er you fall, in the
dead of night, when-
3

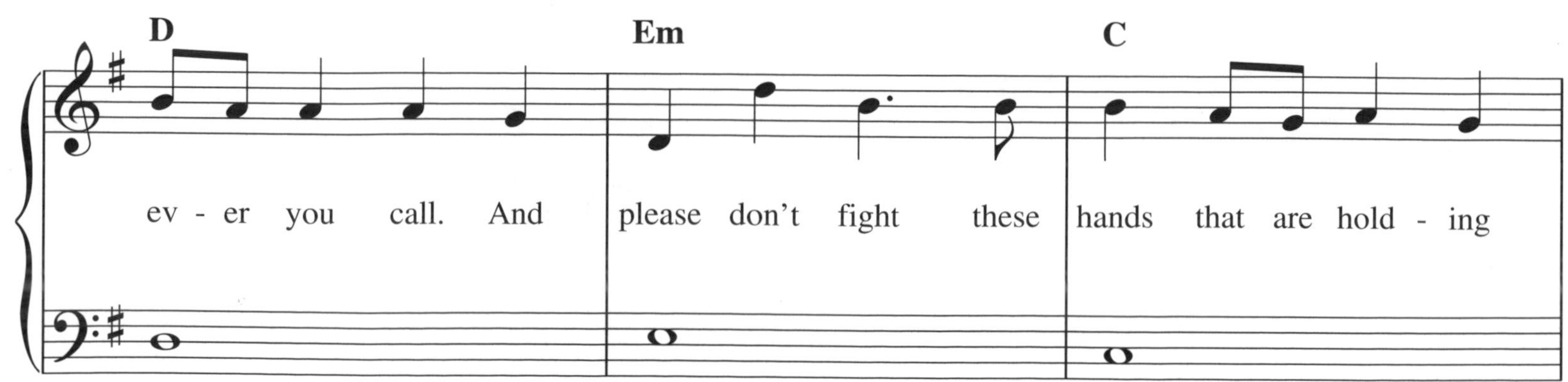
D
Em
C
ev - er you call. And
please don't fight these
hands that are hold - ing

1.
2.
G
D
D
you. And
My hands are hold - ing you
My hands are hold - ing

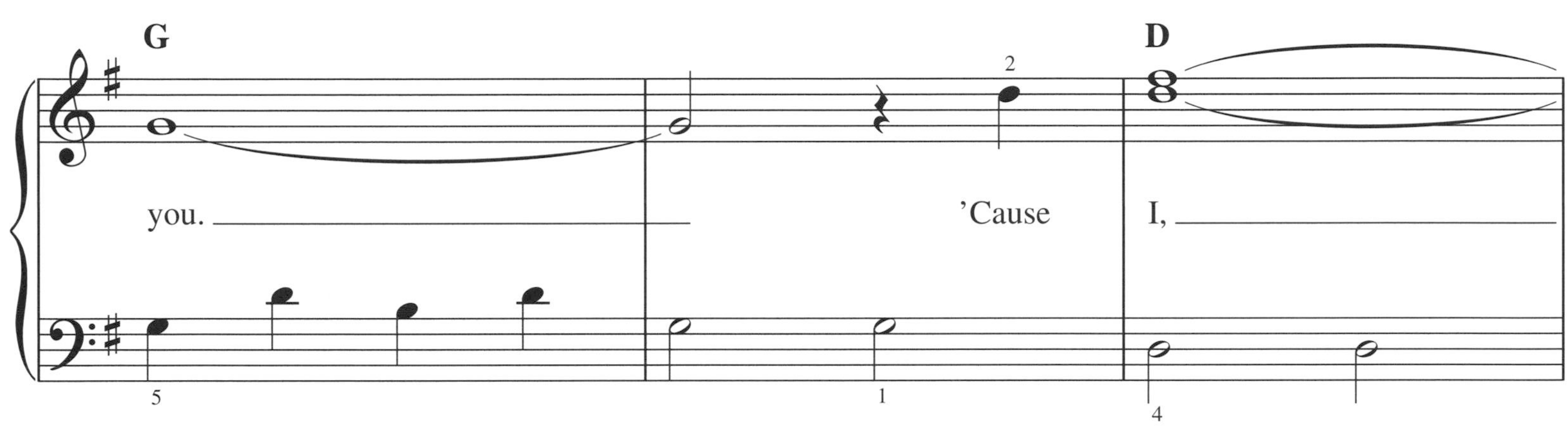
G
D
you.
'Cause
I,

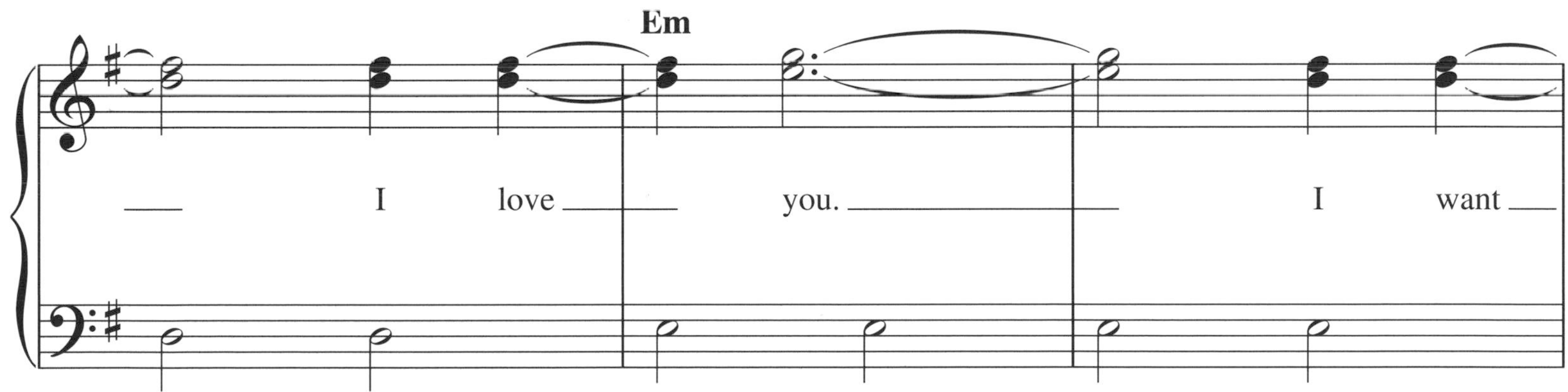
Em
I love
you.
I want

C
D
you
to know

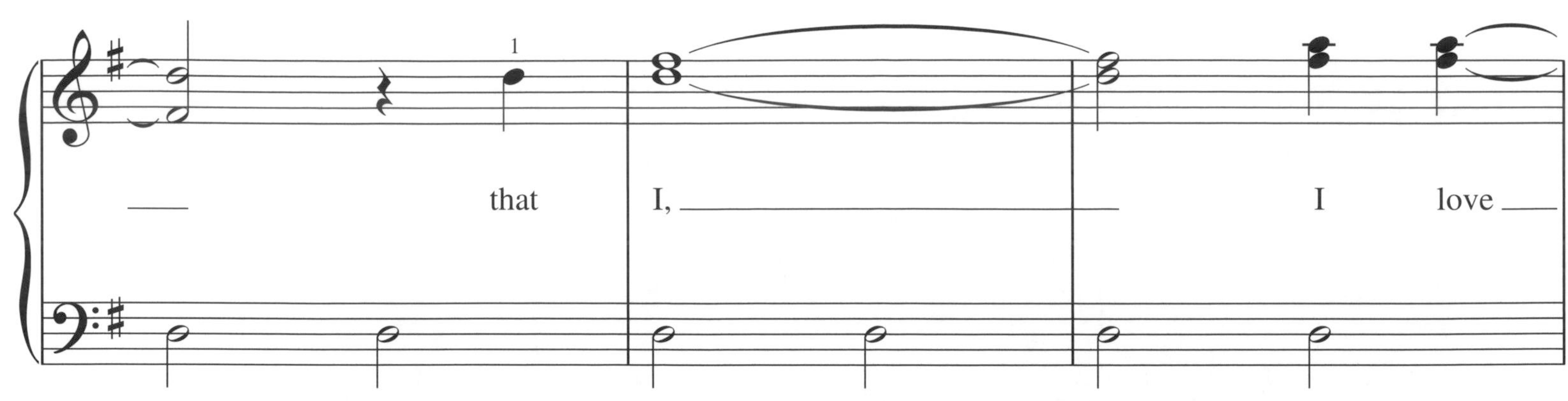
1
that I, I love

Em
C
you. I'll nev - er let

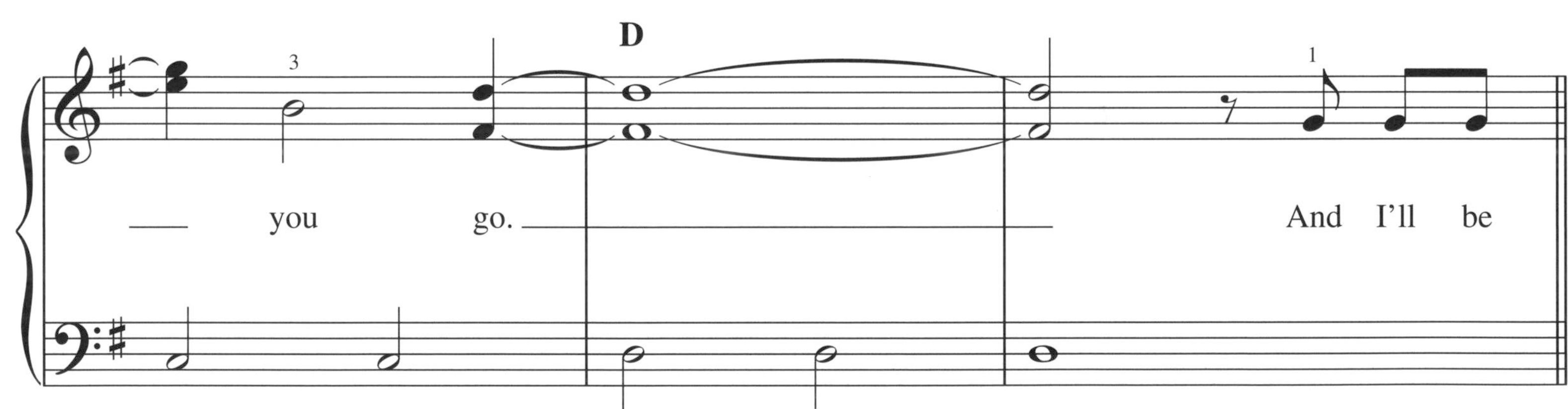
3
D
1
you go. And I'll be

Em
C
G
4
by your side
here at My side,
wher - ev - er you fall, in the dead of night, when -

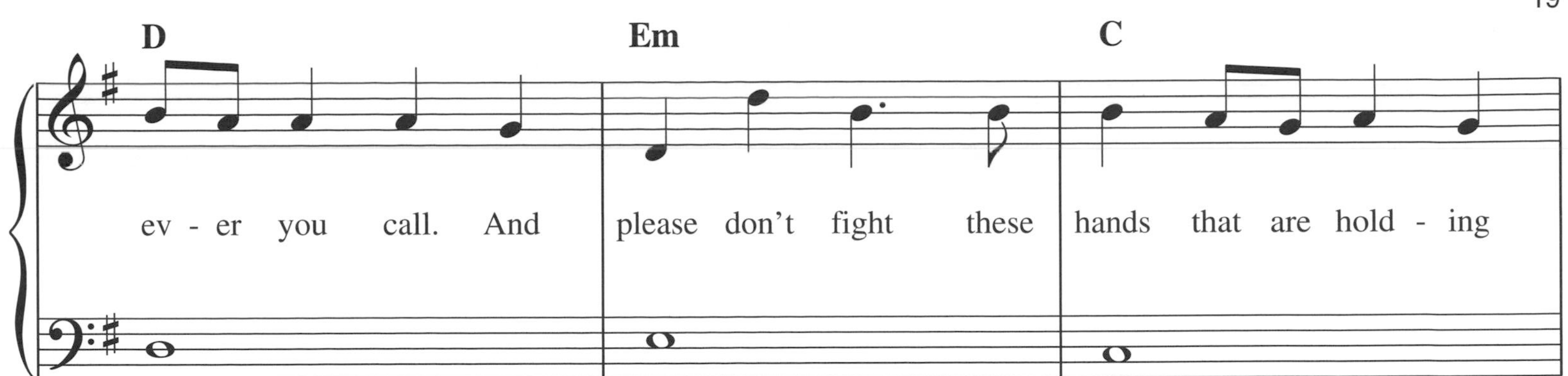
D
Em
C
ev - er you call. And
please don't fight these
hands that are hold - ing

1.
2.
G
D
D
you. And
My hands are hold - ing you
My hands are hold - ing

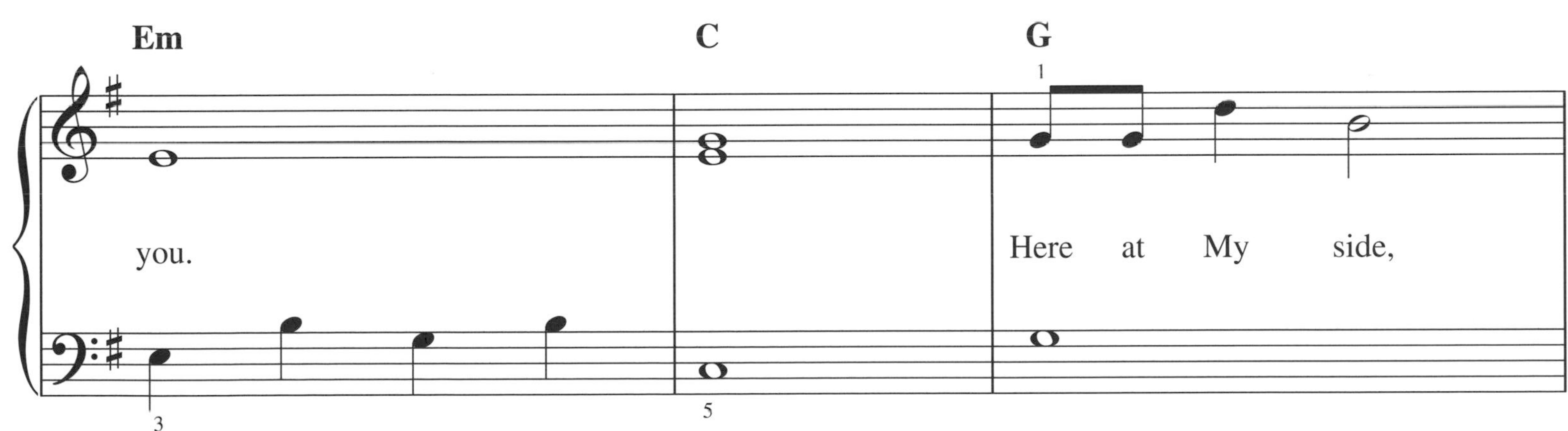
Em
C
G
you.
Here at My side,

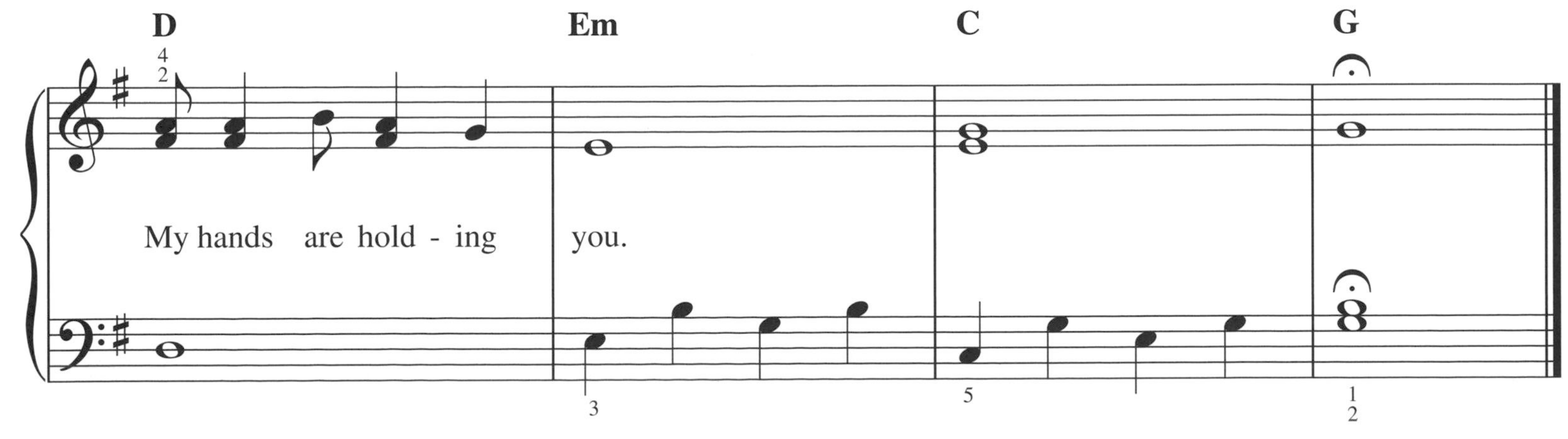
D
Em
C
G
My hands are hold - ing
you.

CALL MY NAME

Words and Music by MAC POWELL,
DAVID CARR, TAI ANDERSON,
BRAD AVERY and MARK LEE

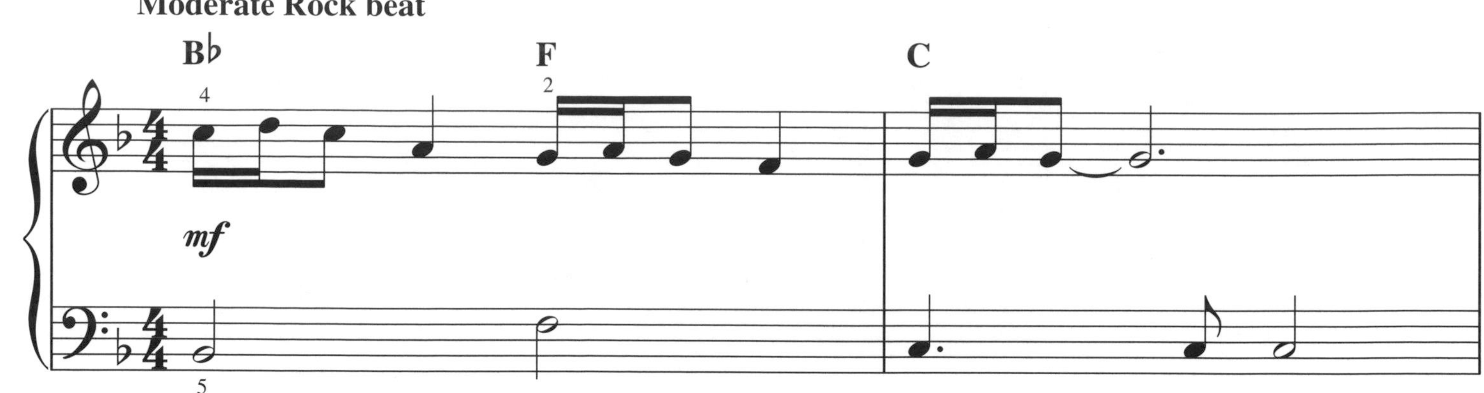

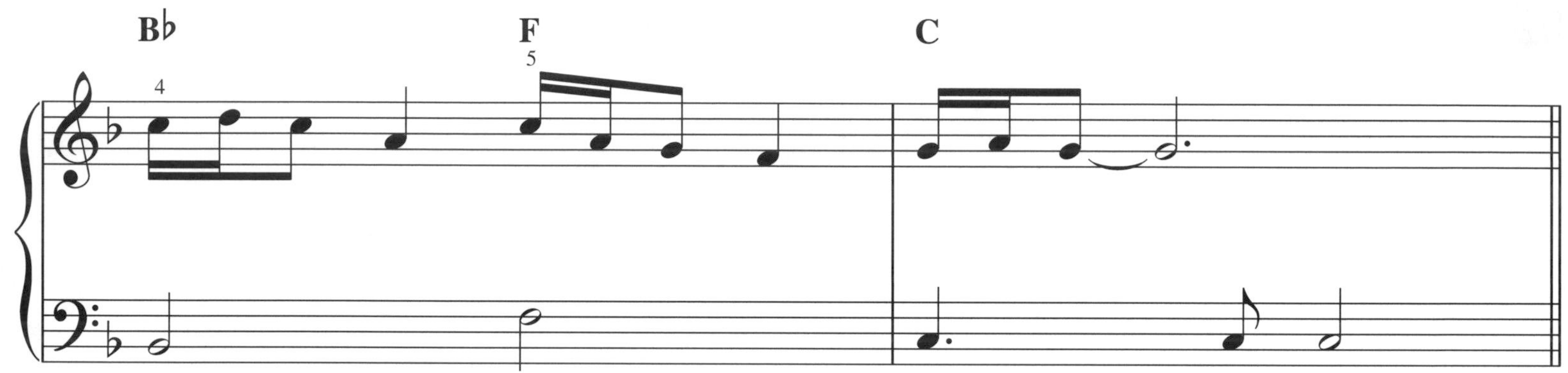

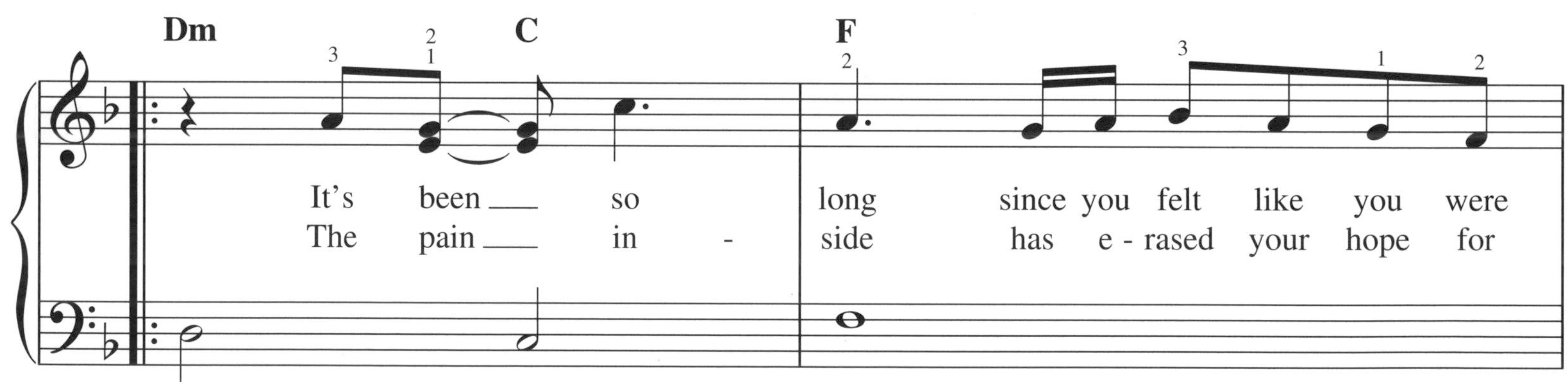

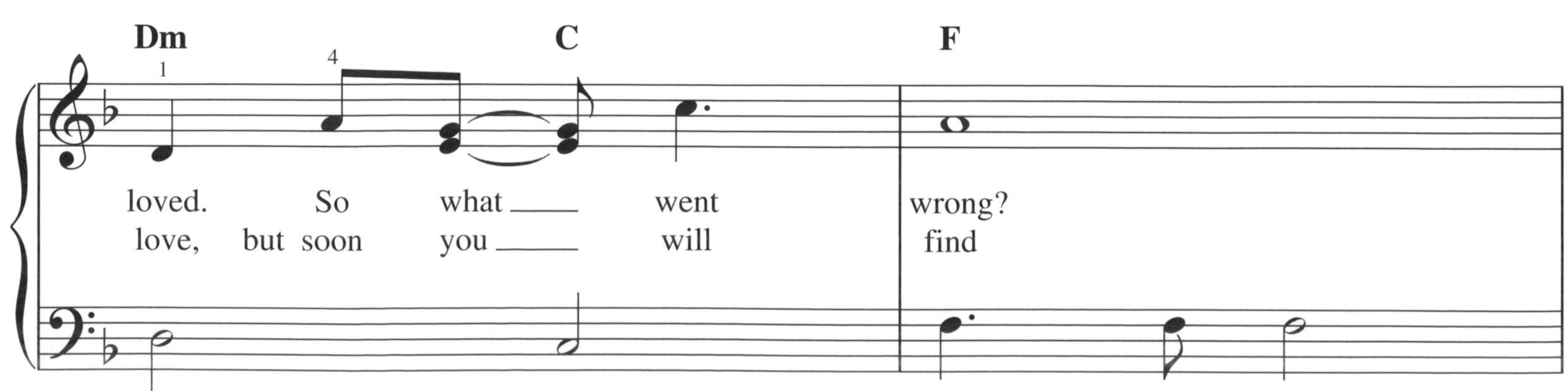

Dm
C
F
But do you know there's a place where you be -
that I'll give you all that your heart could ev - er

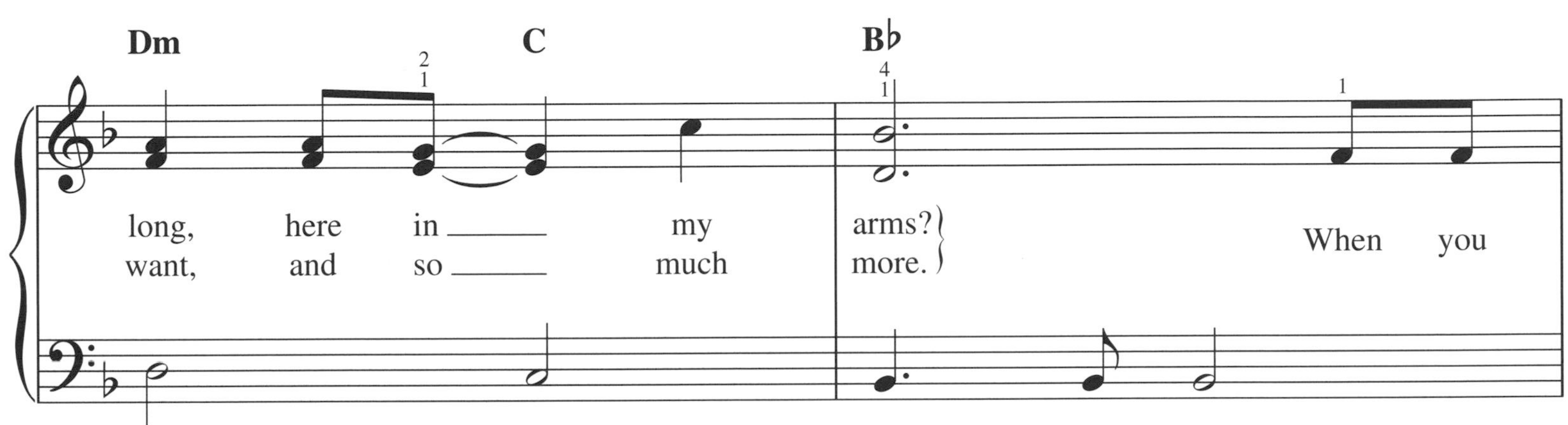
Dm
C
B♭
long, here in my arms?
want, and so much more.
When you

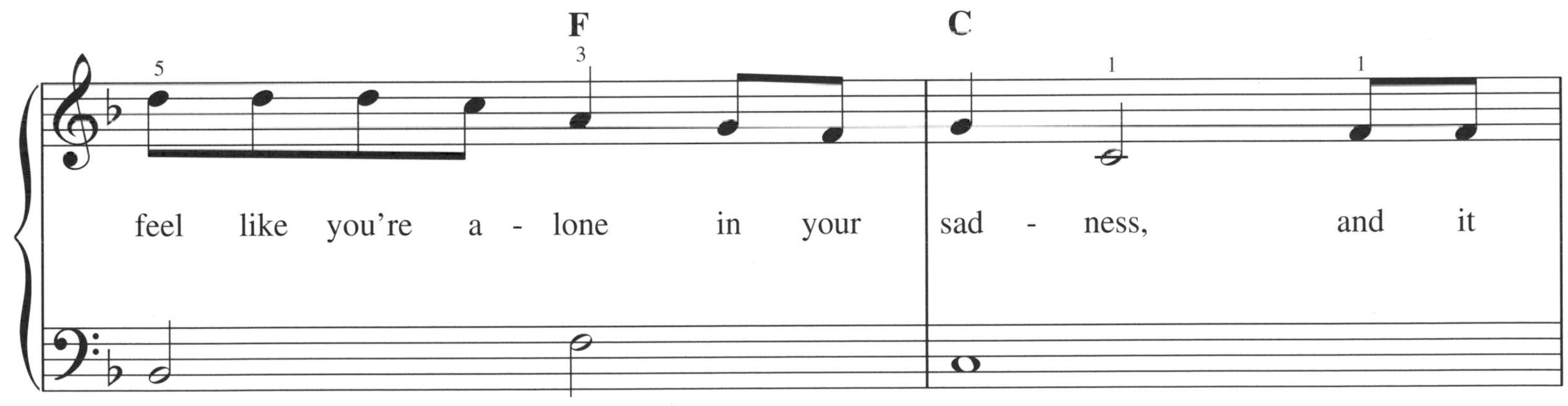
F
C
feel like you're a - lone in your sad - ness, and it

B♭
F
C
seems like no one in this whole world cares, and you

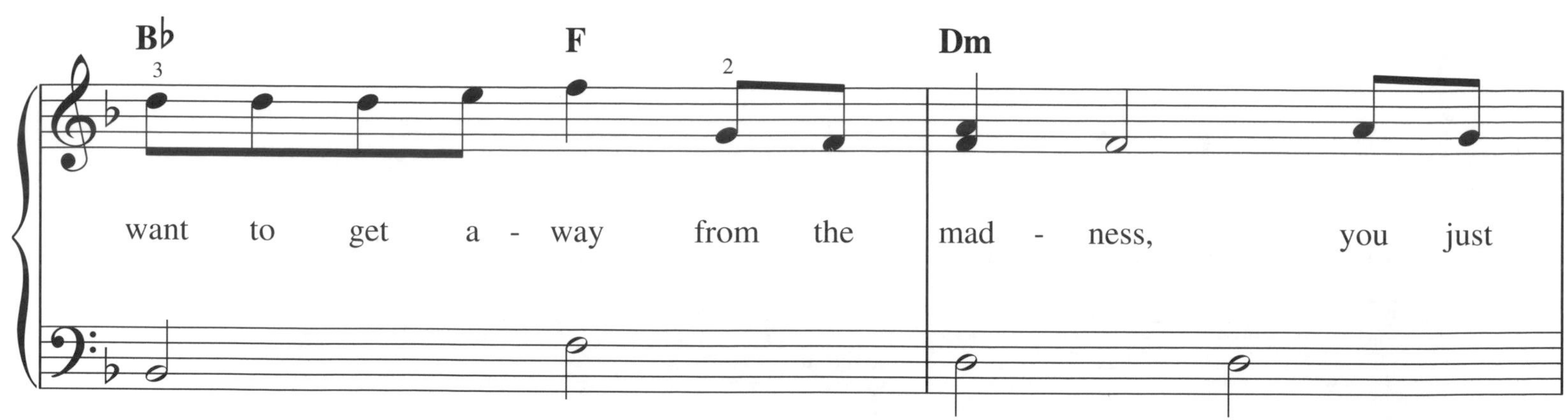
B♭
F
Dm
want to get a - way from the mad - ness, you just

B♭
F
C
Gm
call my name and I'll be there. You just

1.
B♭
F
C
B♭
F
call my name and I'll be there. Na na na na,

C
B♭
F
na na na.
Na na na na, na na na na,

2.
C
Bb
F
C
na na na.
call my name and I'll be

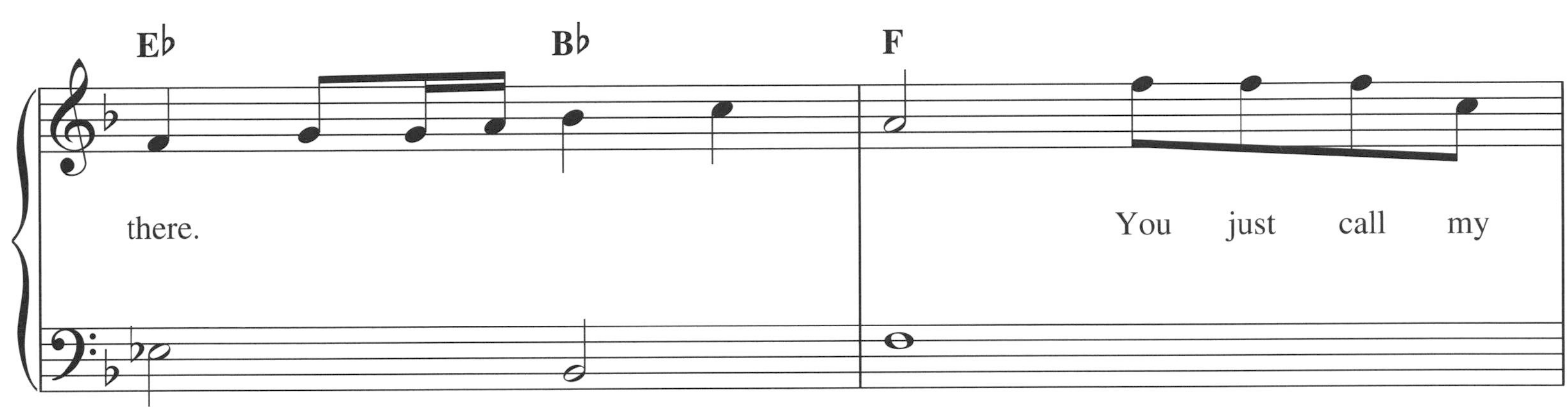
Eb
Bb
F
there.
You just call my

Eb
Bb
F
name,
yeah. You just call my

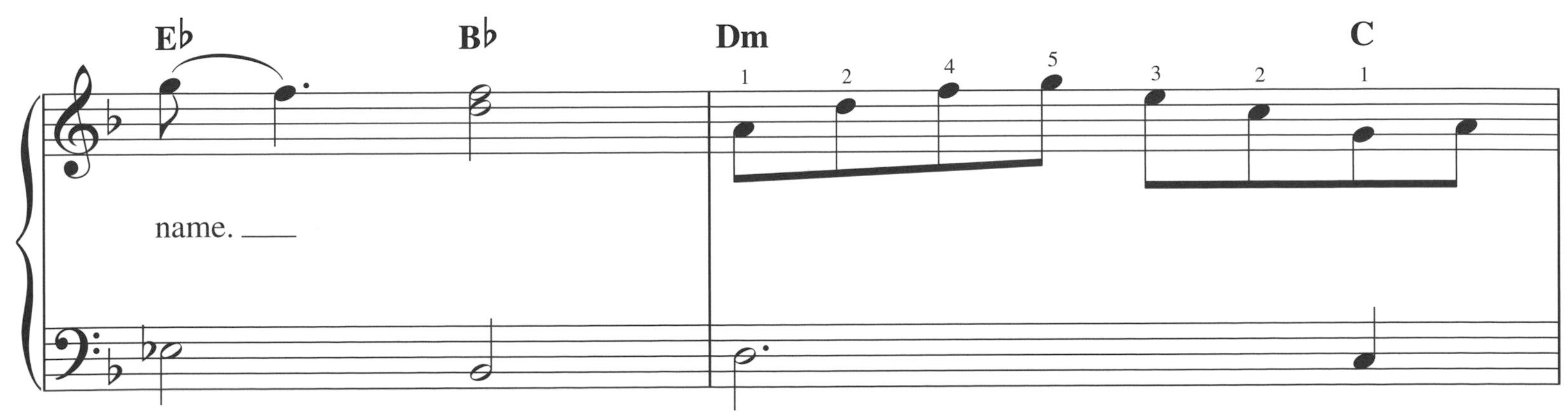
Eb
Bb
Dm
C
name.

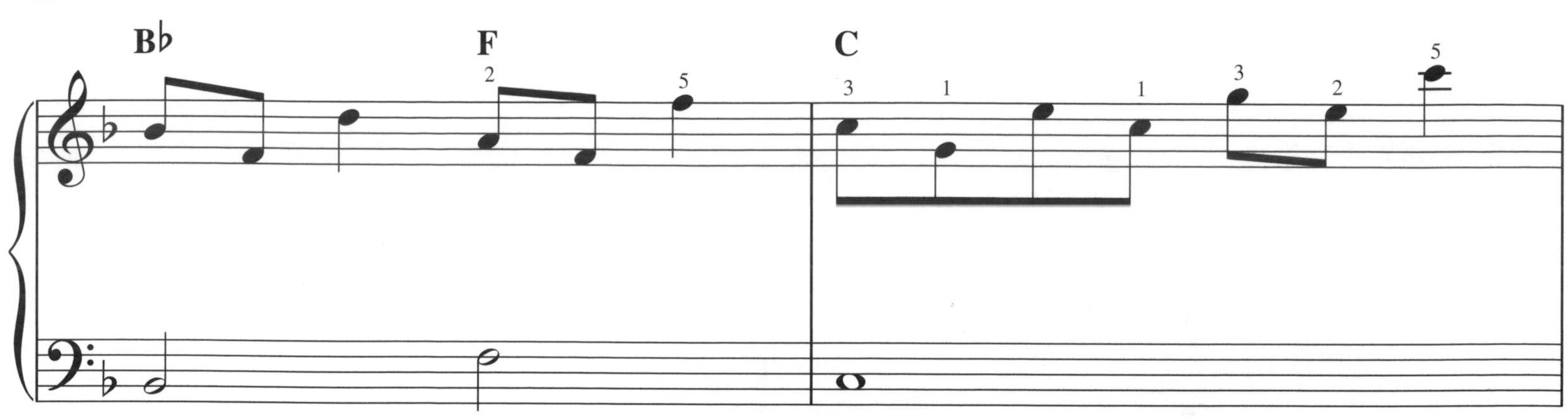
B♭
F
C
2
5
3
1
1
3
2
5

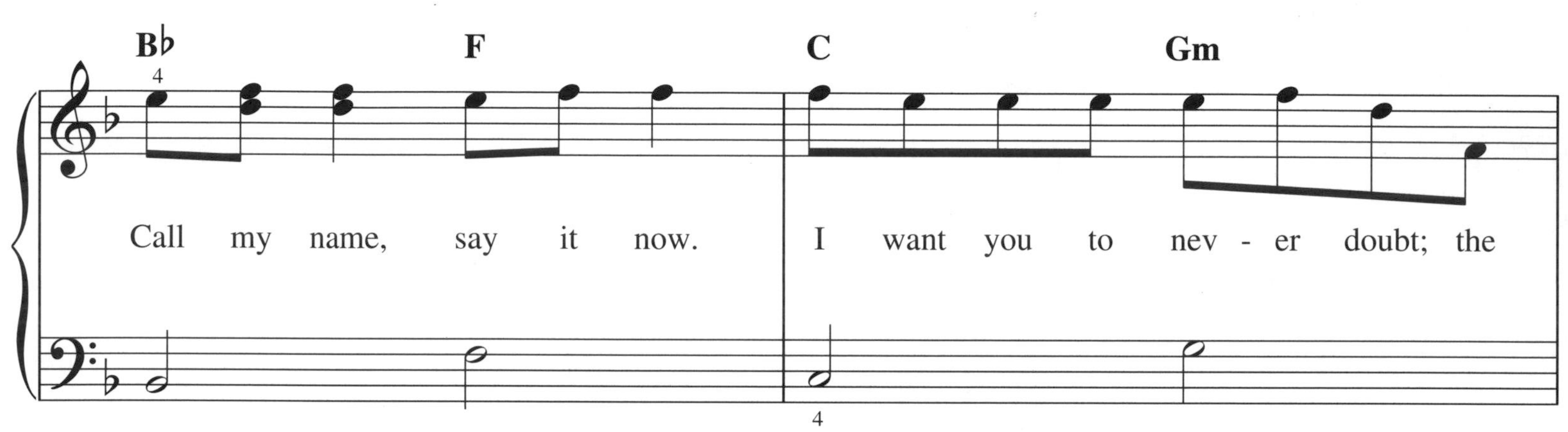
B♭
F
C
Gm
4
Call my name, say it now. I want you to nev - er doubt; the
4

B♭
F
C
4
love I have for you is so a - live.

B♭
F
C
Gm
Call my name, say it now. I want you to nev - er doubt; the

B♭
F
C
1
love I have for you is so a - live.

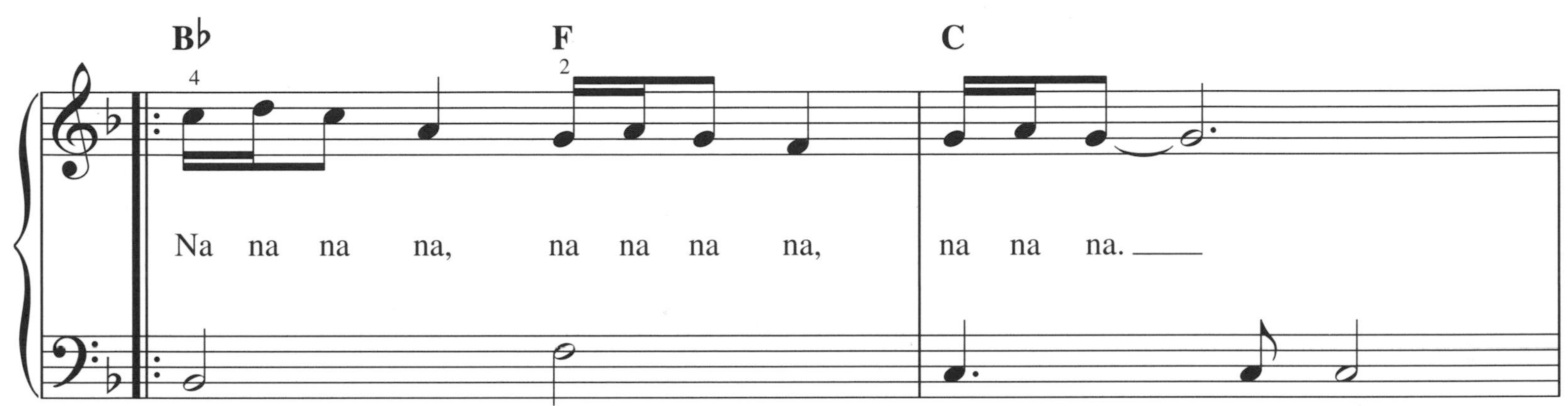
B♭
F
C
4
2
Na na na na, na na na na, na na na.

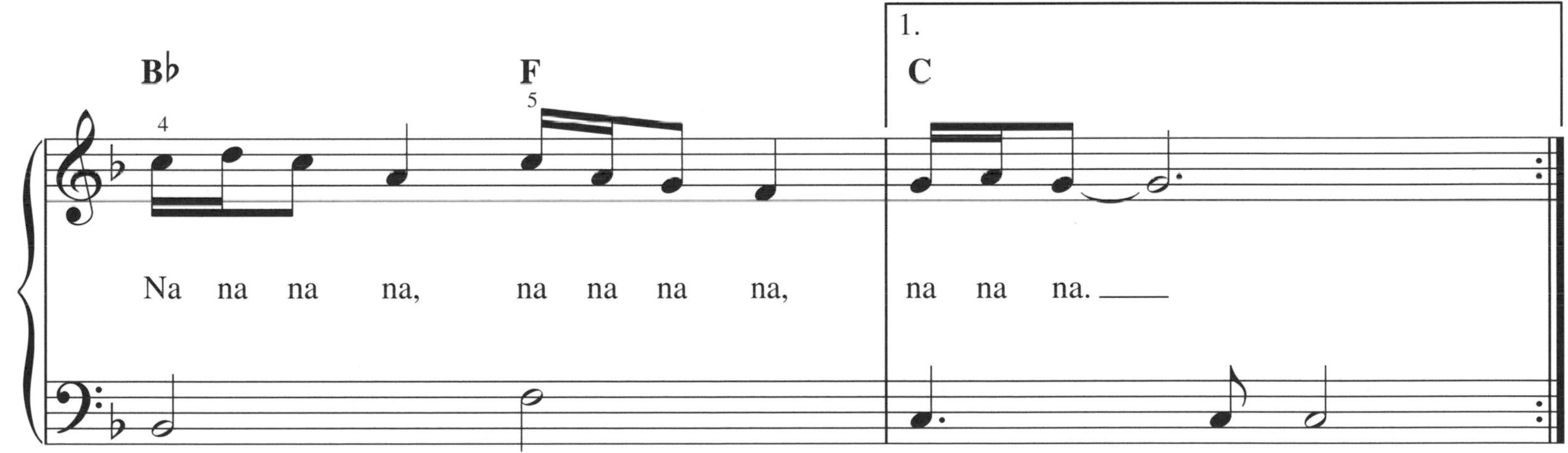
1.
B♭
F
C
4
5
Na na na na, na na na na, na na na.

2.
C
F
5
na na na. You just call my name.
1
2

COUNT ME IN

Words and Music by LEELAND MOORING,
JACK MOORING, MICHAEL DEWAYNE SMITH
and WILLIAM JACOB HOLTZ

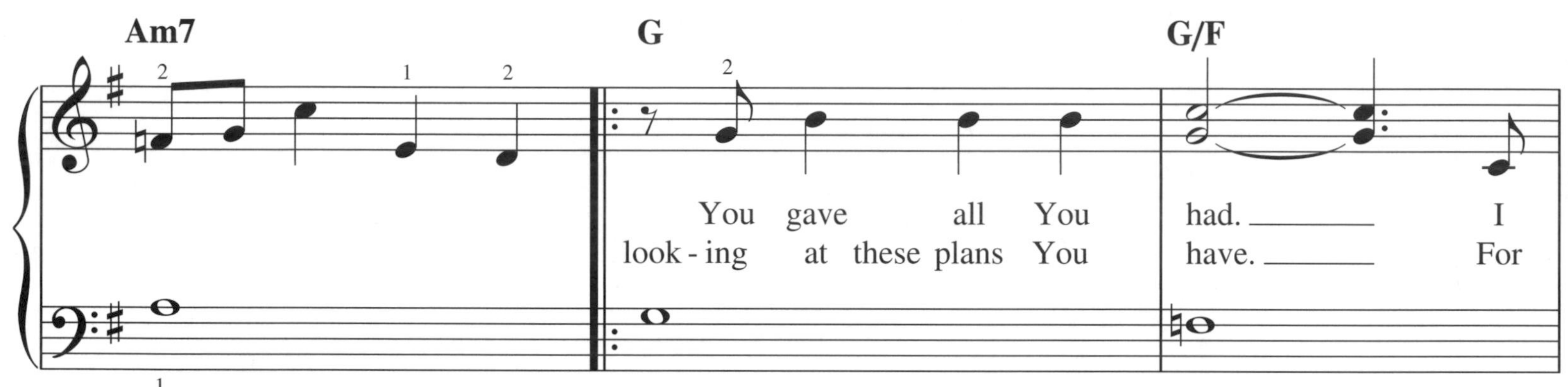

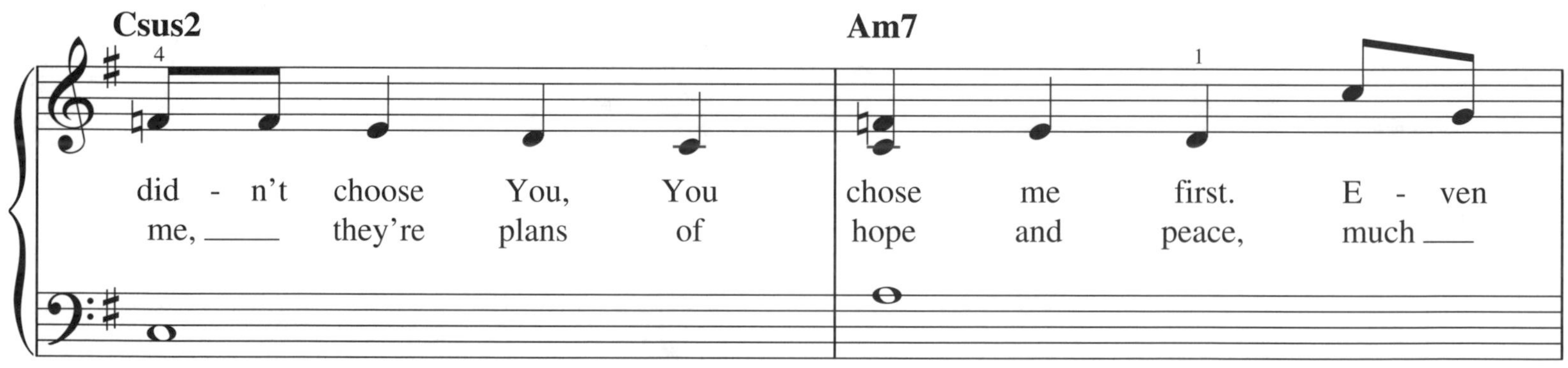

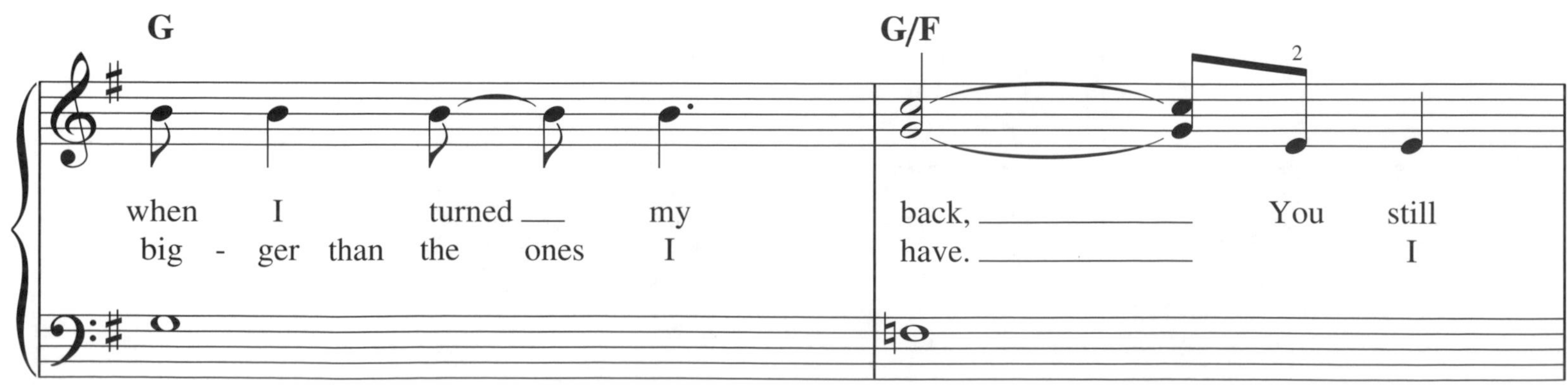

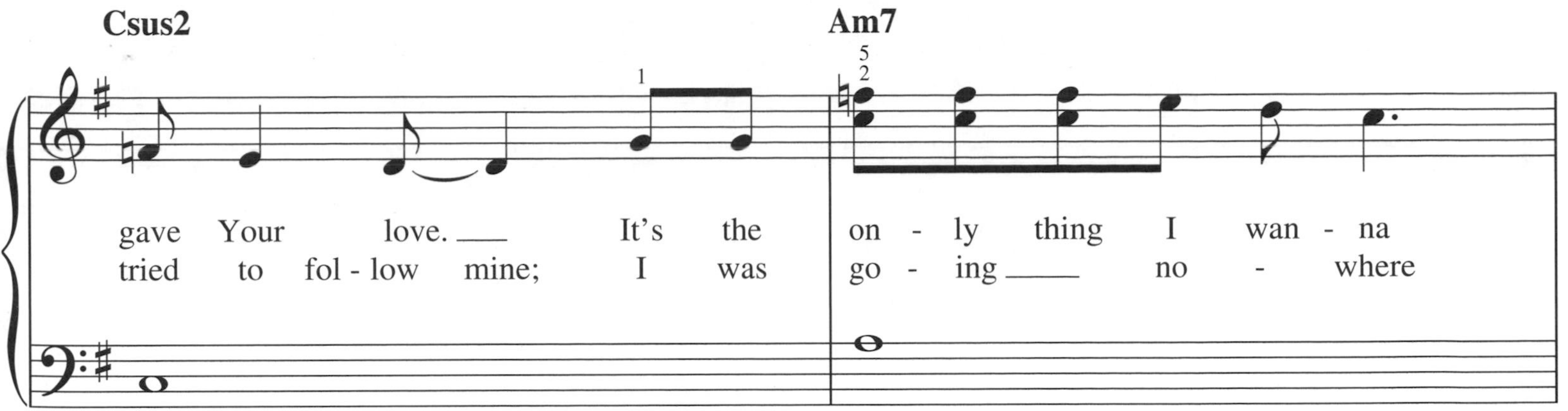
Csus2
Am7
gave Your love. It's the on - ly thing I wan - na
tried to fol - low mine; I was go - ing no - where

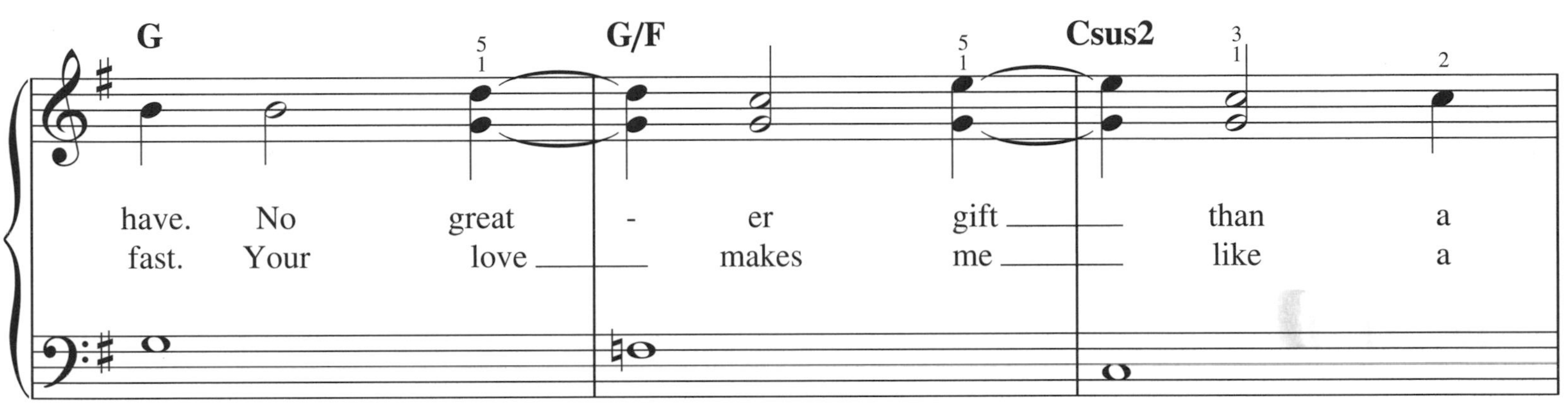
G
G/F
Csus2
have. No great - er gift than a
fast. Your love makes me like a

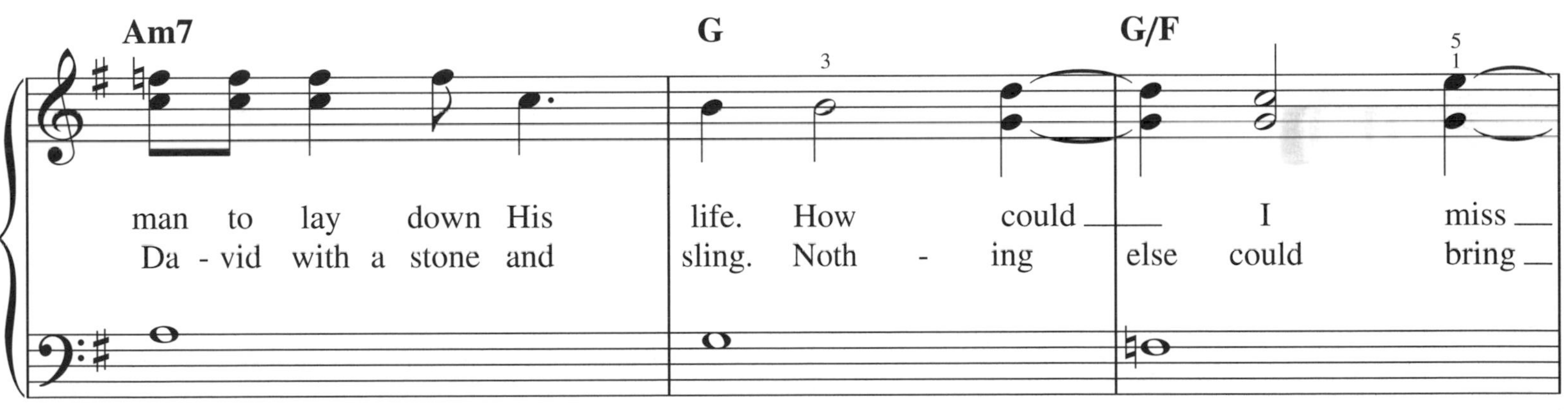
Am7
G
G/F
man to lay down His life. How could I miss
Da - vid with a stone and sling. Noth - ing else could bring

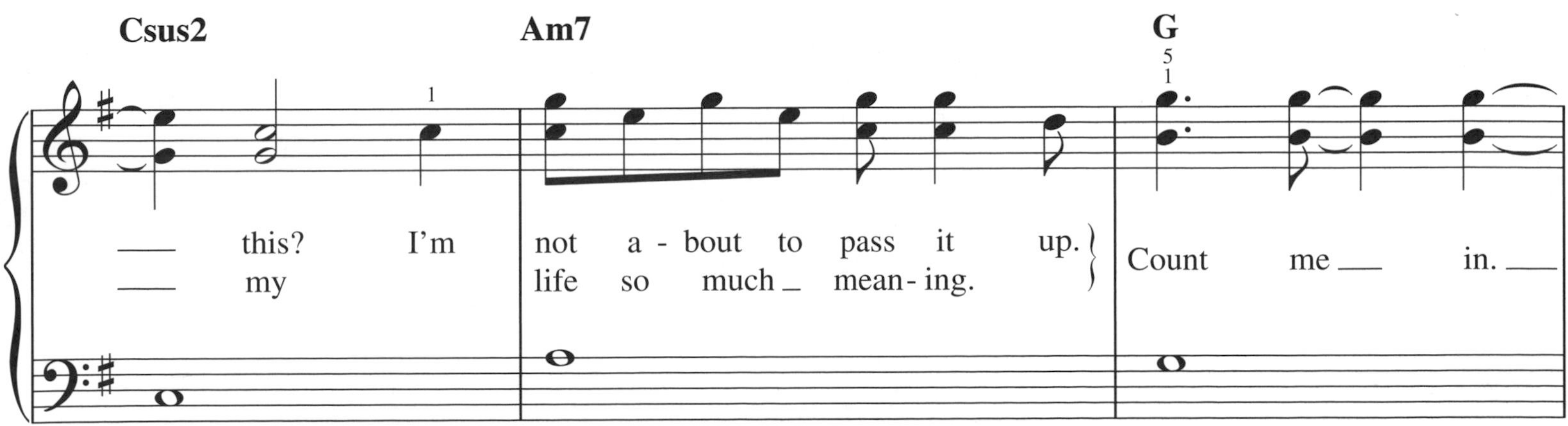
Csus2
Am7
G
this? I'm not a - bout to pass it up.
my life so much mean - ing.
Count me in.

G/F
Csus2
Am7
I'm a - mazed this love is for me, Lord.

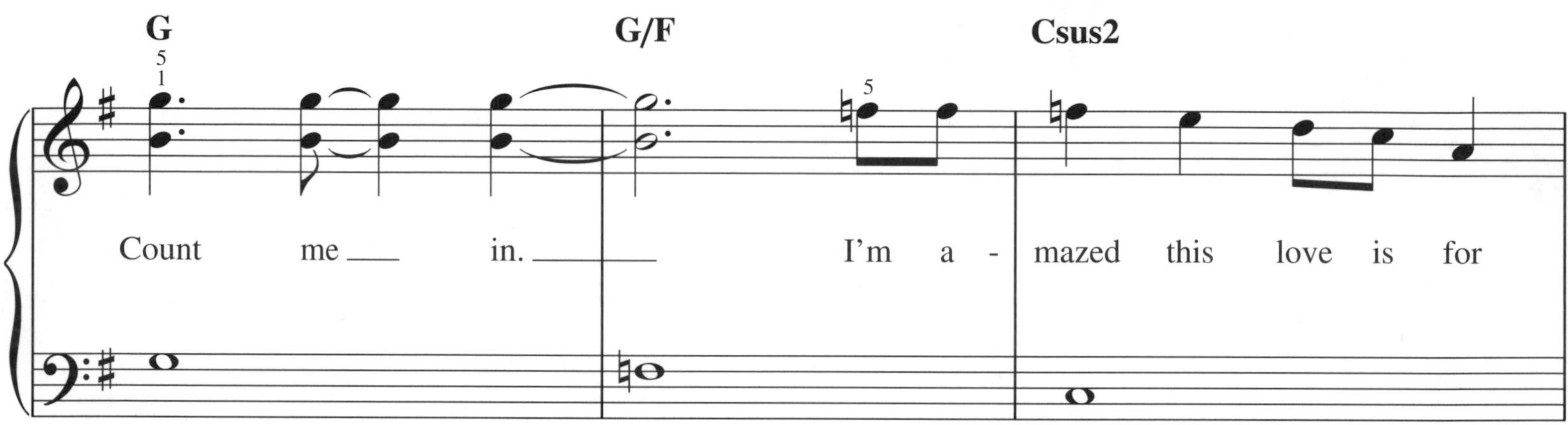
G
G/F
Csus2
Count me in. I'm a - mazed this love is for

Am7
G
G/F
me, Lord. Ooh, ooh, ooh, ooh,

Csus2
Am7
G
ooh, ooh. Sha la la la la la la. Ooh, ooh,

1.
2.
G/F
Csus2
Am7
Am7
ooh, ooh,
ooh, ooh.
I'm

F
C
G
F
C
G
I can't be - lieve it.

F
C
G
I can't be - lieve it.
I can't be - lieve it.

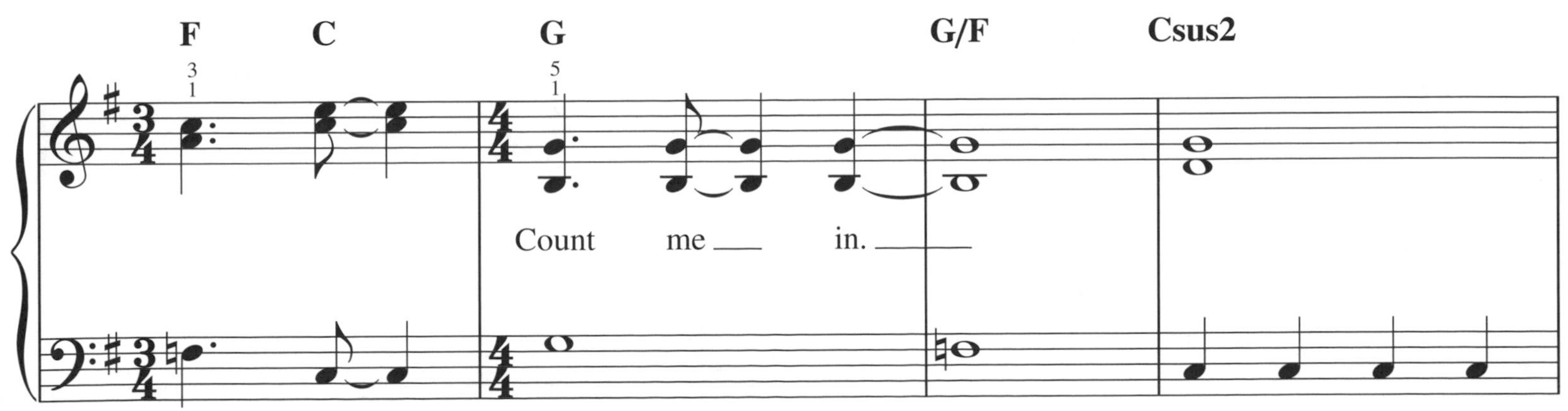
F
C
G
G/F
Csus2
Count me in.

Am7
G
G/F
Csus2
Come on, you can count me in.

Am7
G
G/F
Csus2
And you can count me in.
Vocal ad lib. on repeat

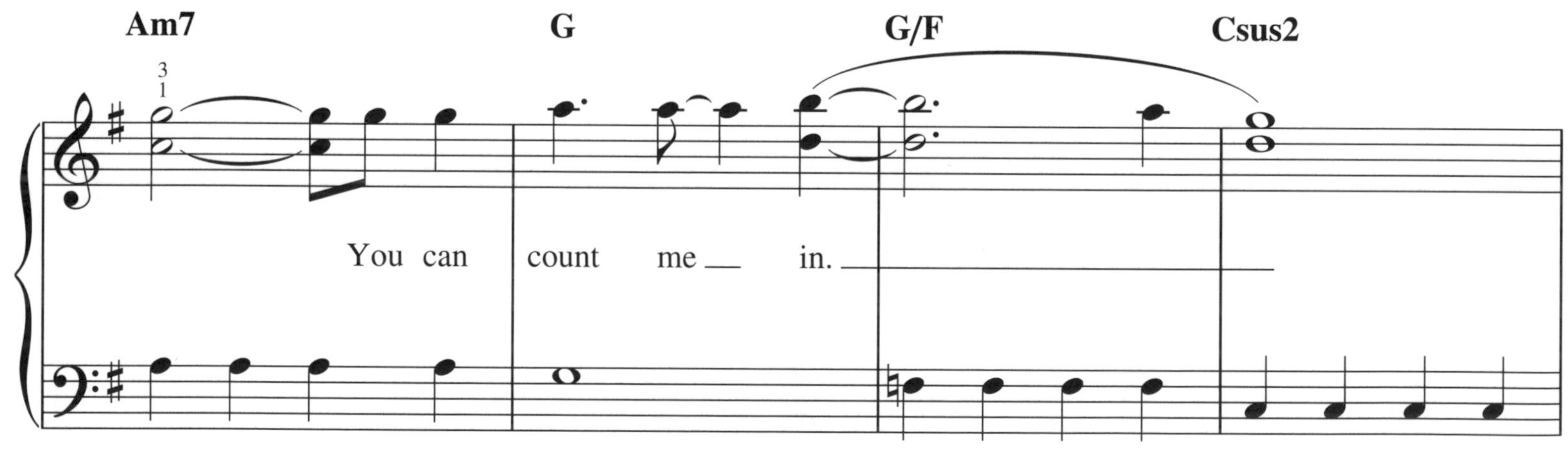
Am7
G
G/F
Csus2
You can count me in.

1.
Am7
2.
Am7
F
C
G

REVELATION

Words by MAC POWELL
Music by THIRD DAY

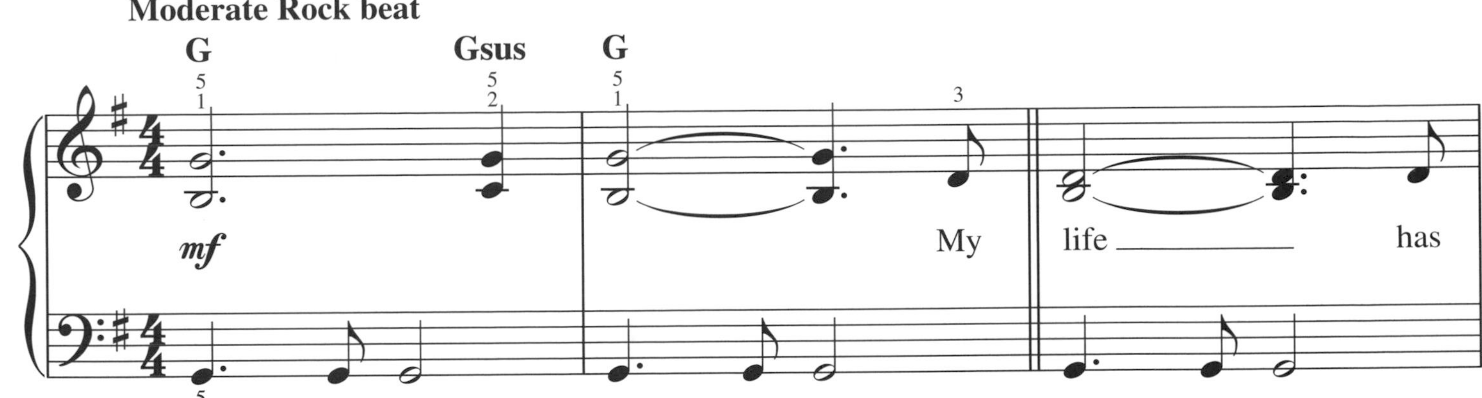

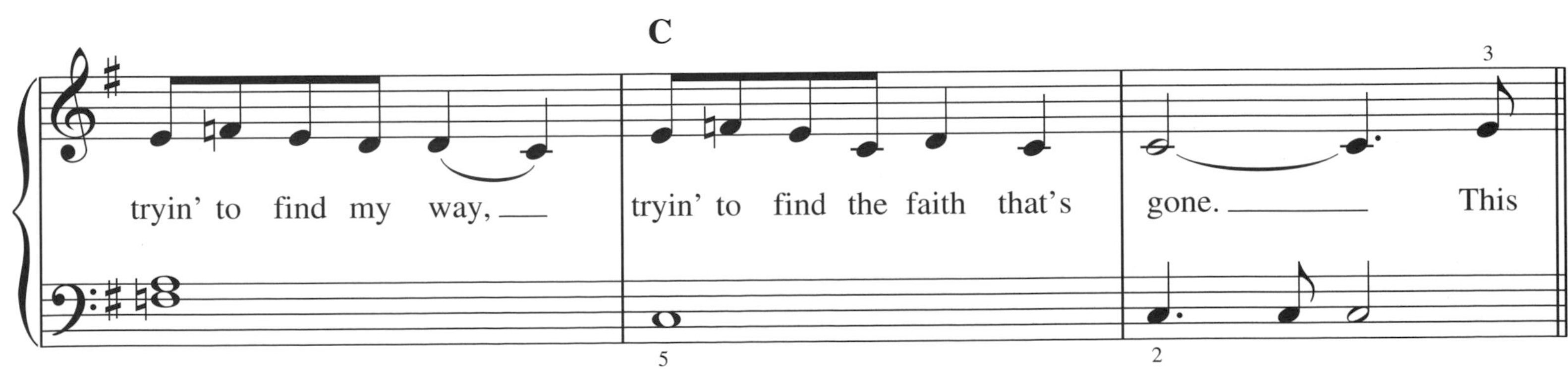

G
2
time, I know that You are hold - ing all the
life has led me down this path that's ev - er
5

D
1 2
an - swers. I'm tired of los - ing hope and tak - ing
wind - ing. Through ev - 'ry twist and turn, I'm al - ways
4

F
chanc - es on roads that nev - er seem to
find - ing that I am lost a - gain.

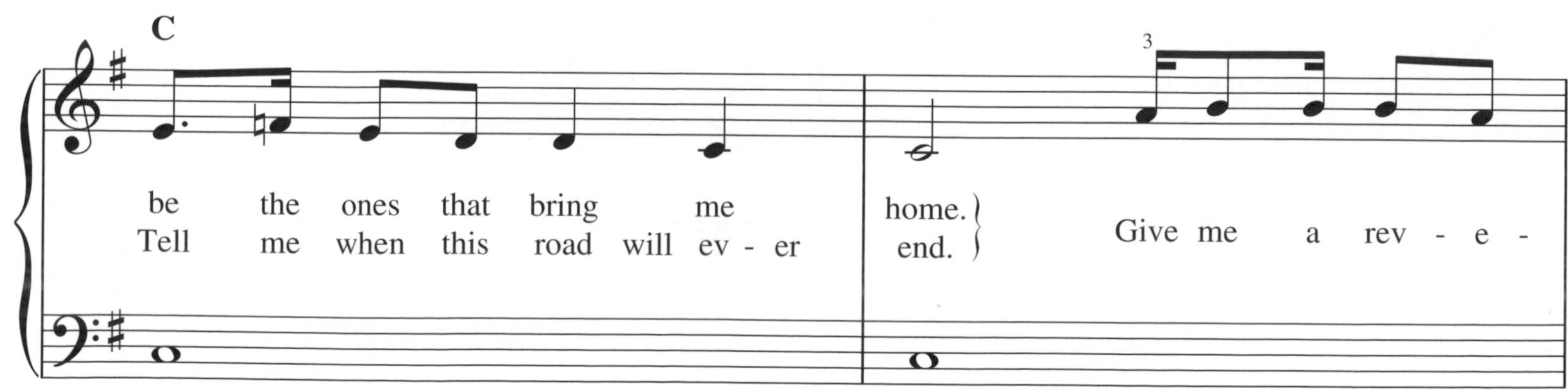
C
3
be the ones that bring me home.
Tell me when this road will ev - er end.
Give me a rev - e -

G
Dm
la - tion, show me what to
do, 'cause I've been tryin' to
2

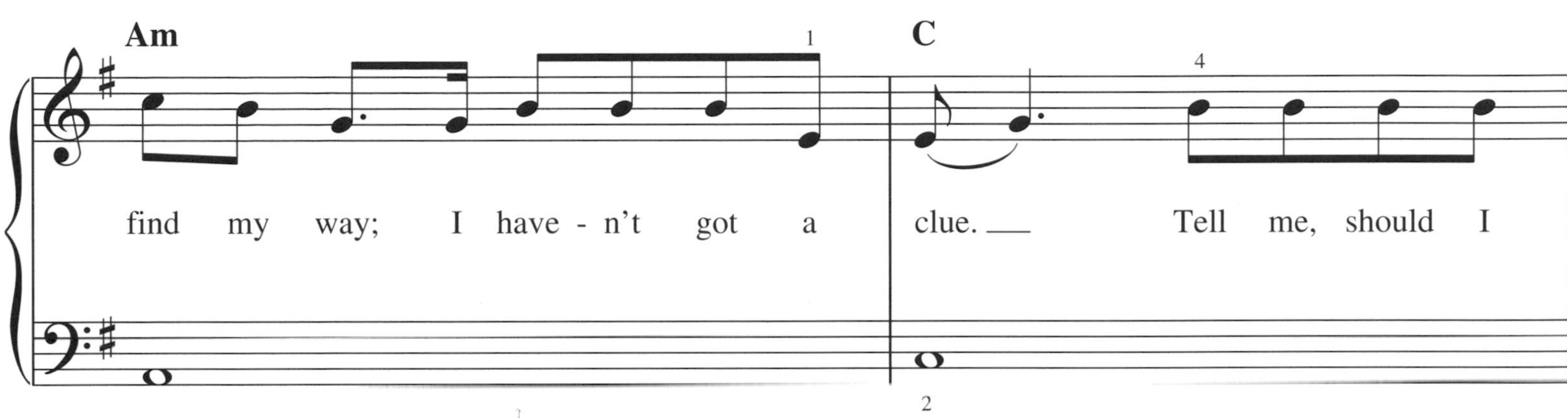
Am
C
1
4
find my way; I have - n't got a
clue. Tell me, should I
2

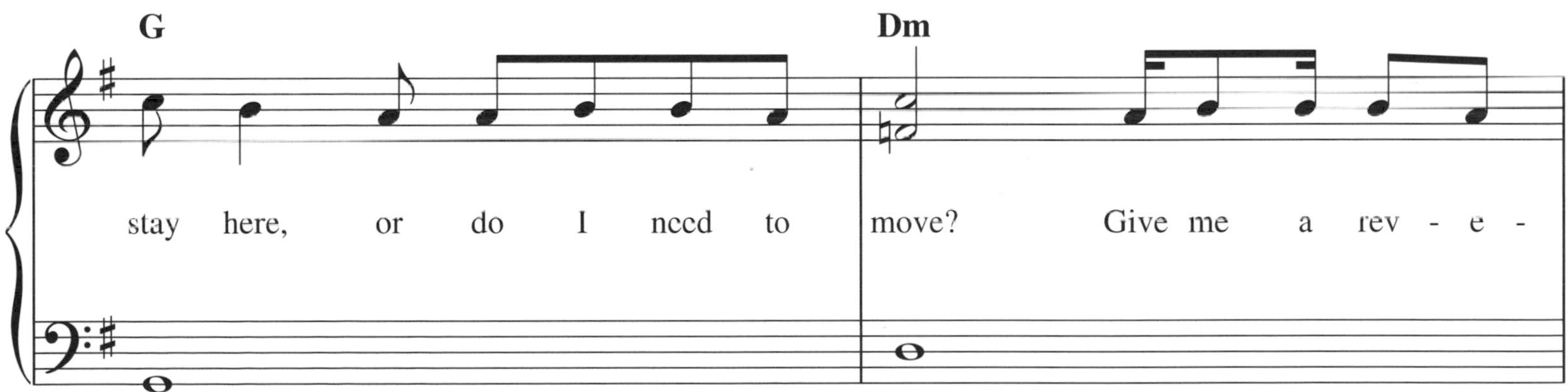
G
Dm
stay here, or do I need to
move? Give me a rev - e -

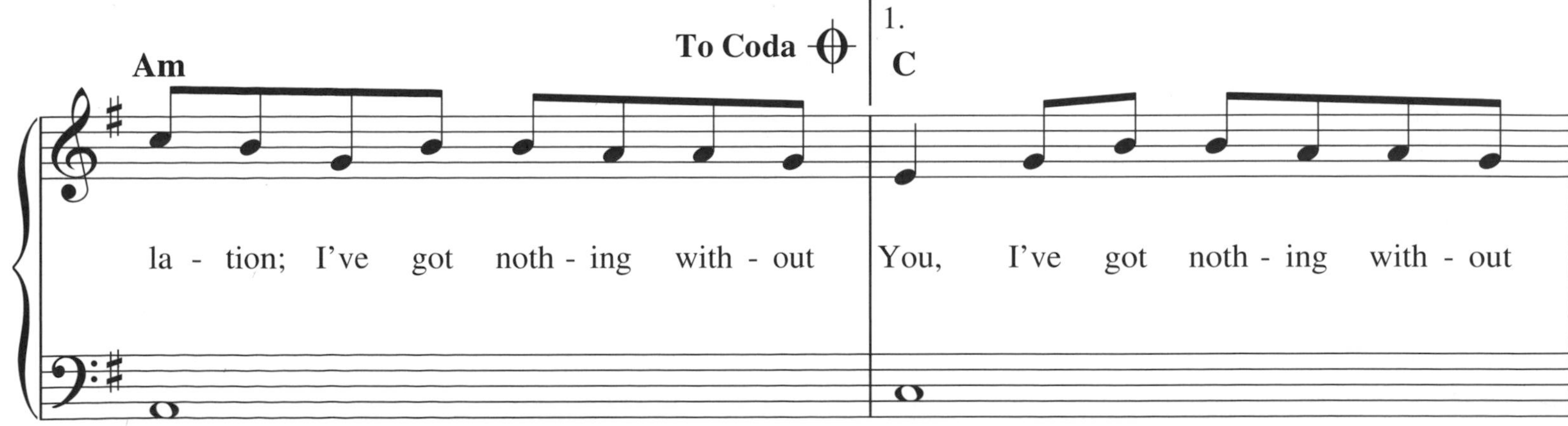
Am
To Coda
1.
C
la - tion; I've got noth - ing with - out
You, I've got noth - ing with - out

G
1
2
4
3
You.
My

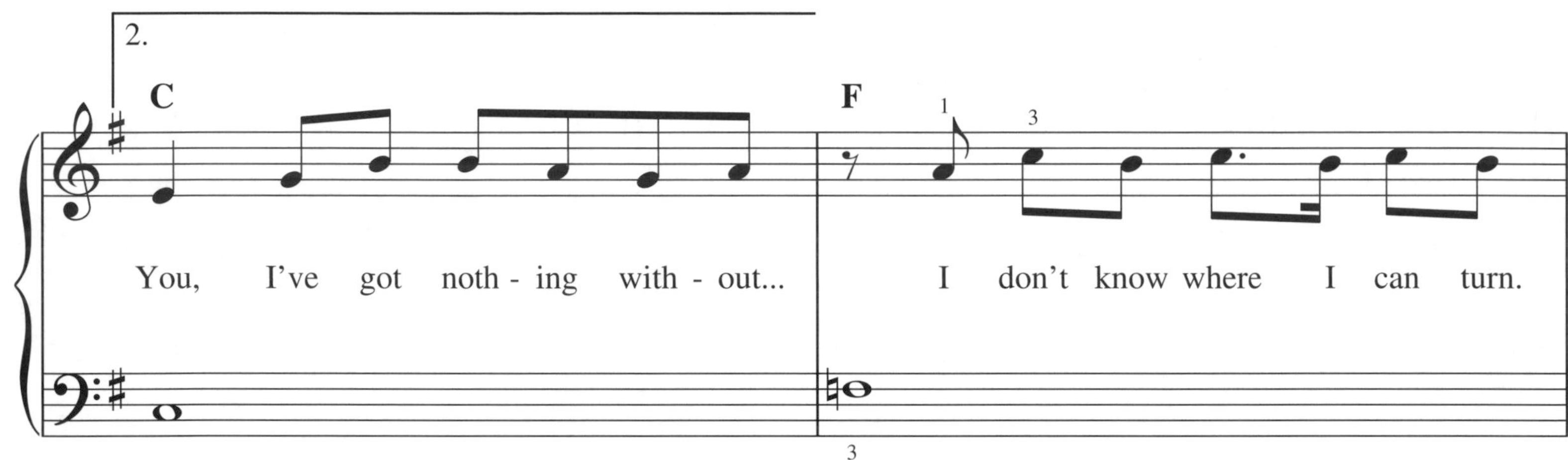
2.
C
F
1
3
You, I've got noth - ing with - out...
I don't know where I can turn.
3

Am
Em
3
1
Tell me, when will I learn?
Won't You show me where I need to

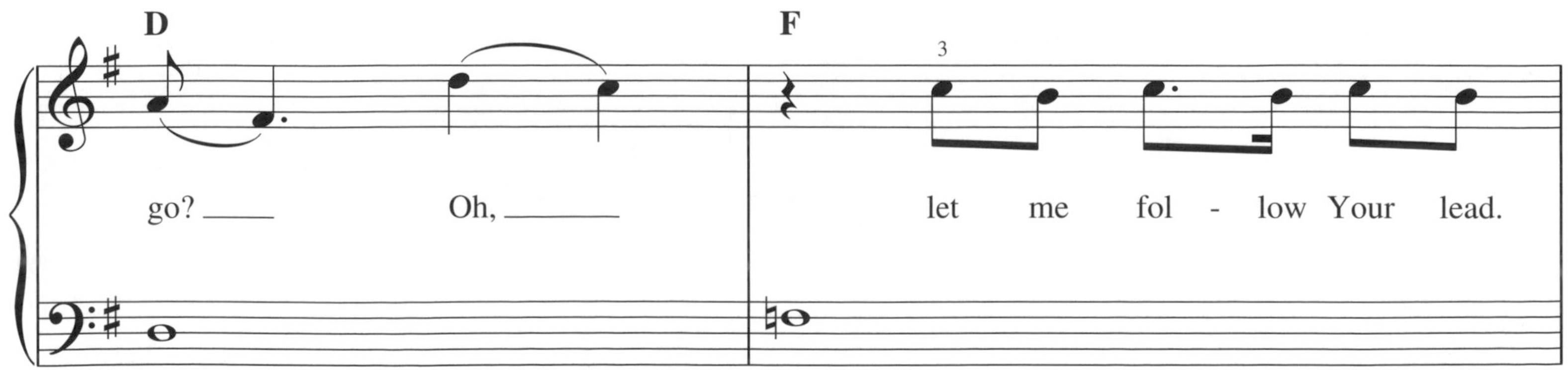
D
F
3
go?
Oh,
let me fol - low Your lead.

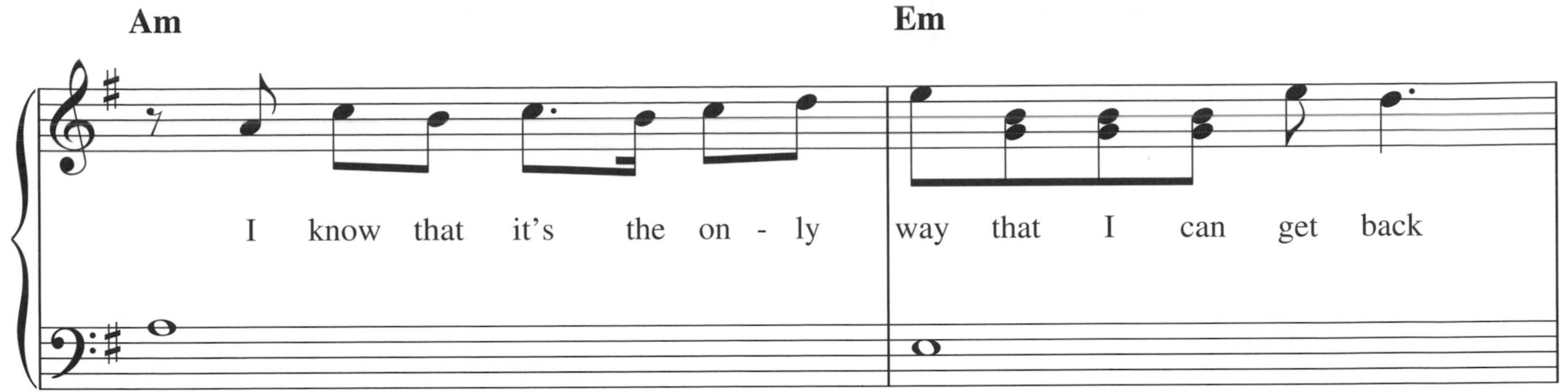

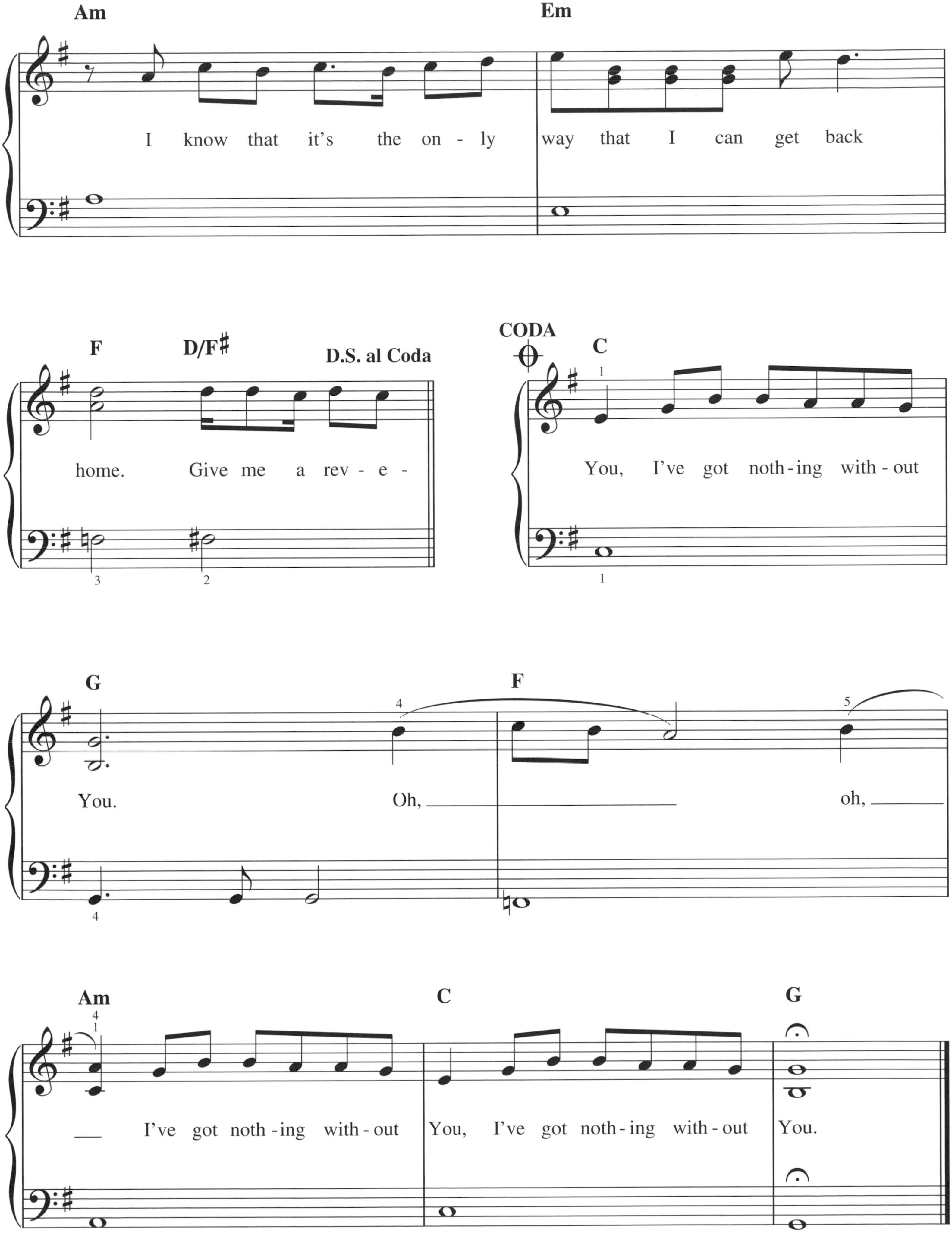

Am
Em
I know that it's the on - ly
way that I can get back
F
D/F#
D.S. al Coda
home. Give me a rev - e -
CODA
C
You, I've got noth - ing with - out
G
F
You. Oh,
oh,
Am
C
G
I've got noth - ing with - out
You, I've got noth - ing with - out
You.

GIVE ME YOUR EYES

Words and Music by JASON INGRAM
and BRANDON HEATH

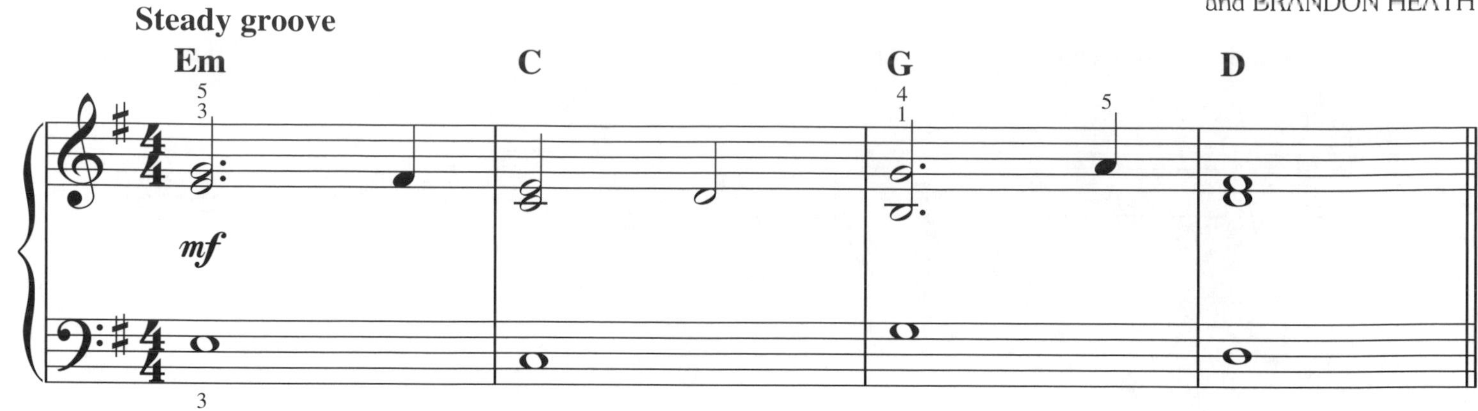

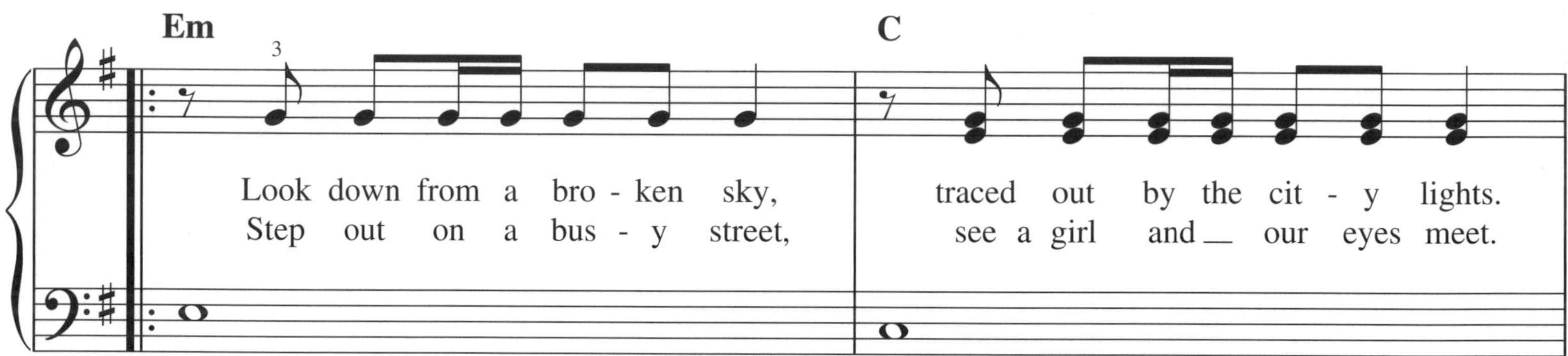

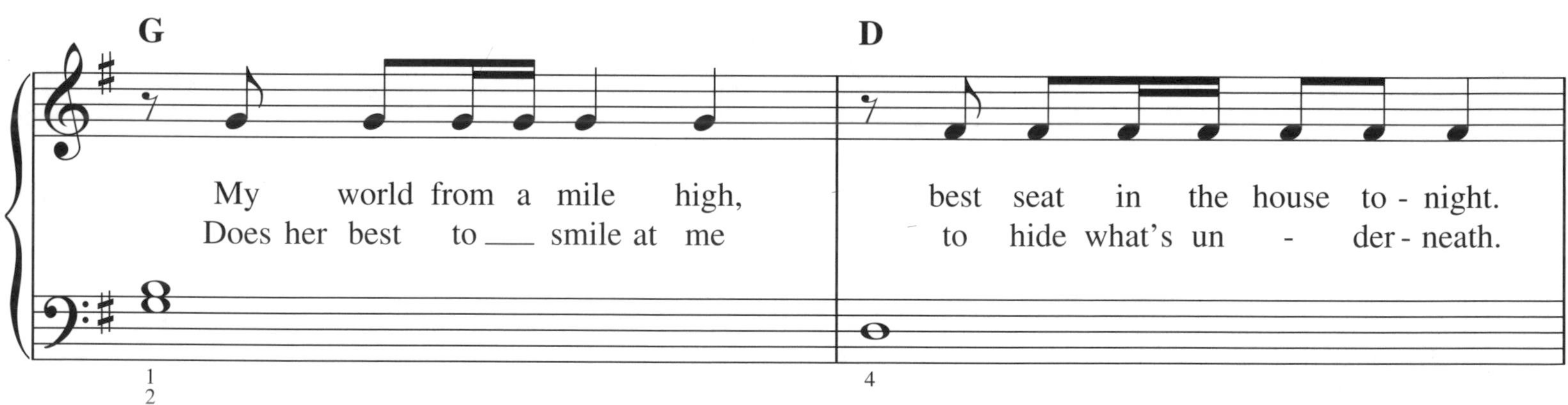

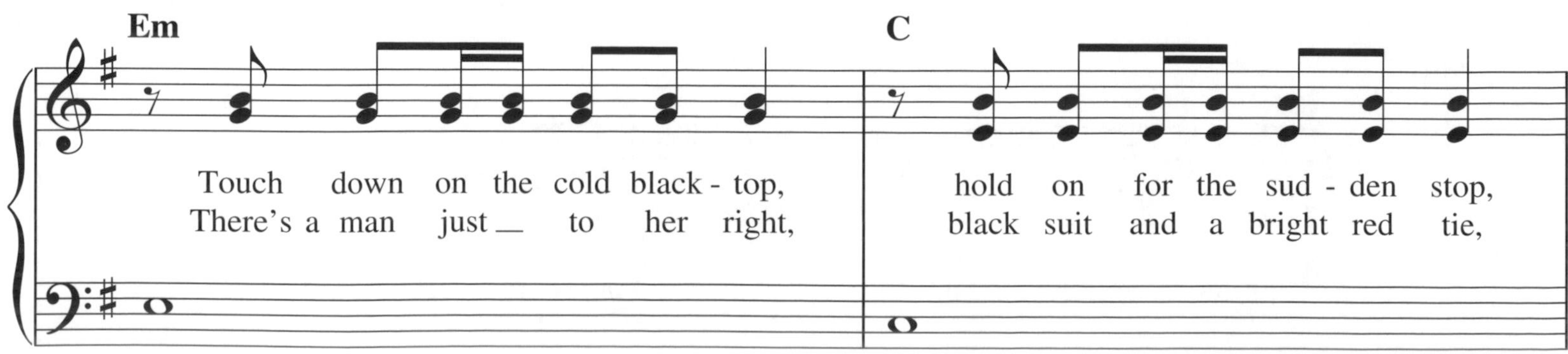

G
D
breathe in the fa - mil - iar shock of con - fu - sion and cha - os.
too a-shamed to tell his wife he's out of work; he's buy - ing time.

Em
C
Am
All those peo - ple go - ing some - where. Why havc I nev - er

Em
cared? Give me Your eyes for just one sec - ond, give me Your

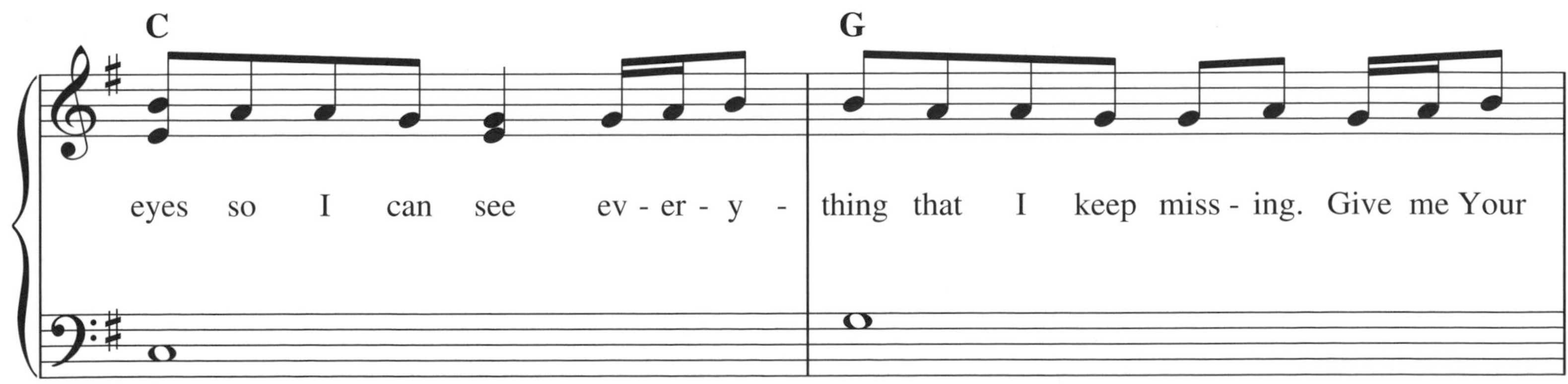
C
G
eyes so I can see ev - er - y - thing that I keep miss - ing. Give me Your

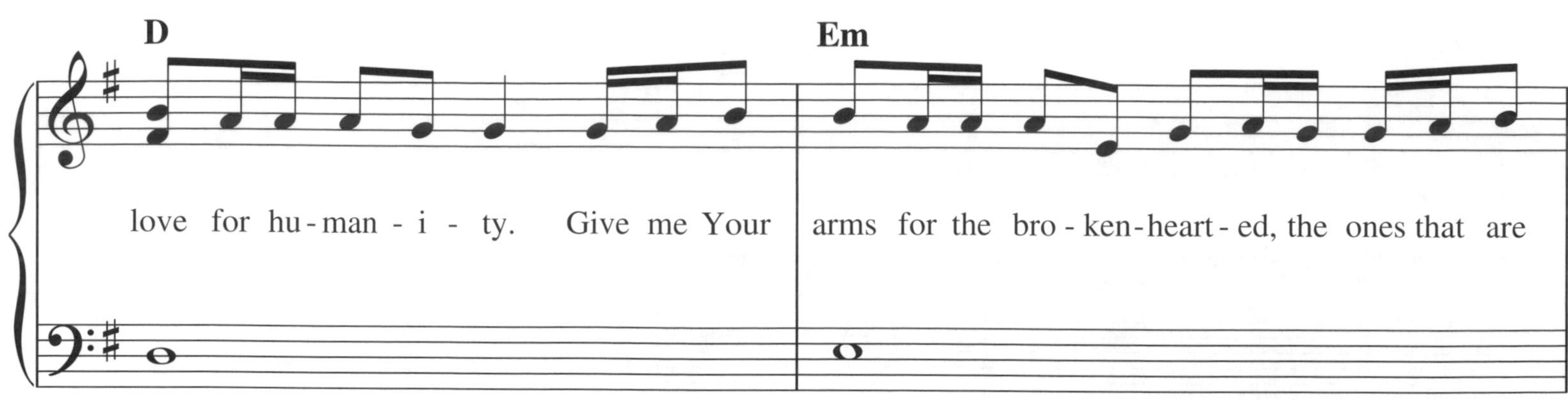
D
Em
love for hu - man - i - ty. Give me Your
arms for the bro - ken-heart - ed, the ones that are

C
G
far be - yond my reach. Give me Your
eyes for the ones for - got - ten, give me Your

D
Em
C
eyes so I can see. Yeah,
yeah,
yeah,

1.
2., 3.
G
D
D
Fine
yeah.
1
2
4
4

C
G
I've been here a mil - lion times;
a cou-ple of mil - lion eyes

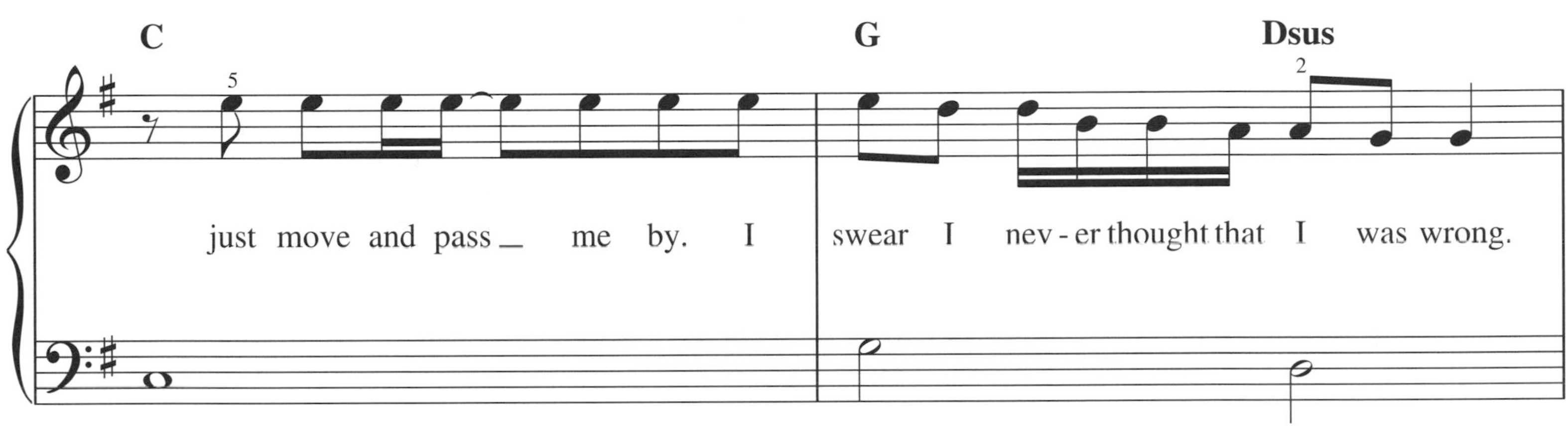
C
G
Dsus
just move and pass me by. I
swear I nev-er thought that I was wrong.

C
G
Well, I want a sec - ond glance,
so give me a sec - ond chance

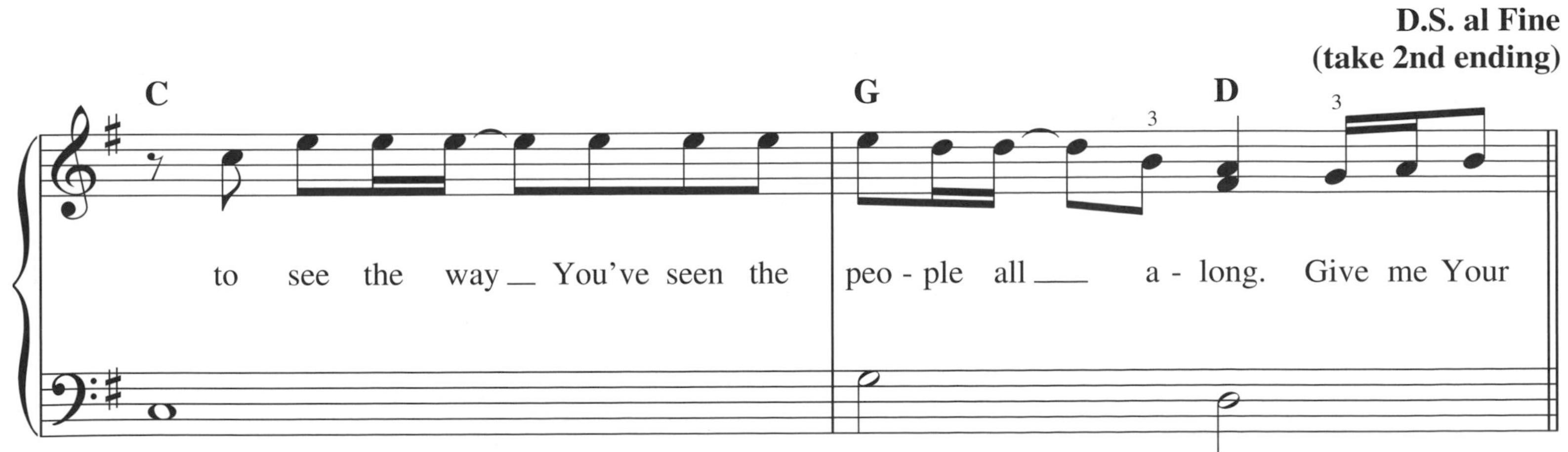
D.S. al Fine
(take 2nd ending)
C
G
D
to see the way You've seen the
peo-ple all a-long. Give me Your

JESUS MESSIAH

Words and Music by CHRIS TOMLIN, JESSE REEVES,
DANIEL CARSON and ED CASH

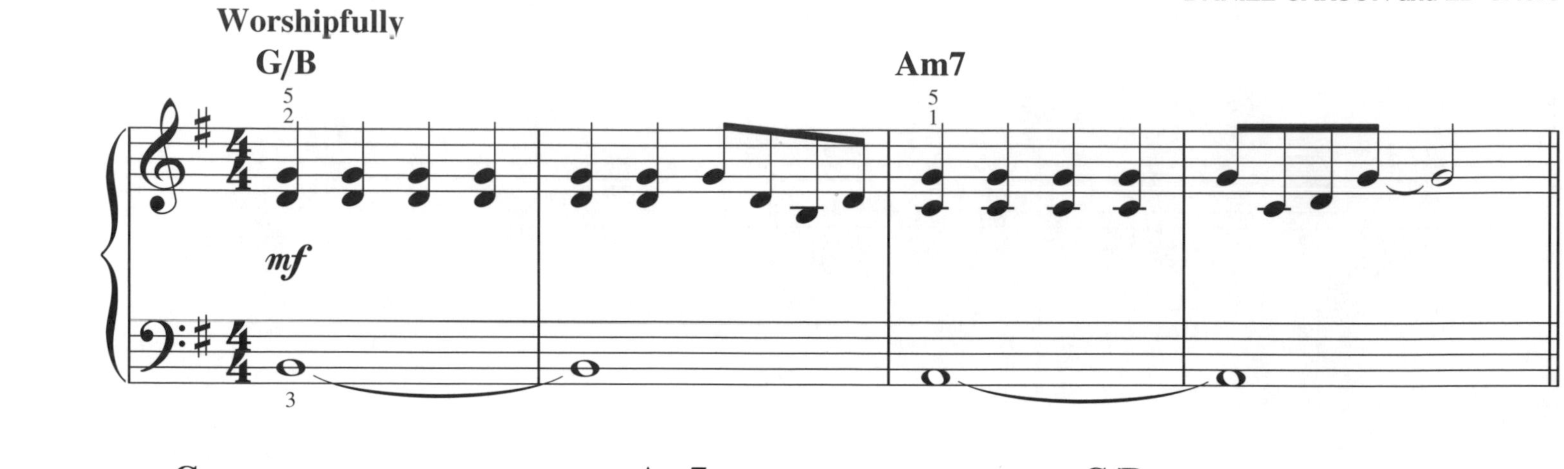

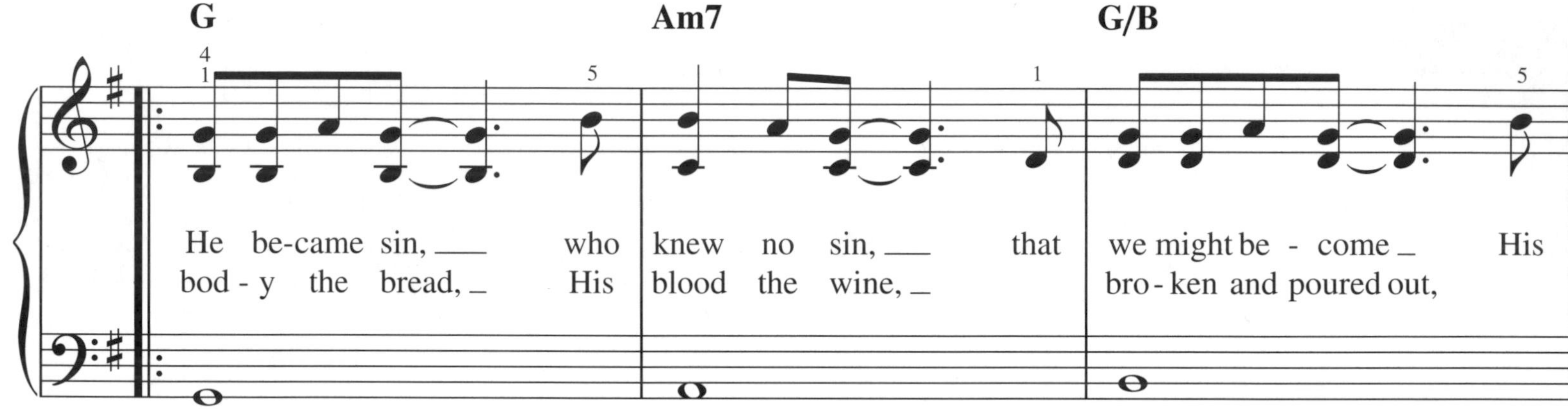

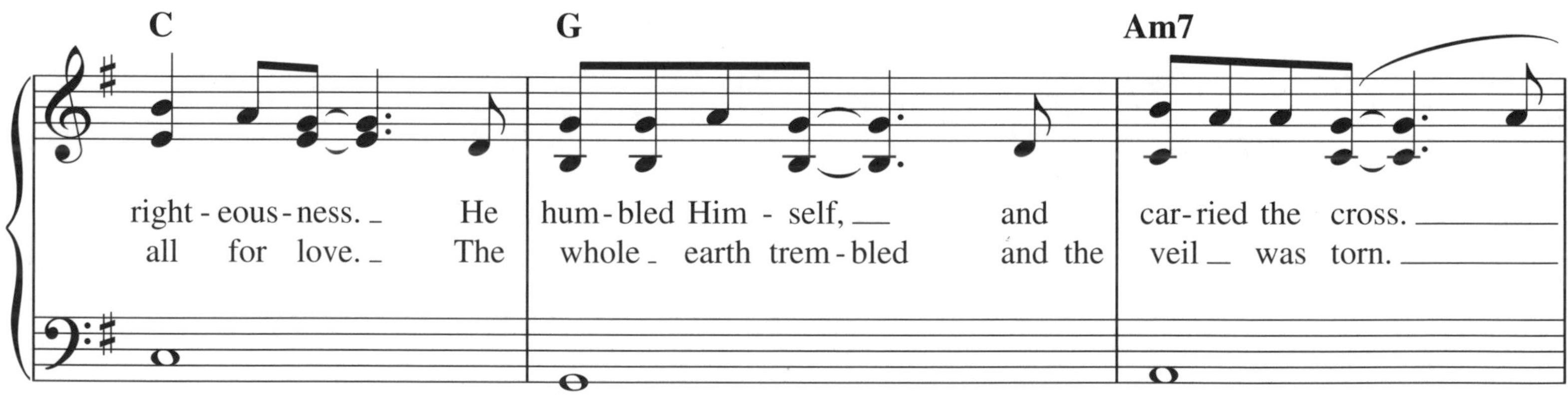

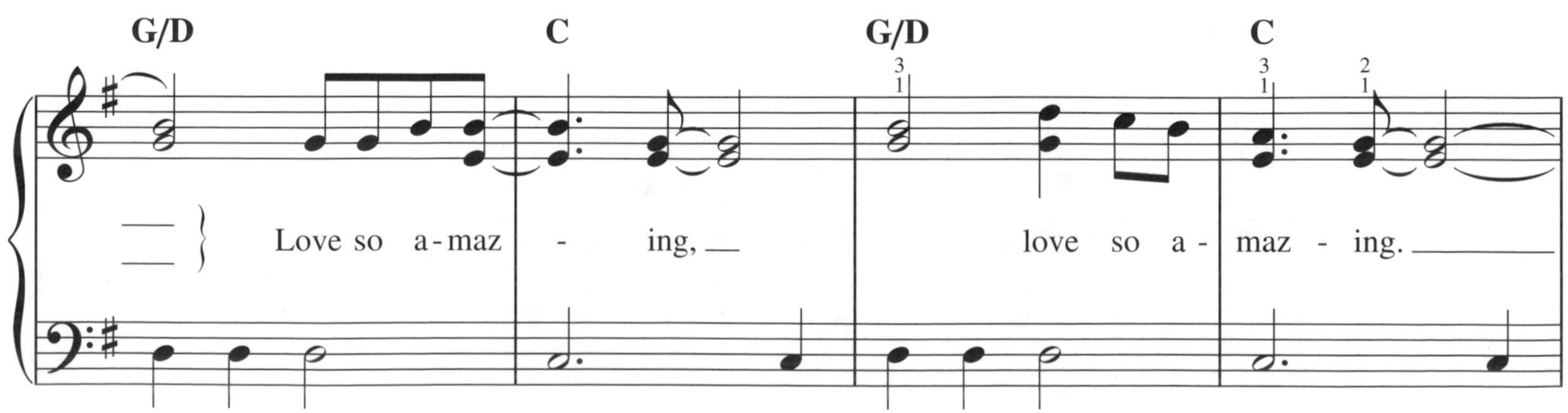

G
Jesus Messiah, Name above all

C
G
names, Blessed Redeemer,

Dsus
D
Emmanuel. The rescue for sin-

G
C
ners, the ransom from Heaven.

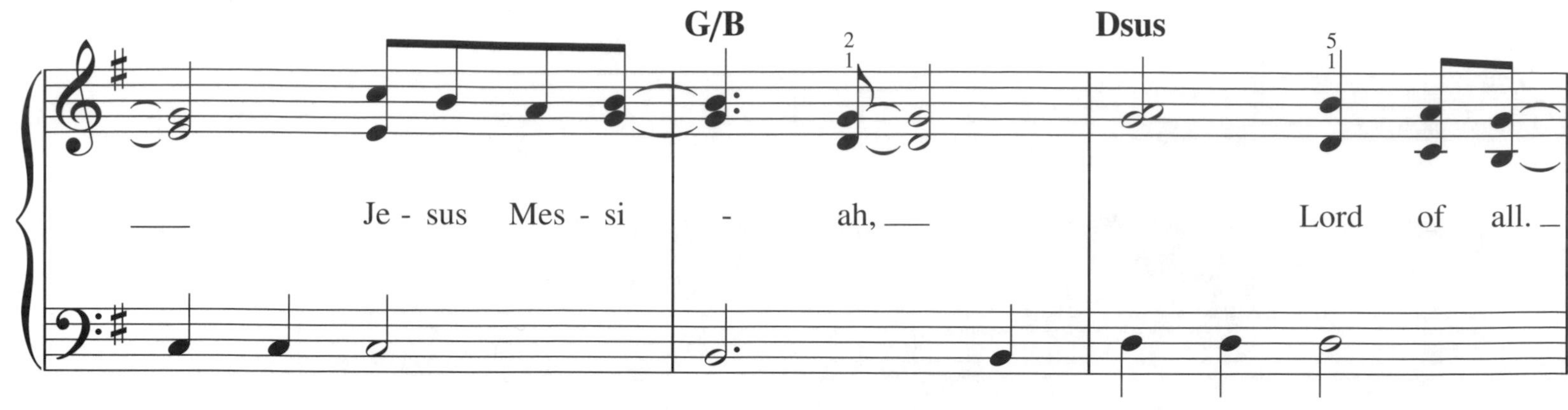
G/B
Dsus
Je - sus Mes - si - ah,
Lord of all.

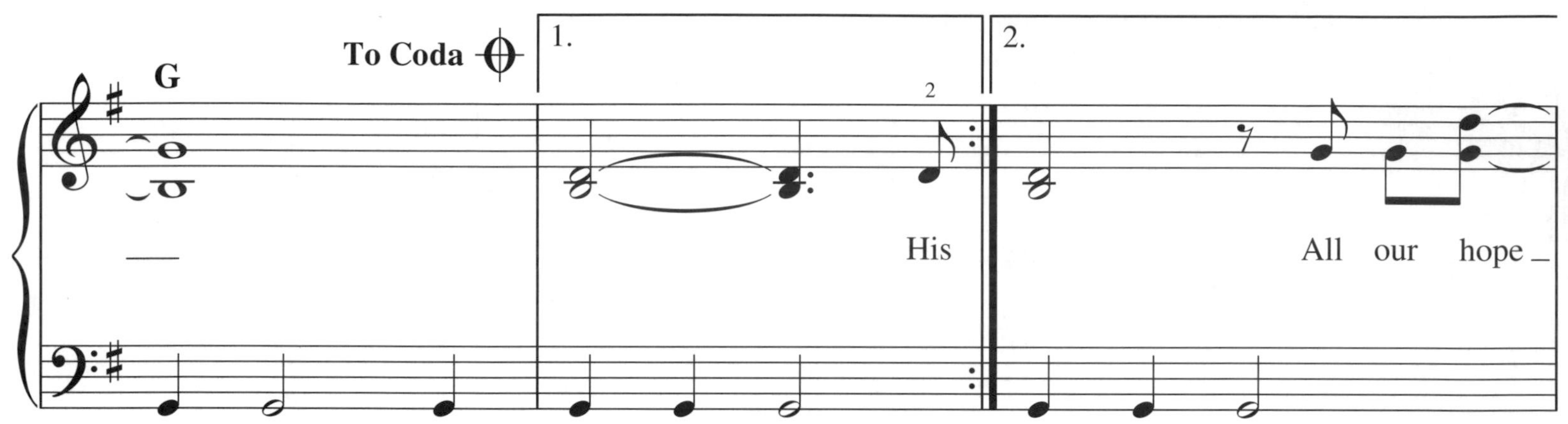
G
To Coda
1.
2.
His
All our hope

Am7
G/B
C
is in You,
all our hope
is in You.

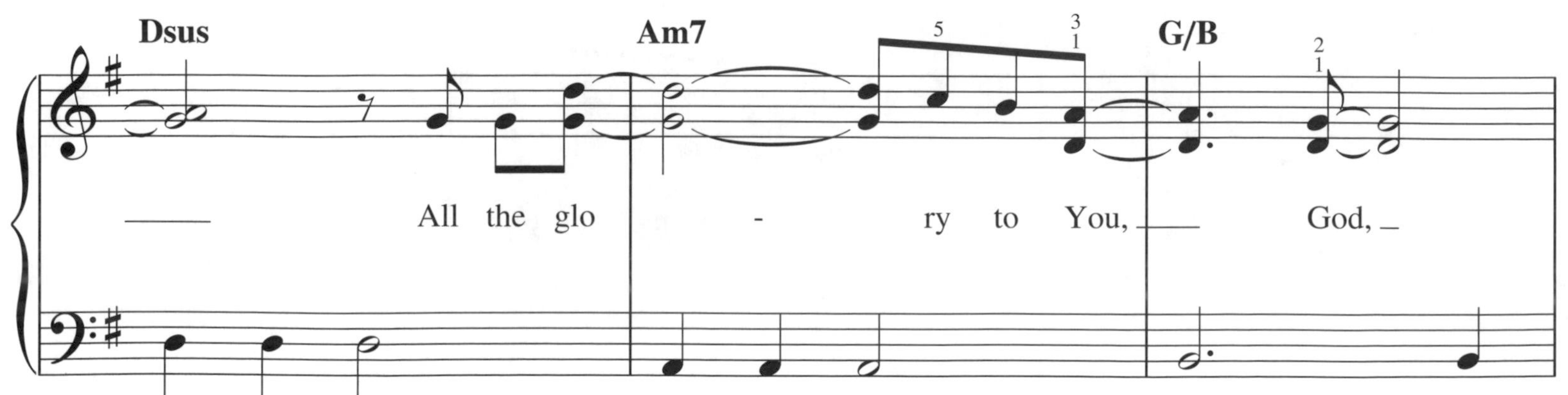
Dsus
Am7
G/B
All the glo - ry to You,
God,

C
Dsus
D
D.S. al Coda
3
the Light of the world.
Je - sus Mes - si -

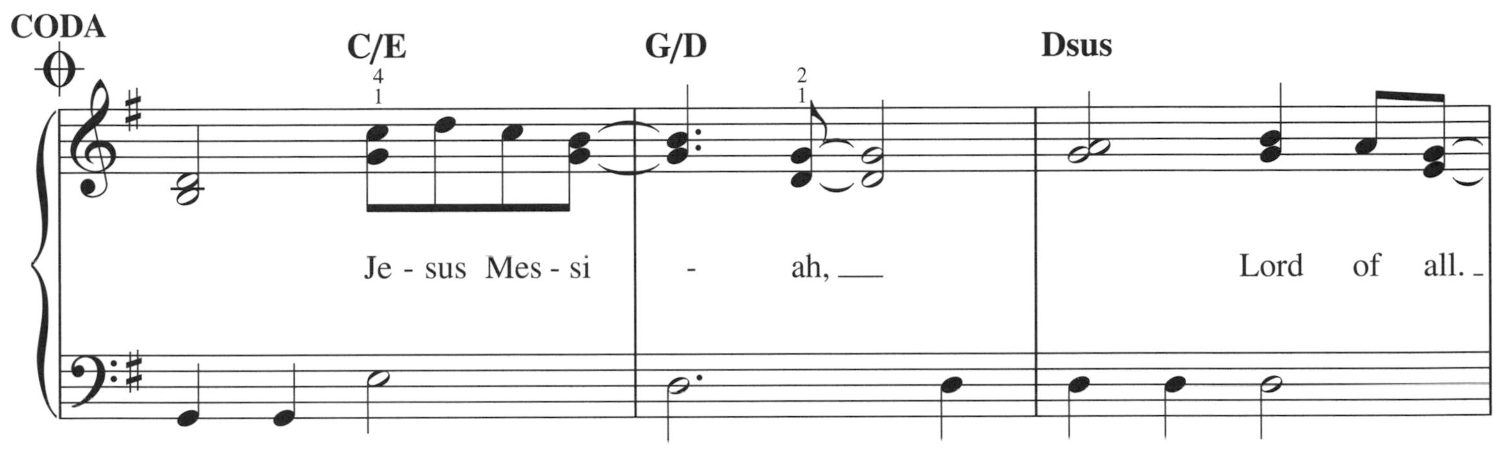
CODA
C/E
G/D
Dsus
Je - sus Mes - si - ah,
Lord of all.

C
3
You're the Lord of all,

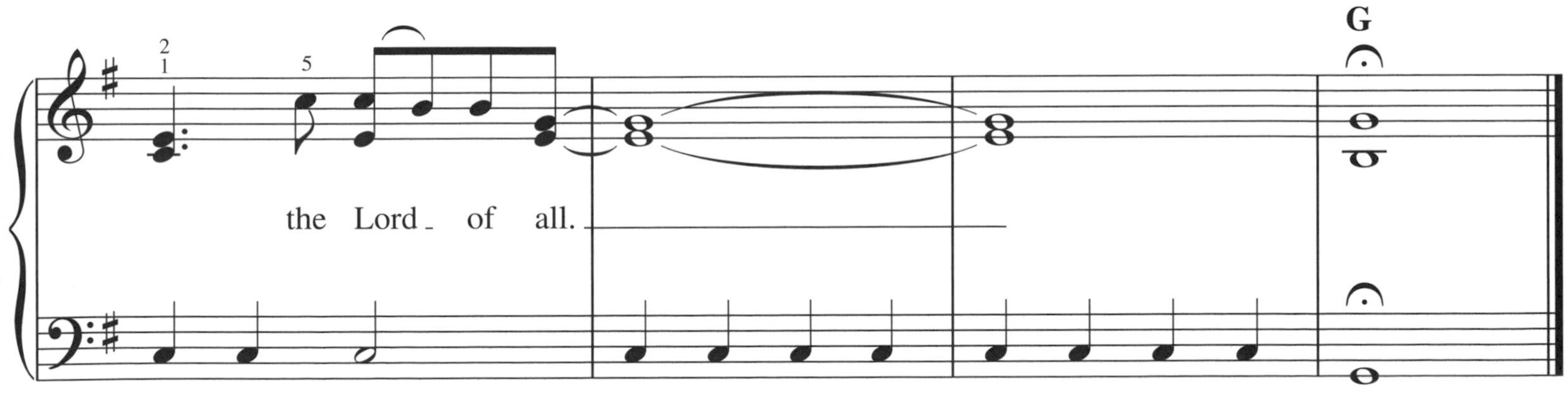
G
5
the Lord of all.

MIGHTY TO SAVE

Words and Music by BEN FIELDING
and REUBEN MORGAN

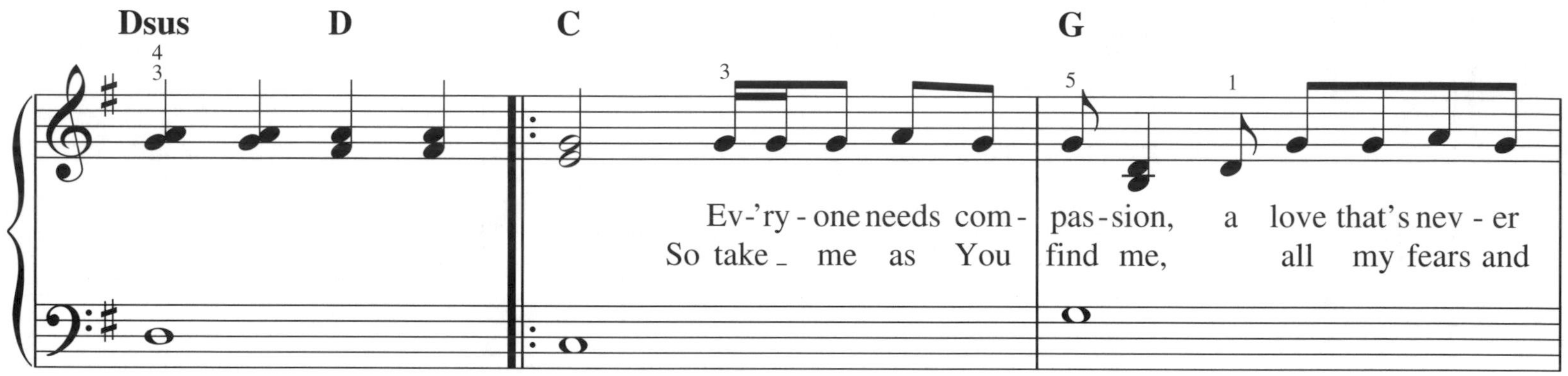

C
Dsus
C/E
D/F♯
G
Sav - ior, He can move the

D
C
G
Em
D
moun- tains. My God is
might-y to save, He is
might-y to save. For-

G
D
C
G
ev - er Au-thor of sal -
va - tion, He rose and
con-quered the grave, Je - sus

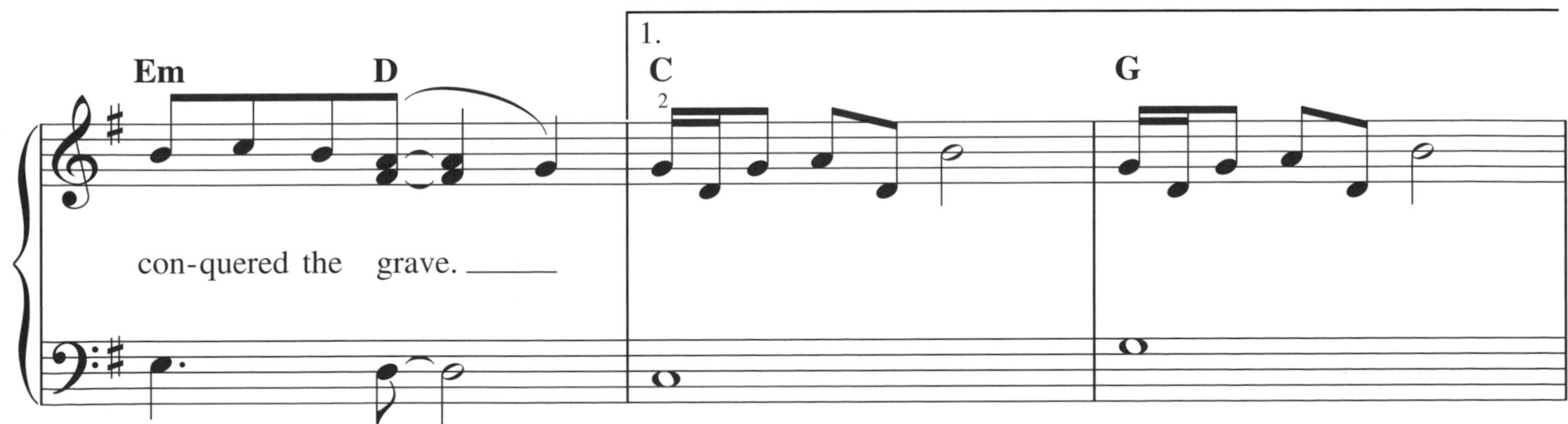
Em
D
1.
C
G
con-quered the grave.

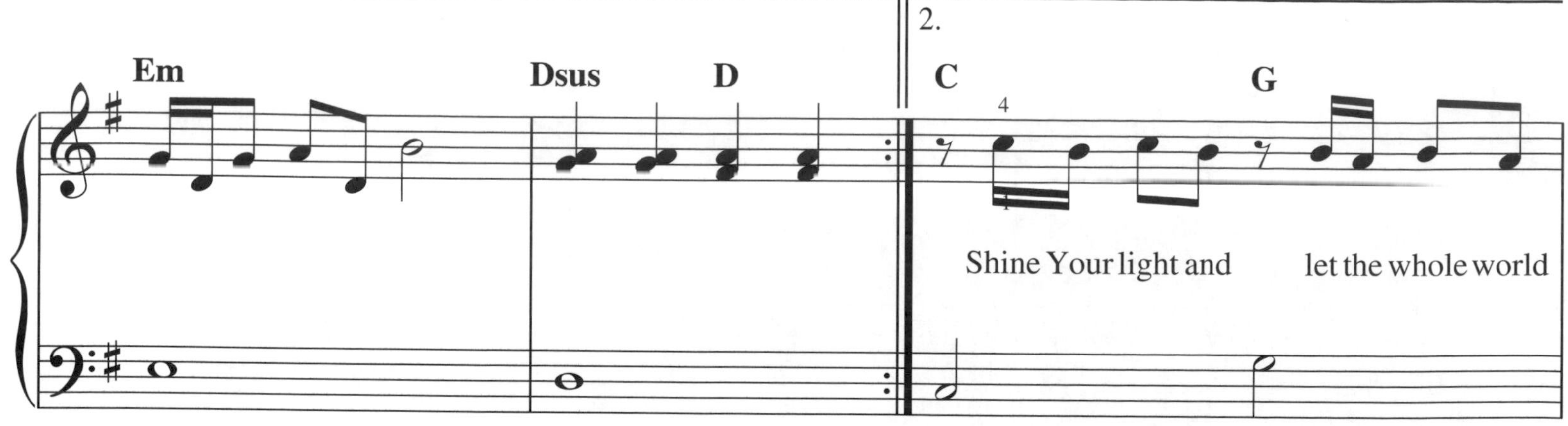
Em
Dsus
D
2.
C
G
Shine Your light and
let the whole world

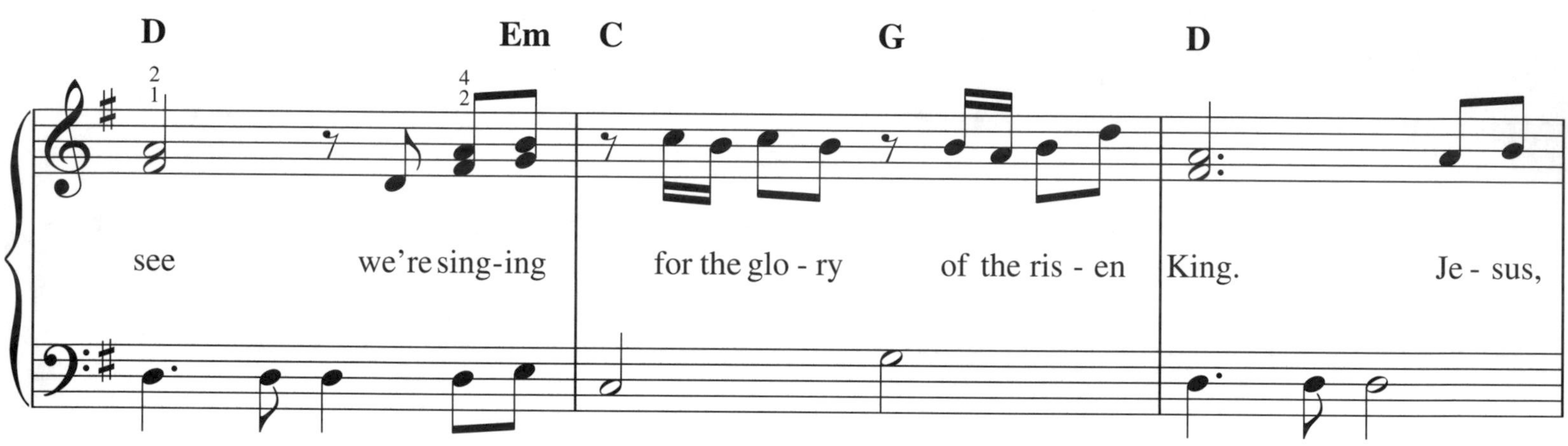
D
Em
C
G
D
see
we're sing-ing
for the glo - ry
of the ris - en
King.
Je - sus,

C
G
D
Em
shine Your light and
let the whole world
see
we're sing - ing

C
G
D
G
for the glo - ry
of the ris - en
King.
Sav - ior, He can move the
Sav - ior, You can move the

D
C
G
Em
D
moun- tains. My God is might-y to save, He is might-y to save. For-
moun- tains. God, You are might-y to save, You are might-y to save. For-

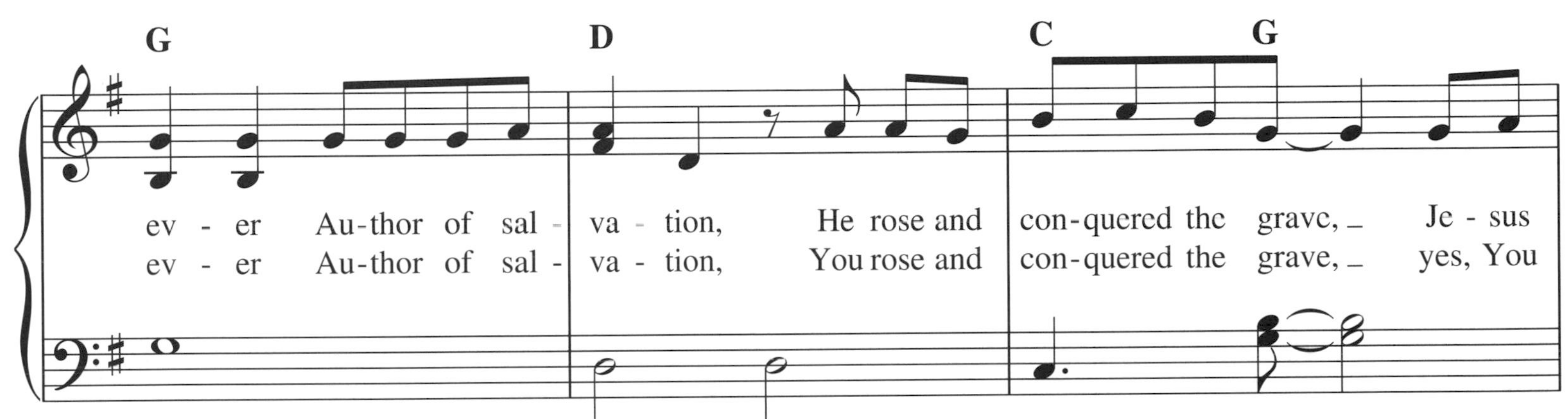
G
D
C
G
ev - er Au-thor of sal - va - tion, He rose and con-quered the grave, Je - sus
ev - er Au-thor of sal - va - tion, You rose and con-quered the grave, yes, You

1.
2.
Em
D
Em
D
C
con-quered the grave. You're my
con-quered the grave.

G
C
G/D
D7
G
You are might - y to save.
rit.

A NEW HALLELUJAH

Words and Music by PAUL BALOCHE,
MICHAEL W. SMITH and DEBBIE SMITH

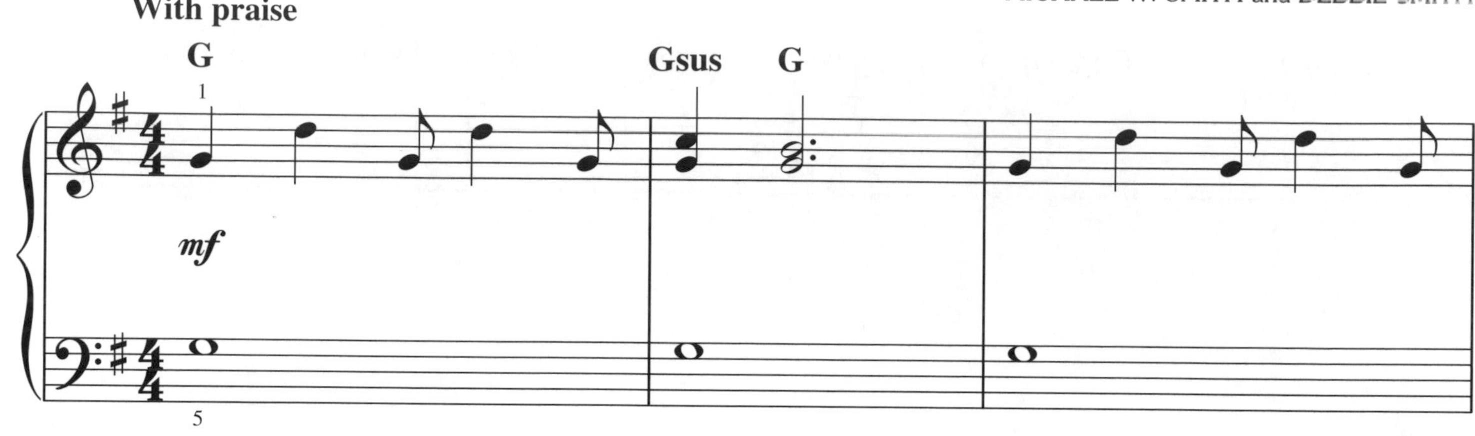

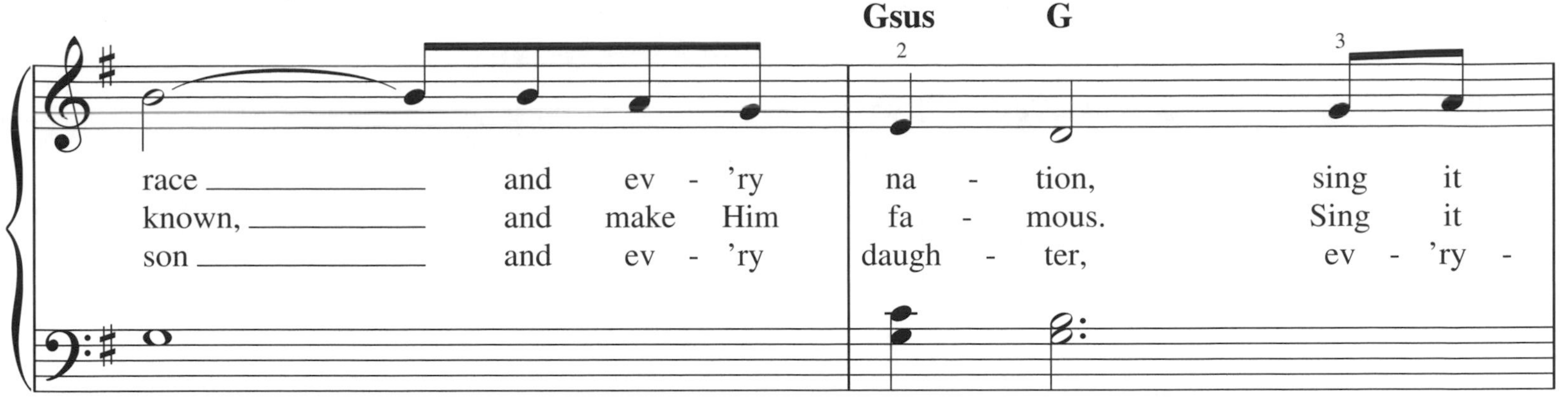
Gsus G
race and ev - 'ry na - tion, sing it
known, and make Him fa - mous. Sing it
son and ev - 'ry daugh - ter, ev - 'ry -

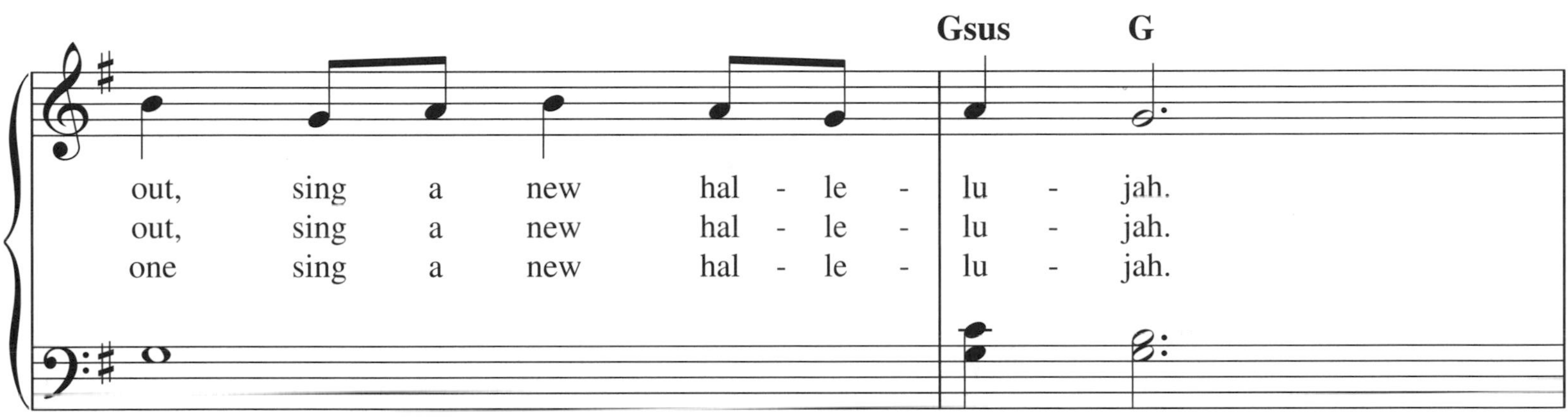
Gsus G
out, sing a new hal - le - lu - jah.
out, sing a new hal - le - lu - jah.
one sing a new hal - le - lu - jah.

1.
Gsus G
Let us
2., 3.
Gsus G

Gsus G
C
A - rise,

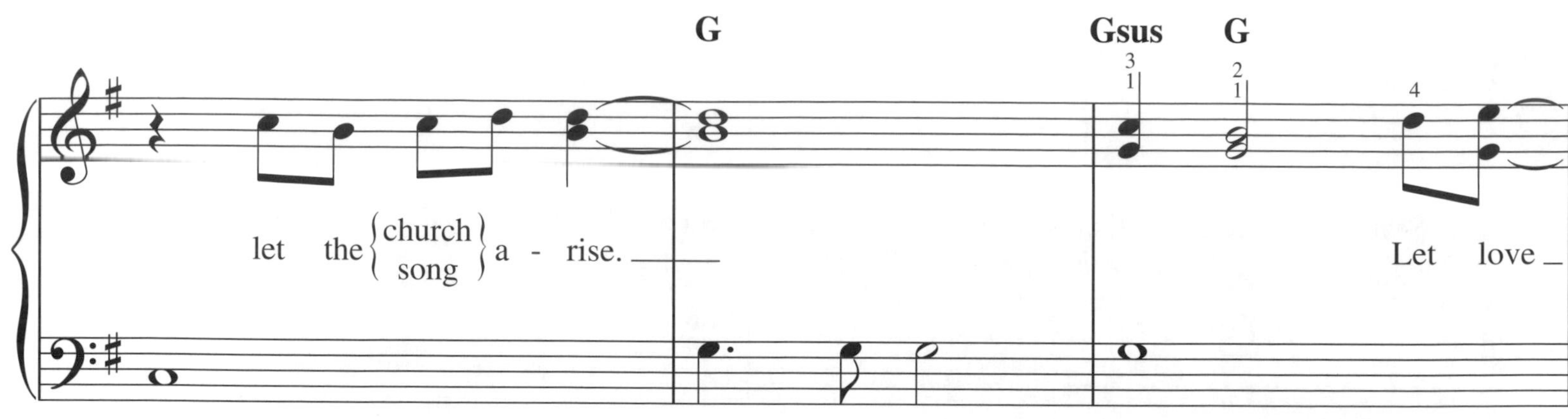
G
Gsus G
3
1
2
1
4
let the church song a - rise.
Let love

C
G
reach to the oth - er side.

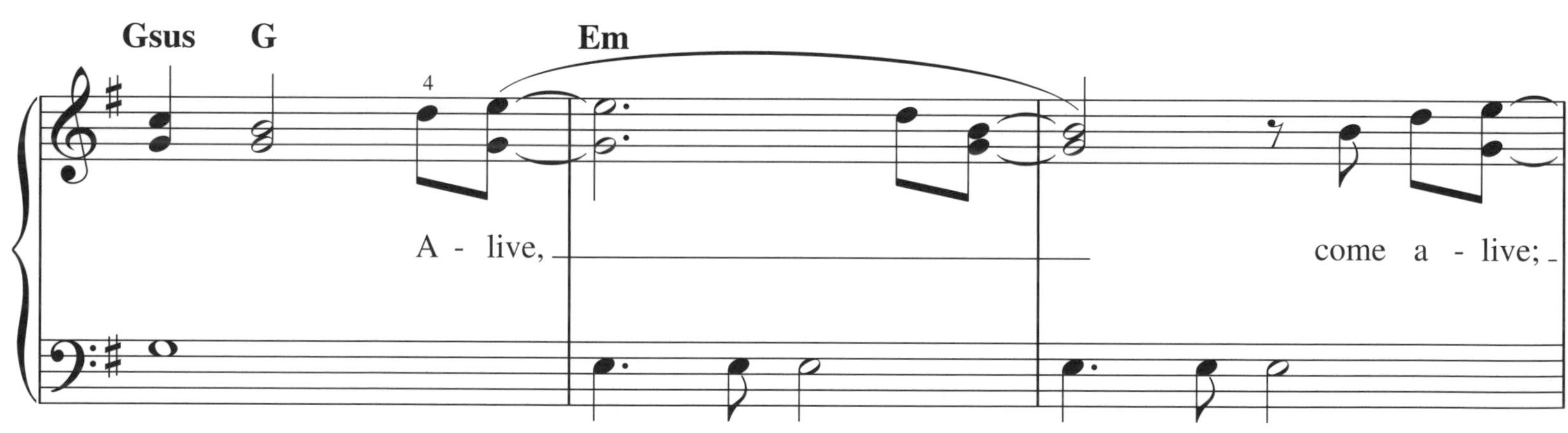
Gsus G
Em
4
A - live,
come a - live;

C
G
5
let the song a - rise.

To Coda
D.S. al Coda
(take 2nd ending)
Gsus
G
Gsus
G
Af - ri -

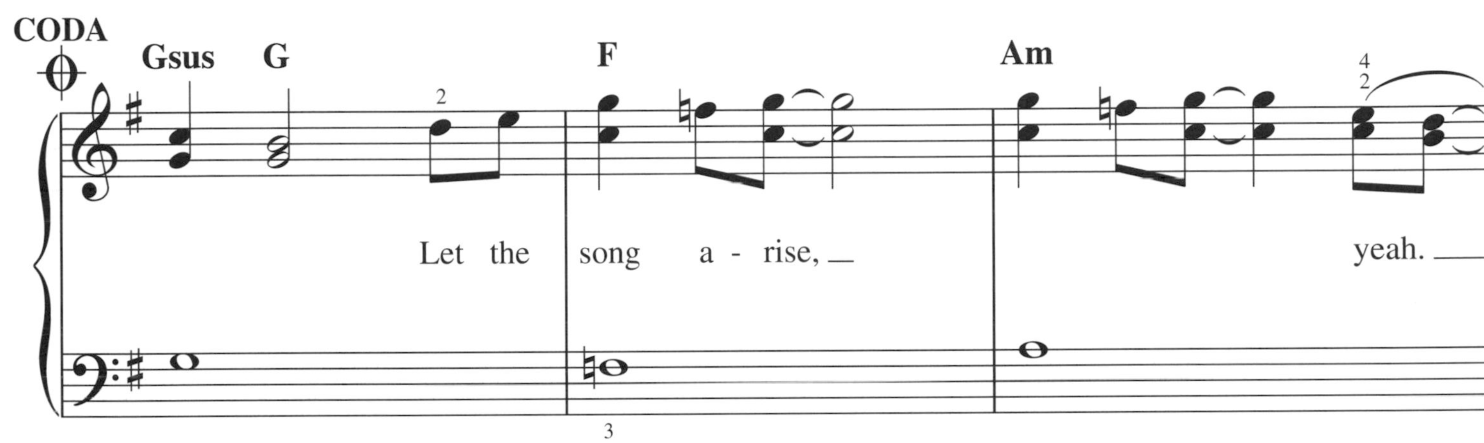
CODA
Gsus
G
F
Am
Let the song a - rise,
yeah.

G
F
Let the song a - rise.

Am
G
Gsus
G

Gsus G C
A - rise,

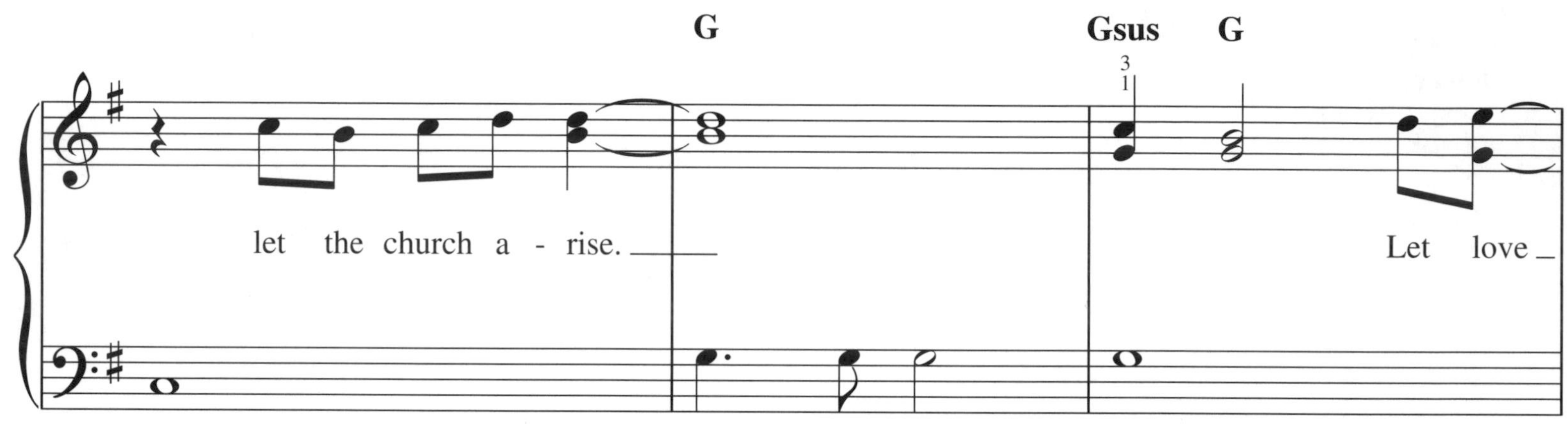
G Gsus G
let the church a - rise.
Let love

C G
reach to the oth - er side.

Gsus G Em
A - live,
come a - live;

C
G
let the song a - rise.

Gsus G
Gsus G
Ev - 'ry -
5

Gsus G
one sing a new hal - le - lu - jah. Ev - 'ry -

Gsus G
one sing a new hal - le - lu - jah.

SLOW FADE

Words and Music by
MARK HALL

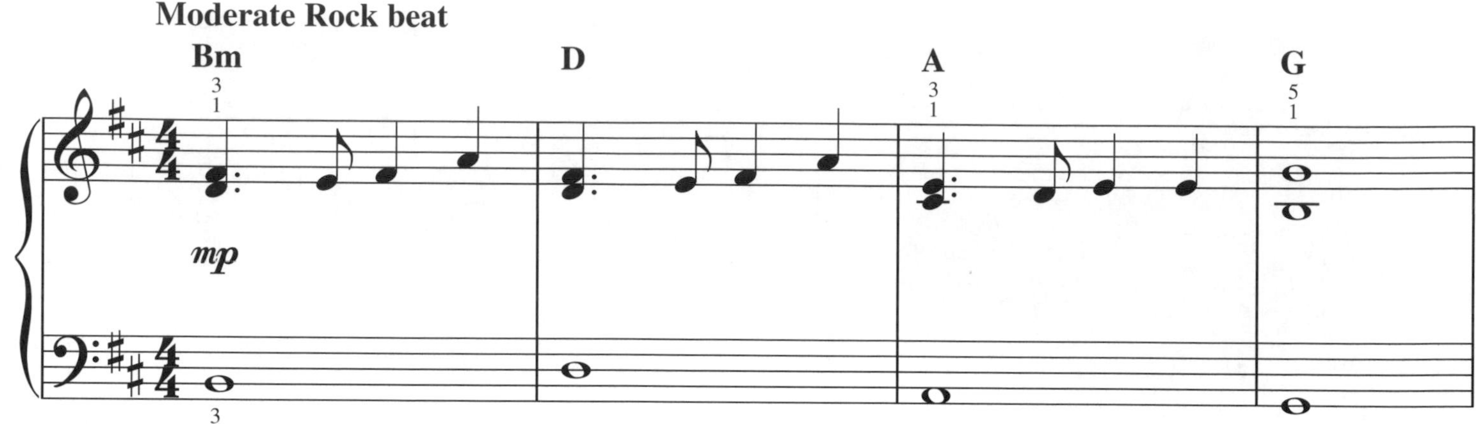

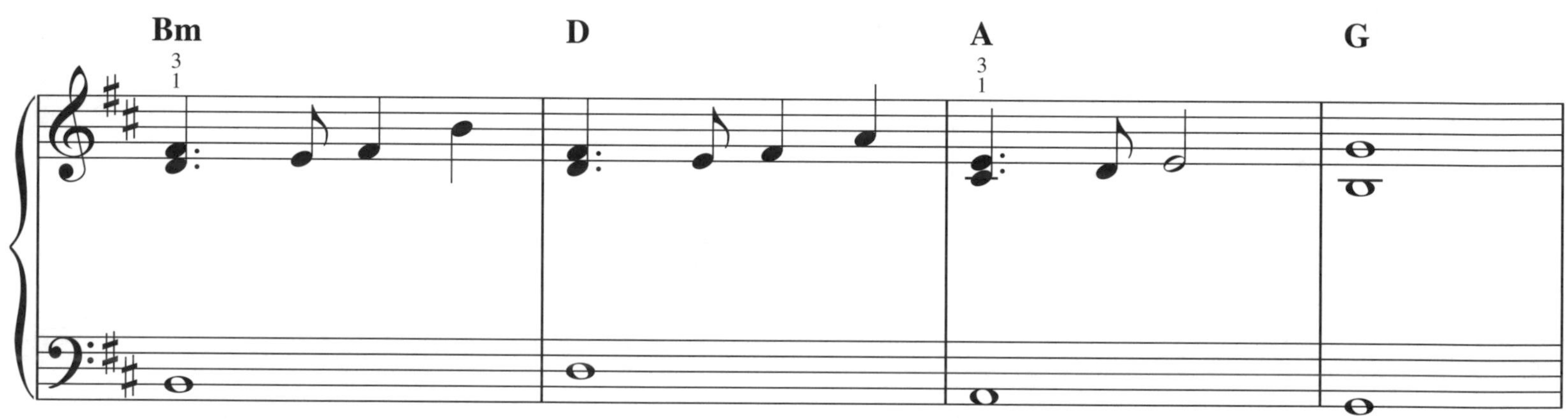

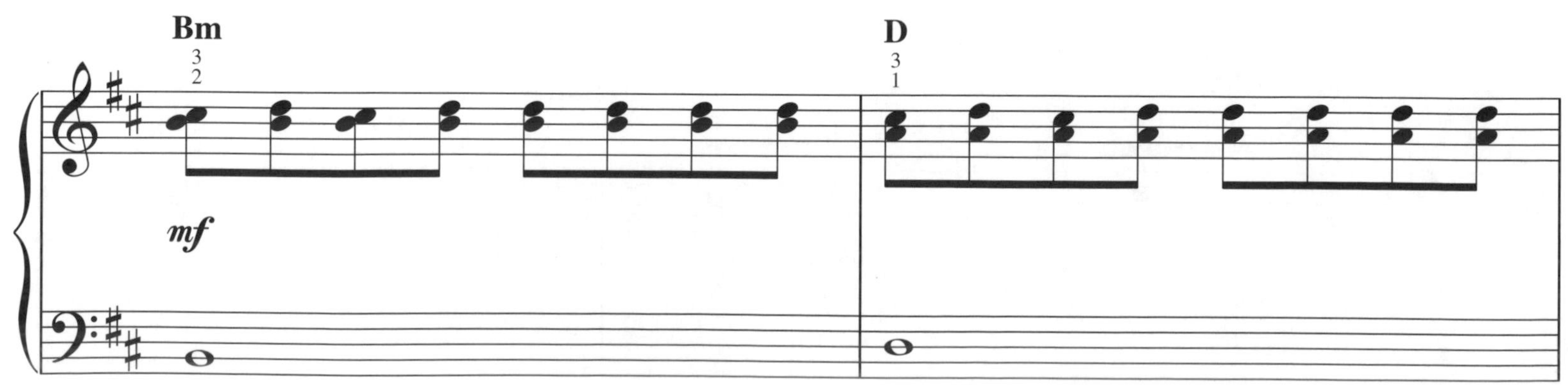

Asus
G
Be

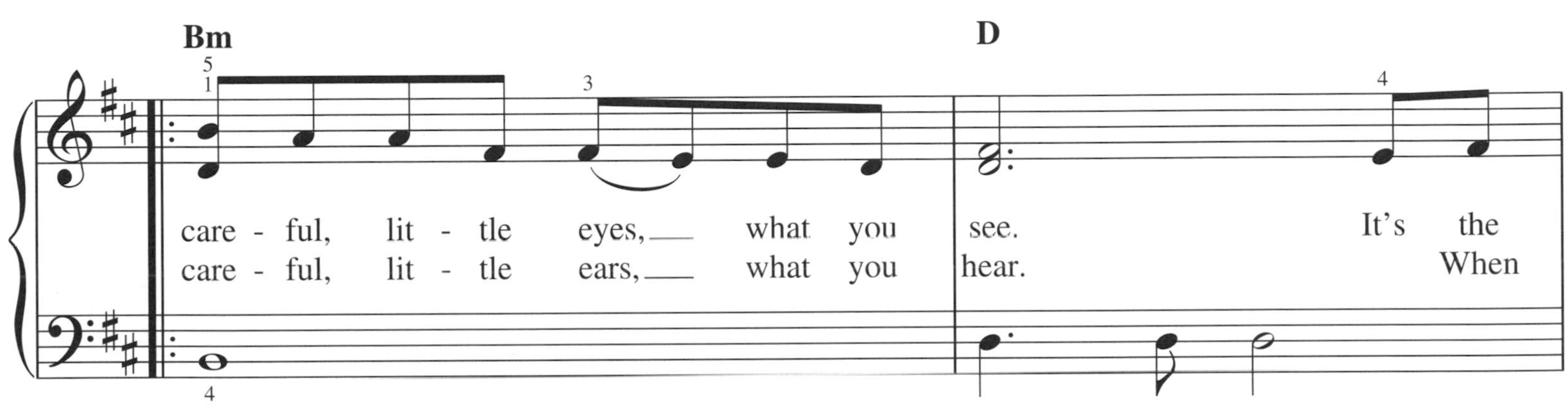
Bm
D
care - ful, lit - tle eyes, what you see. It's the
care - ful, lit - tle ears, what you hear. When

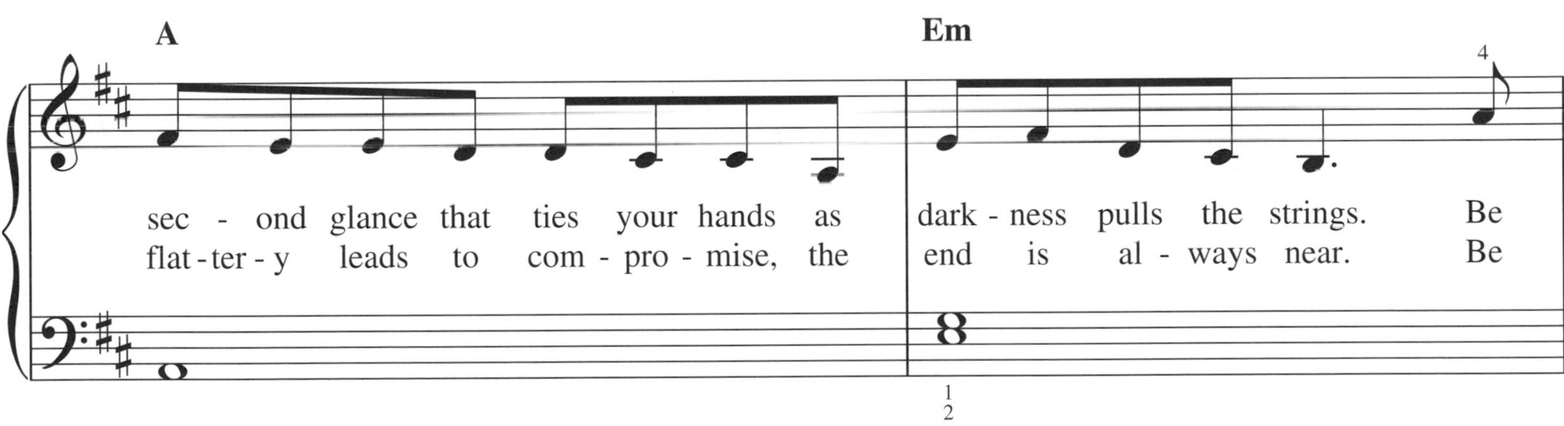
A
Em
sec - ond glance that ties your hands as dark - ness pulls the strings. Be
flat - ter - y leads to com - pro - mise, the end is al - ways near. Be

Bm
D
care - ful, lit - tle feet, where you go, for it's the
care - ful, lit - tle lips, what you say, for

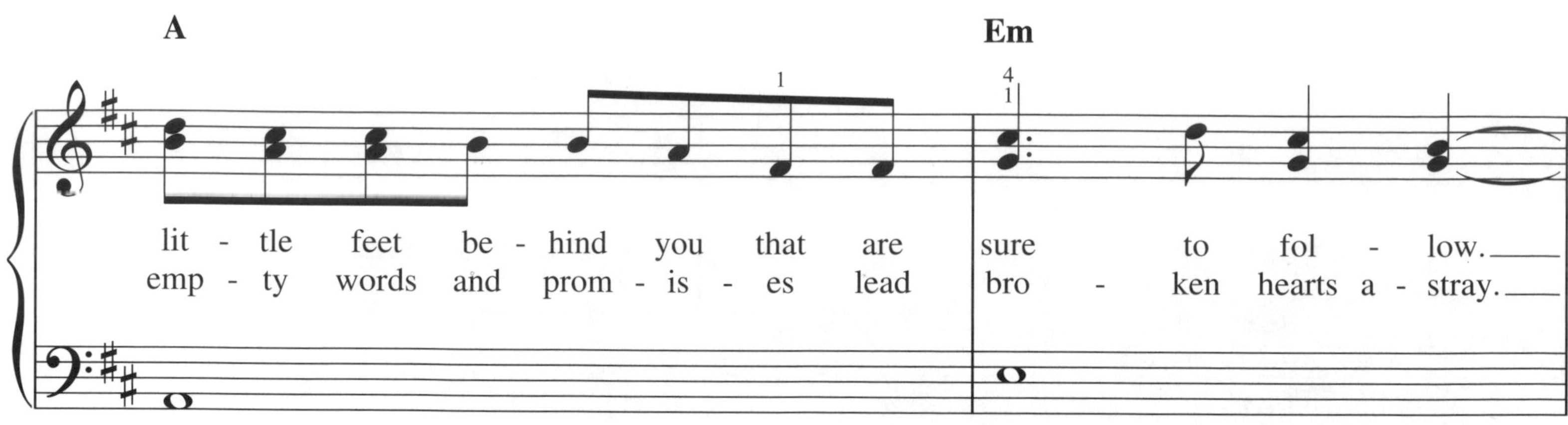
A
Em
lit - tle feet be - hind you that are sure to fol - low.
emp - ty words and prom - is - es lead bro - ken hearts a - stray.

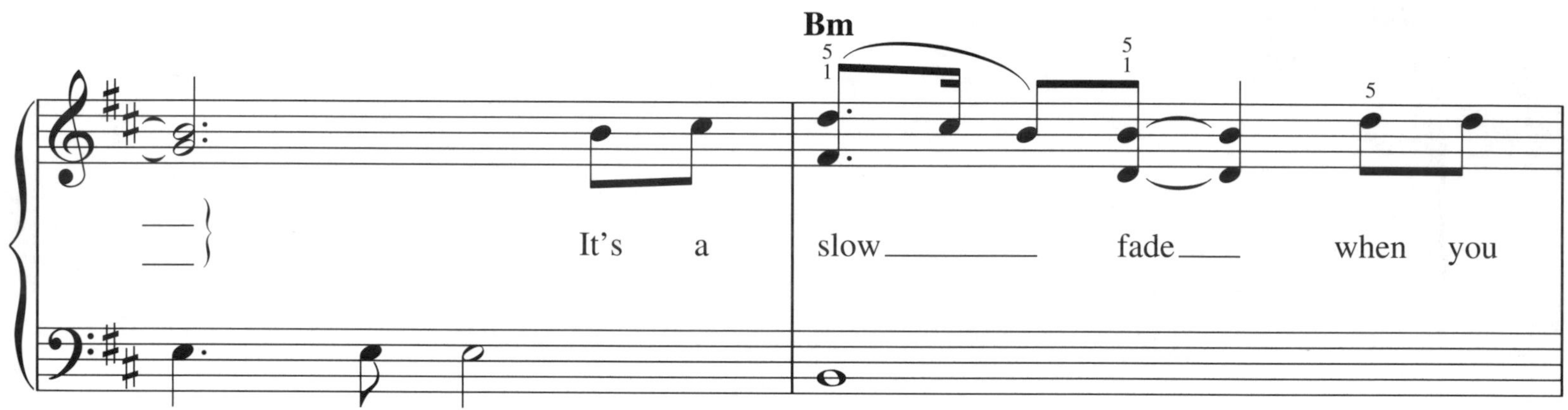
Bm
It's a slow fade when you

A
Em
give your - self a - way. It's a slow fade when

G
Bm
black and white have turned to gray, and thoughts in - vade,

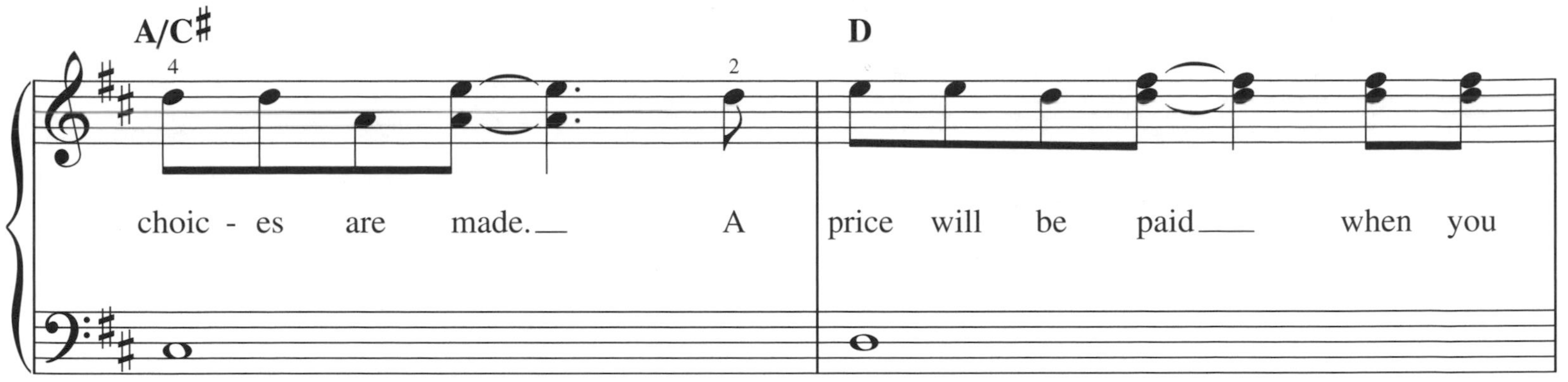
A/C♯
D
choic - es are made. A price will be paid when you

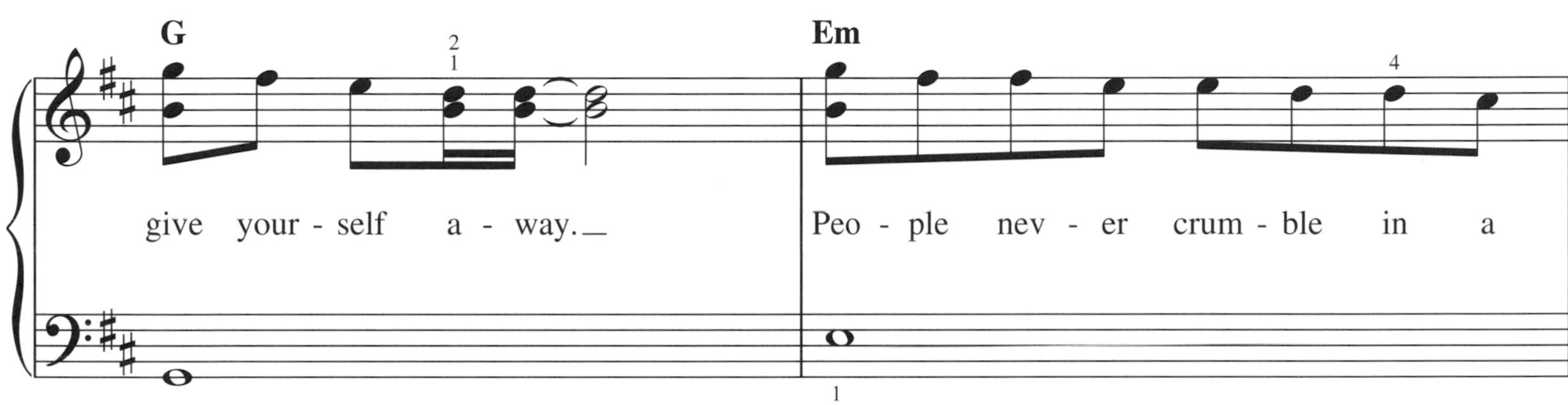
G
Em
give your - self a - way. Peo - ple nev - er crum - ble in a

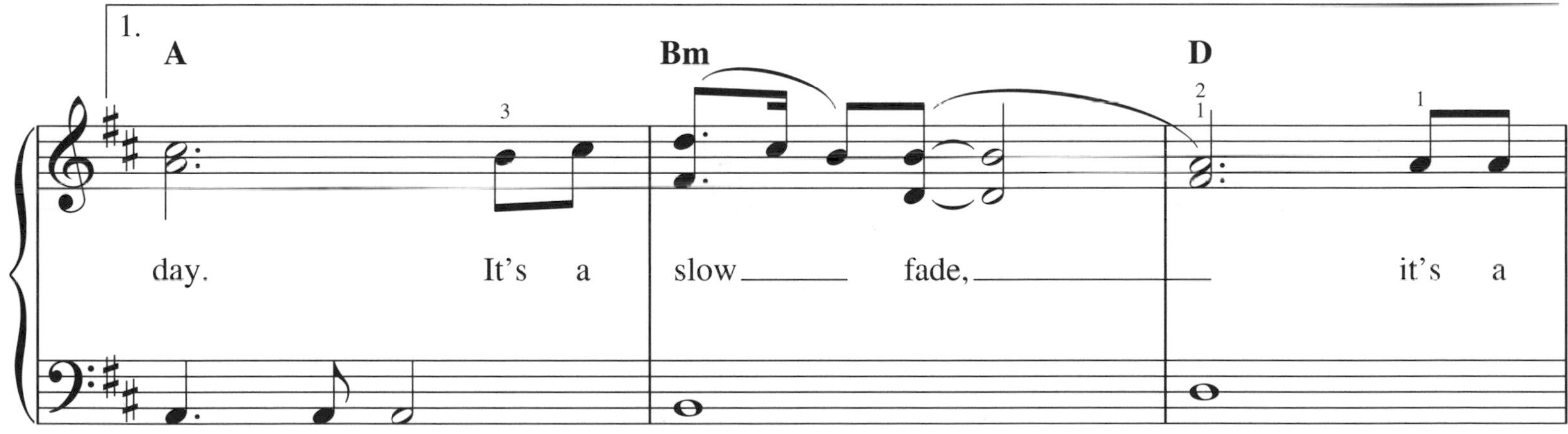
1.
A
Bm
D
day. It's a slow fade, it's a

2.
A
G
A
slow fade. Be day. The

Em
G
2
1
jour - ney from your mind to your hands is short - er than you're
5

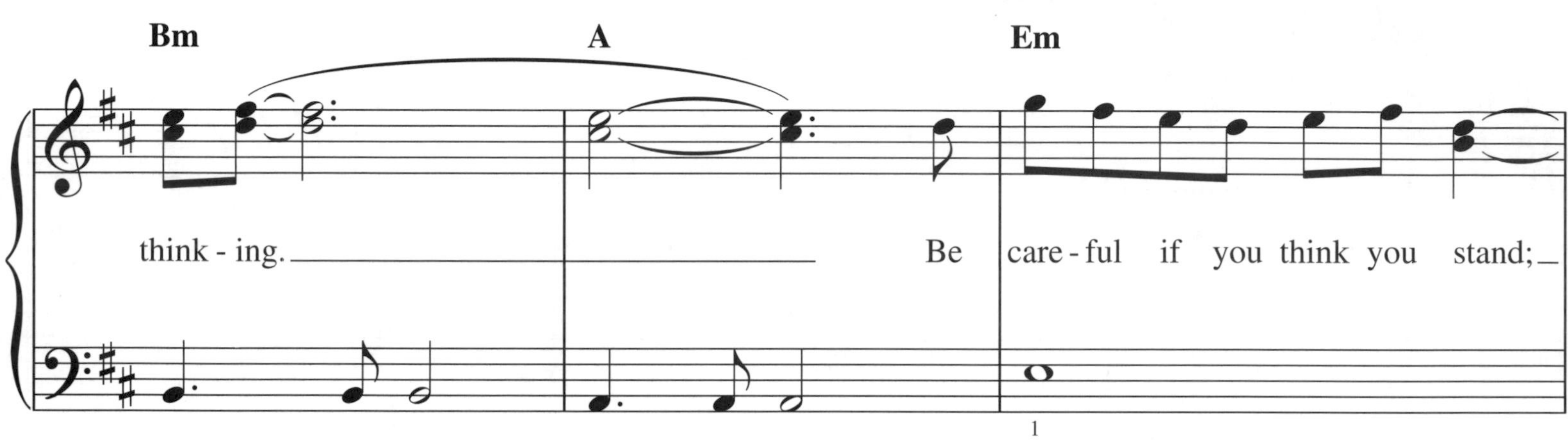
Bm
A
Em
think - ing.
Be
care - ful if you think you stand;
1

G
D
G
you just might be sink - ing.
5

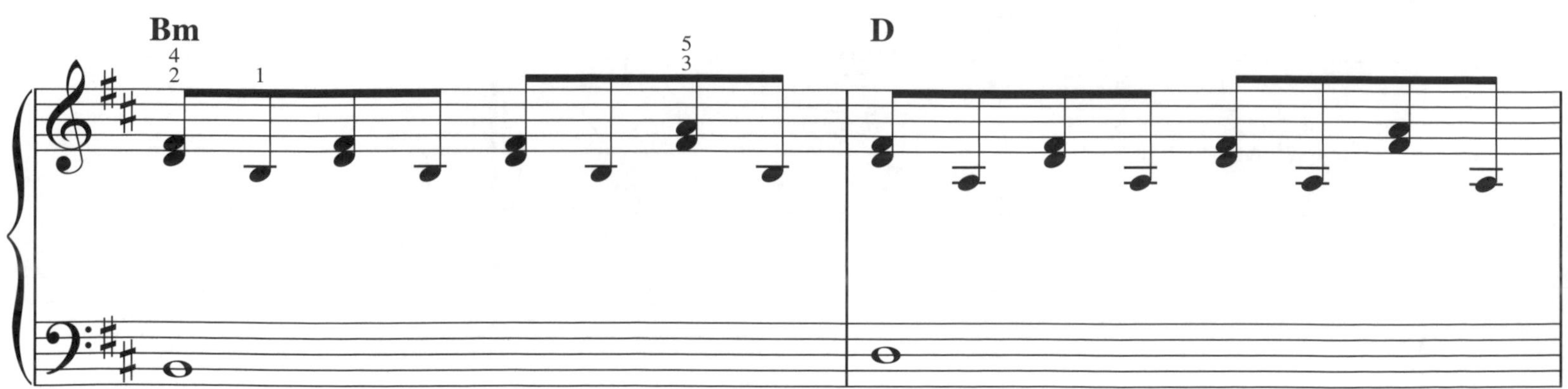
Bm
4
2
1
5
3
D

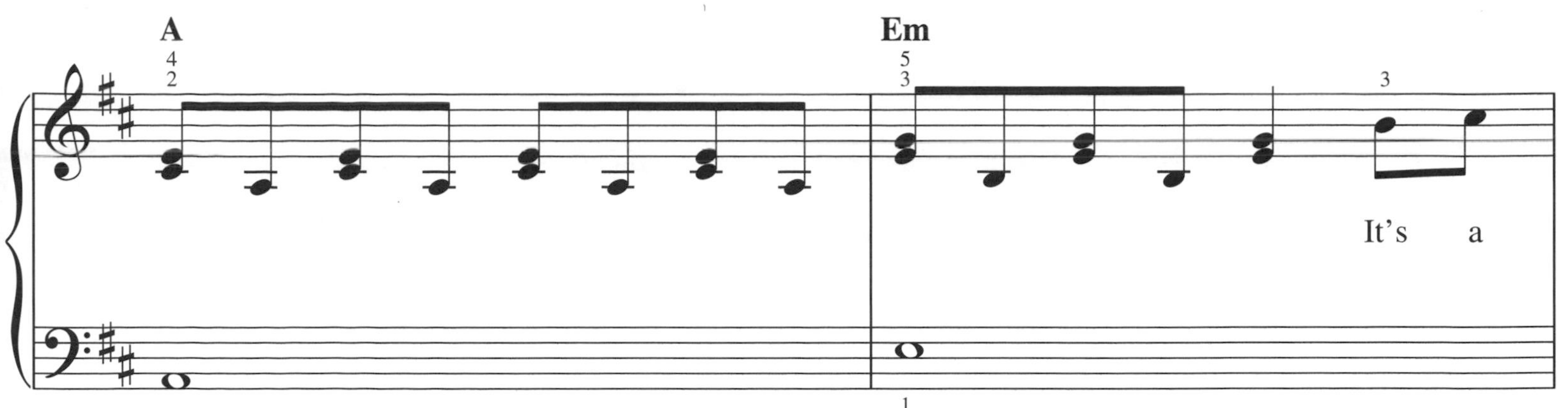
A
Em
It's a

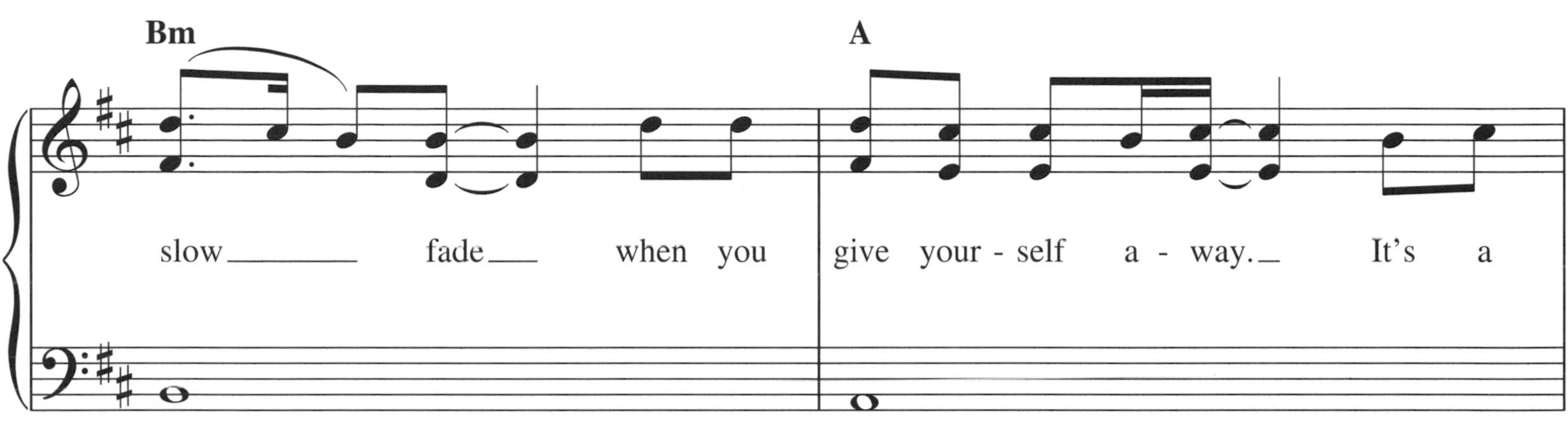
Bm
A
slow fade when you give your - self a - way. It's a

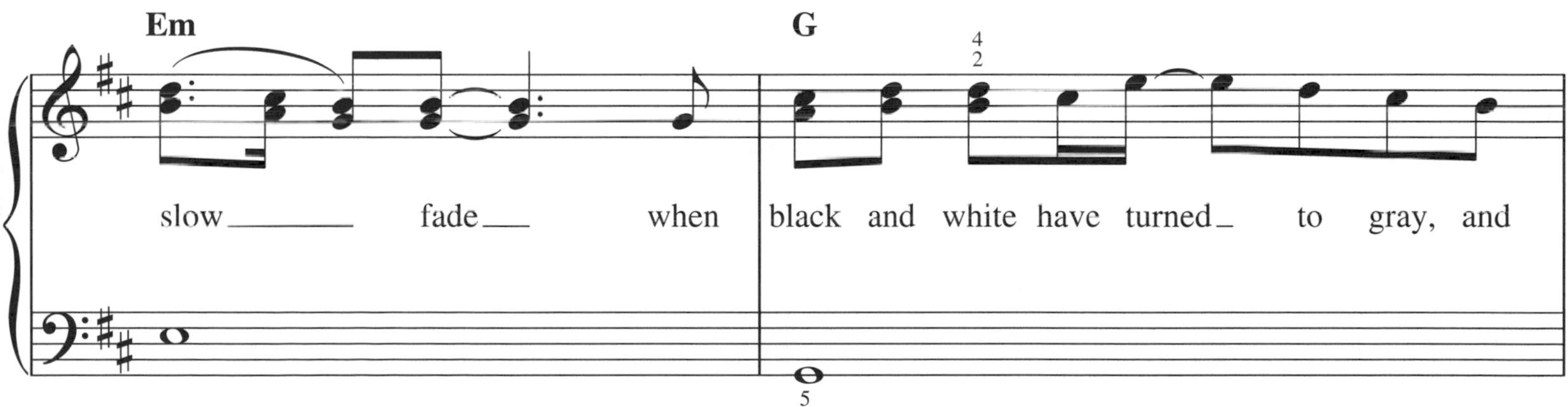
Em
G
slow fade when black and white have turned to gray, and

Bm
A/C♯
thoughts in - vade, choic - es are made. A

D
G
price will be paid___ when you
give your - self a - way.___

Em
A
Peo - ple nev - er crum - ble in a
day,

Em
A
dad - dies nev - er crum - ble in a
day,

Em
G
fam - 'lies nev - er crum - ble in a
day. Child: Oh, be
mp

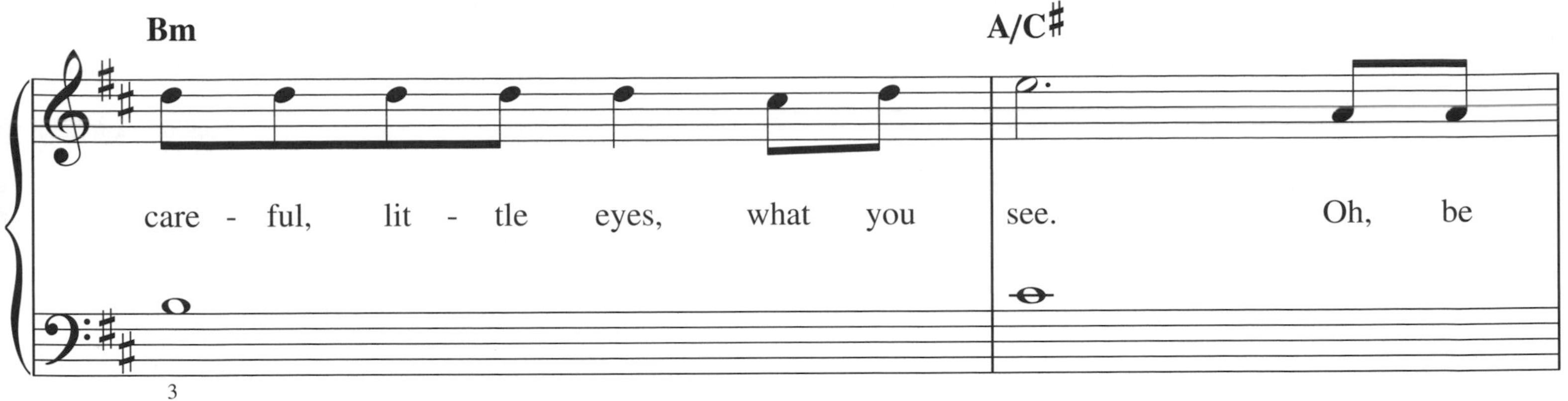
Bm
A/C♯
care - ful, lit - tle eyes, what you see. Oh, be
3

D(add2)
Gmaj7
3
care - ful, lit - tle eyes, what you see, for the

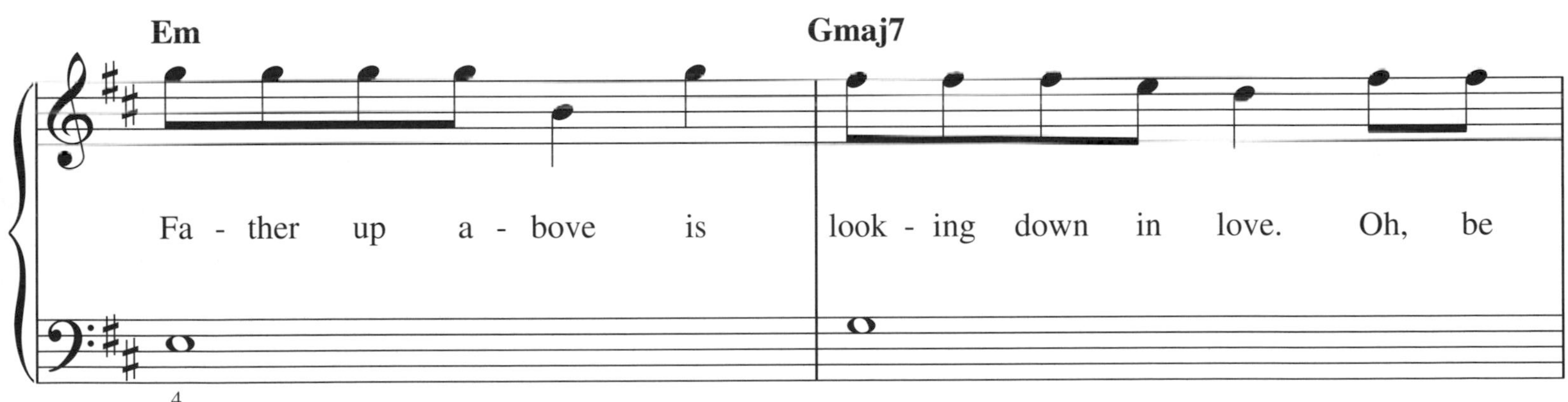
Em
Gmaj7
Fa - ther up a - bove is look - ing down in love. Oh, be
4

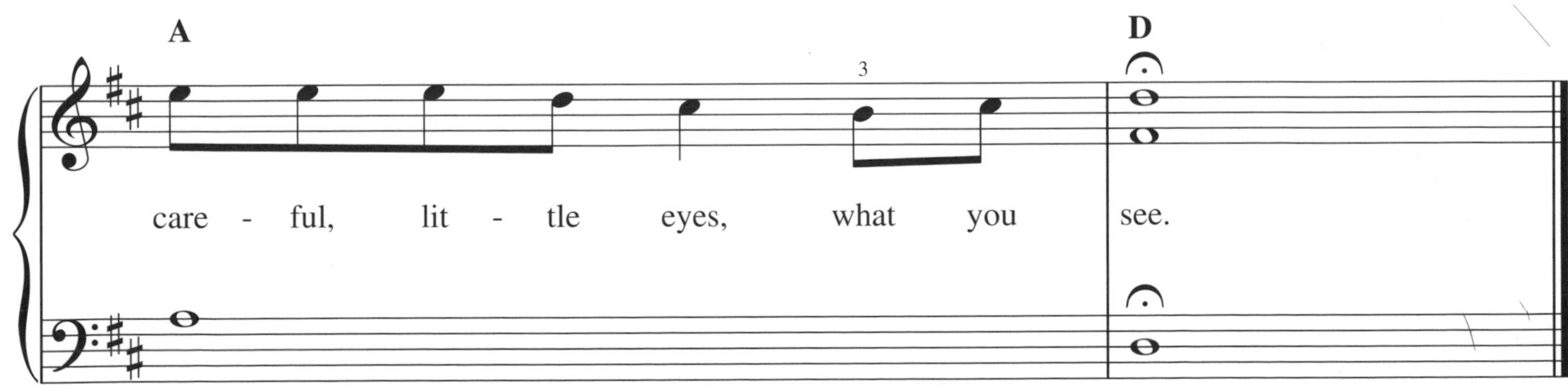
A
D
3
care - ful, lit - tle eyes, what you see.

SOUND OF YOUR NAME

Words and Music by
MICHAEL WATSON

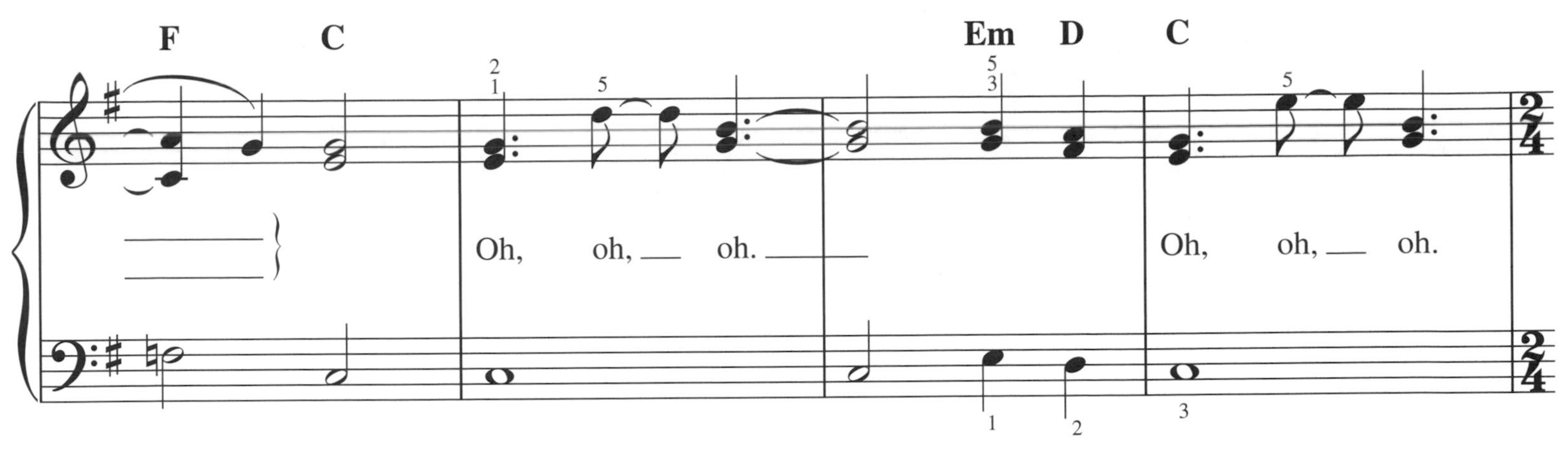
F C Em D C
Oh, oh, oh.
Oh, oh, oh.

Em D G D
Tow - ers fall and king - doms crum - ble, the

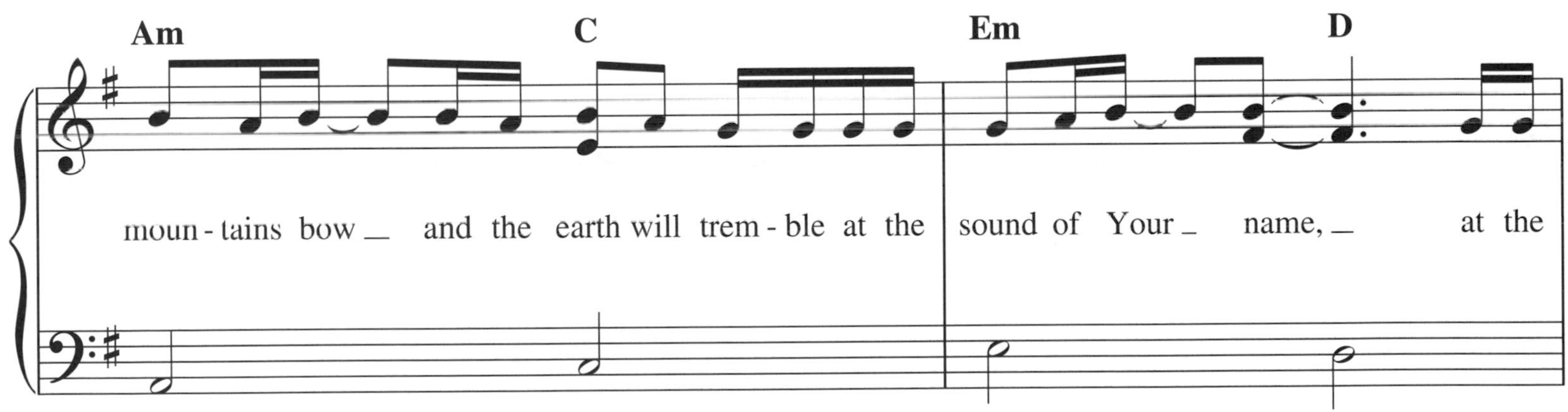
Am C Em D
moun - tains bow and the earth will trem - ble at the sound of Your name, at the

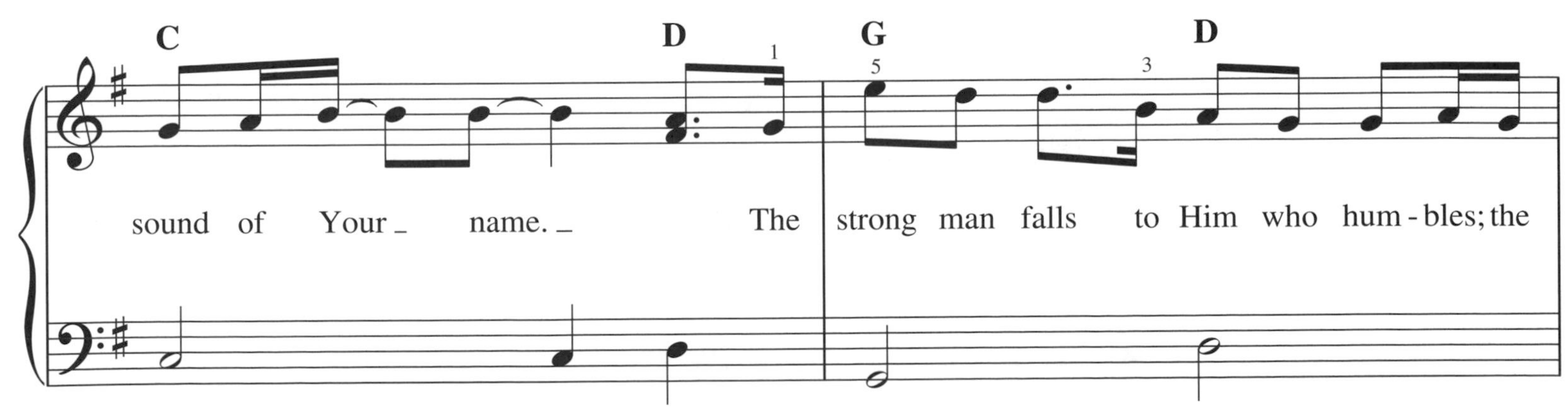
C D G D
sound of Your name. The strong man falls to Him who hum - bles; the

Am
C
1.
Em
D
plans he made were bound to stum - ble.
On - ly You re - main,
C
Em
D
C
on - ly You re - main.
Oh, oh, oh.
2.
C
Em
D
F
Am
On - ly You re - main.
So man can reach the
G
C
G/B
Dm
C
sky if he builds his own de - vice, but still he's far a - way from

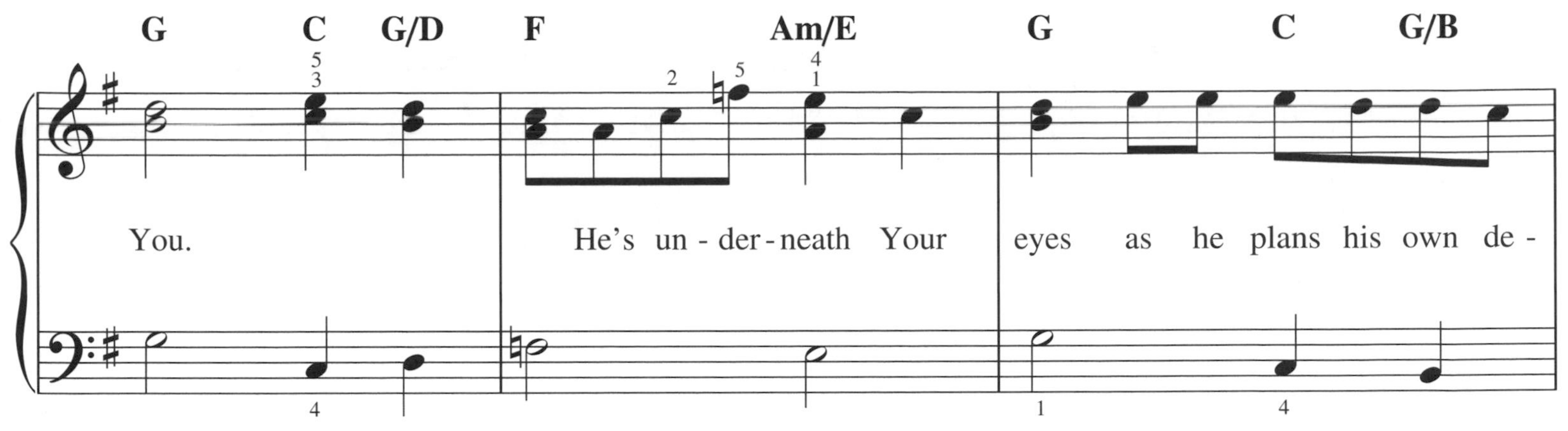
G C G/D F Am/E G C G/B
You. He's un - der - neath Your eyes as he plans his own de -

Dm C/E G Bm
mise. What's new to him is old to You. Oh, oh, oh.

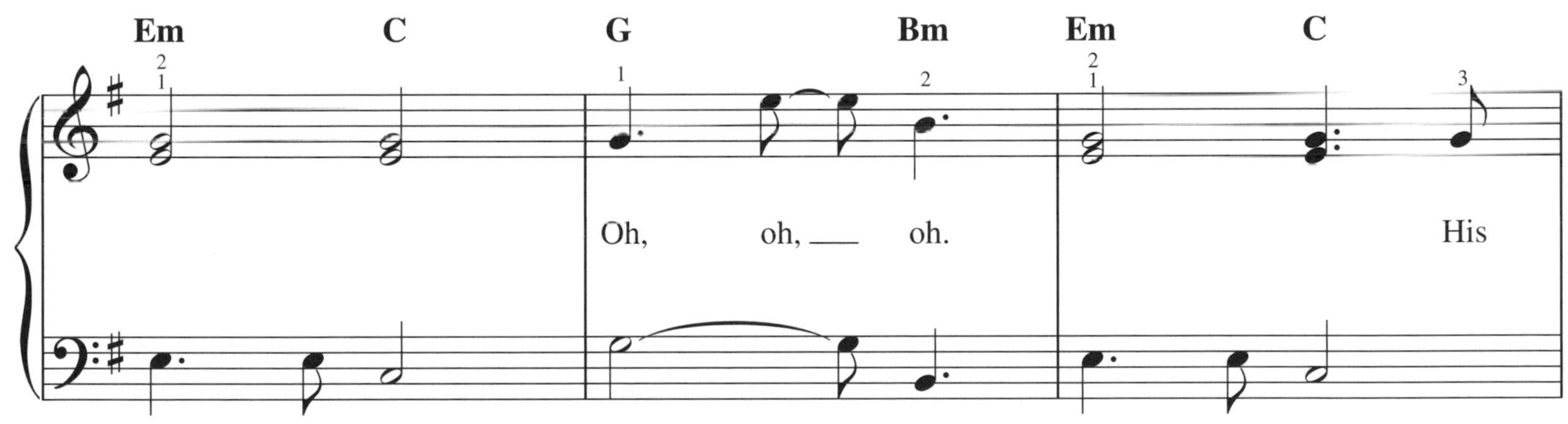
Em C G Bm Em C
Oh, oh, oh. His

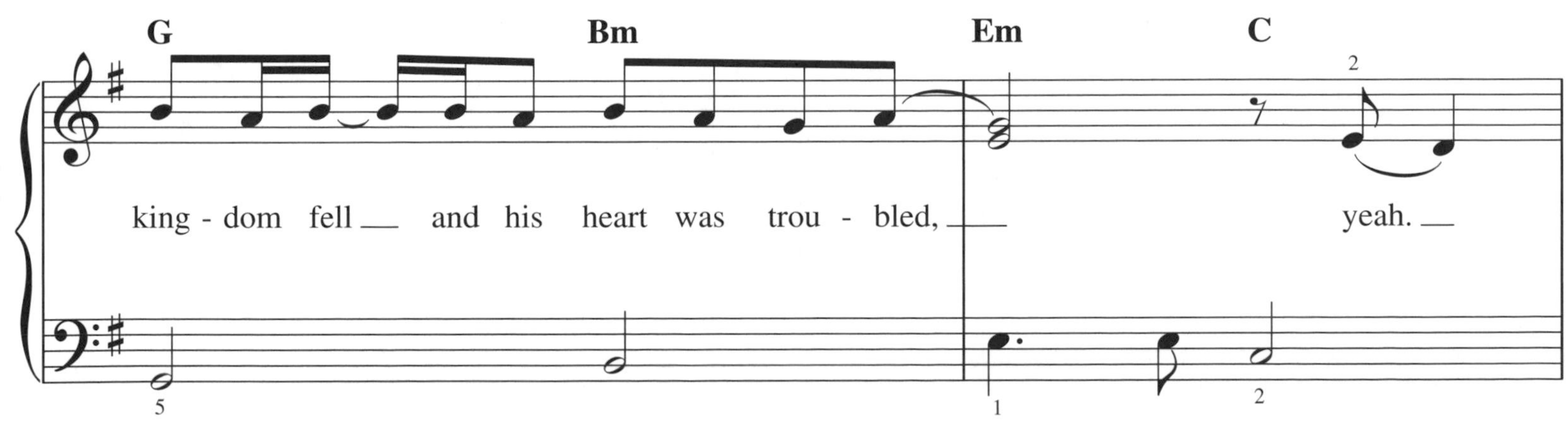
G Bm Em C
king - dom fell and his heart was trou - bled, yeah.

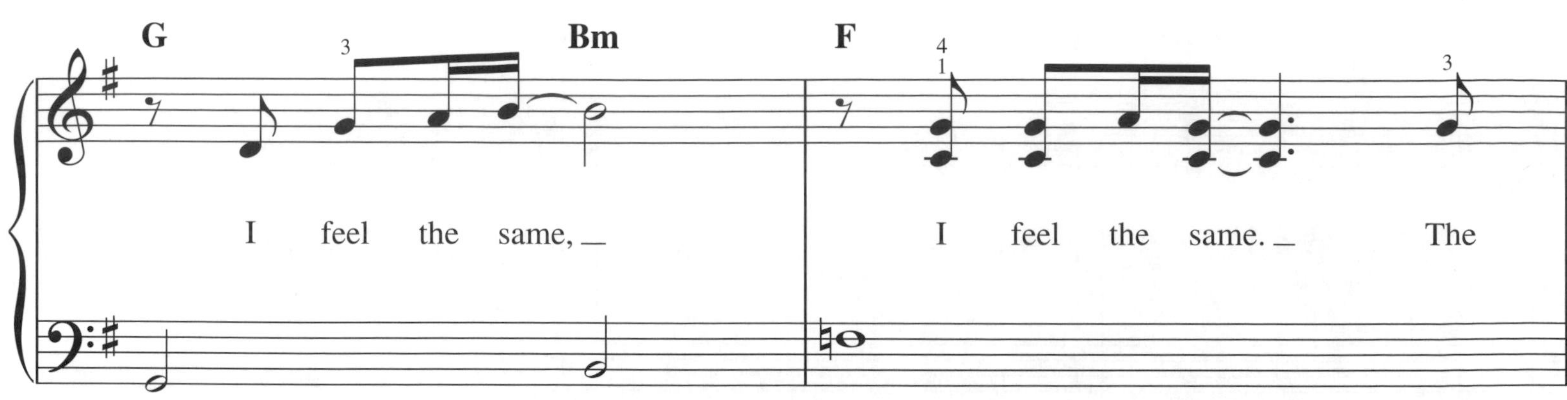
G
Bm
F
I feel the same,
I feel the same.
The

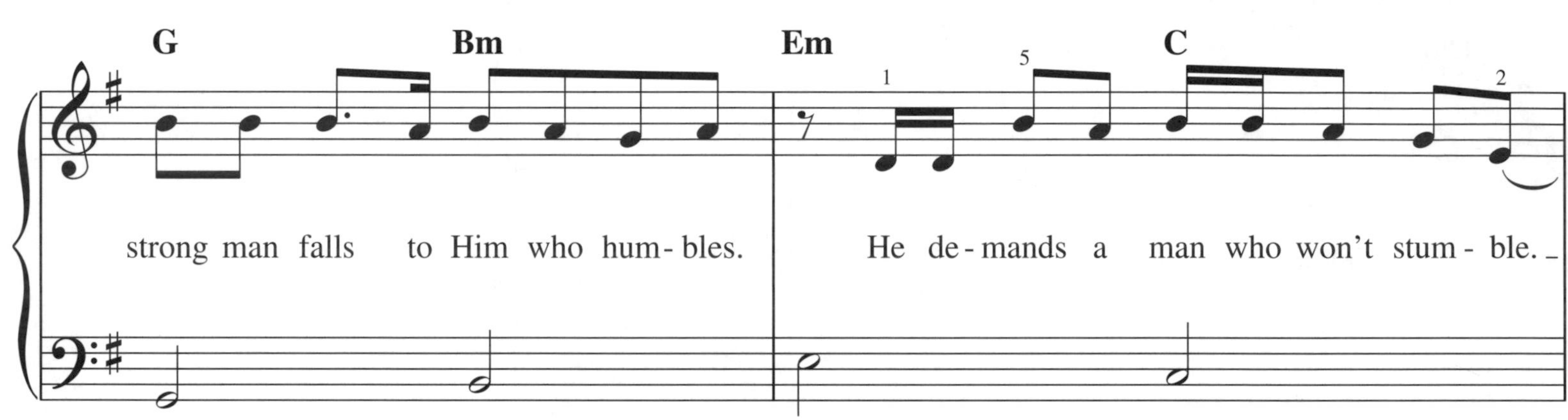
G
Bm
Em
C
strong man falls to Him who hum-bles.
He de-mands a man who won't stum-ble.

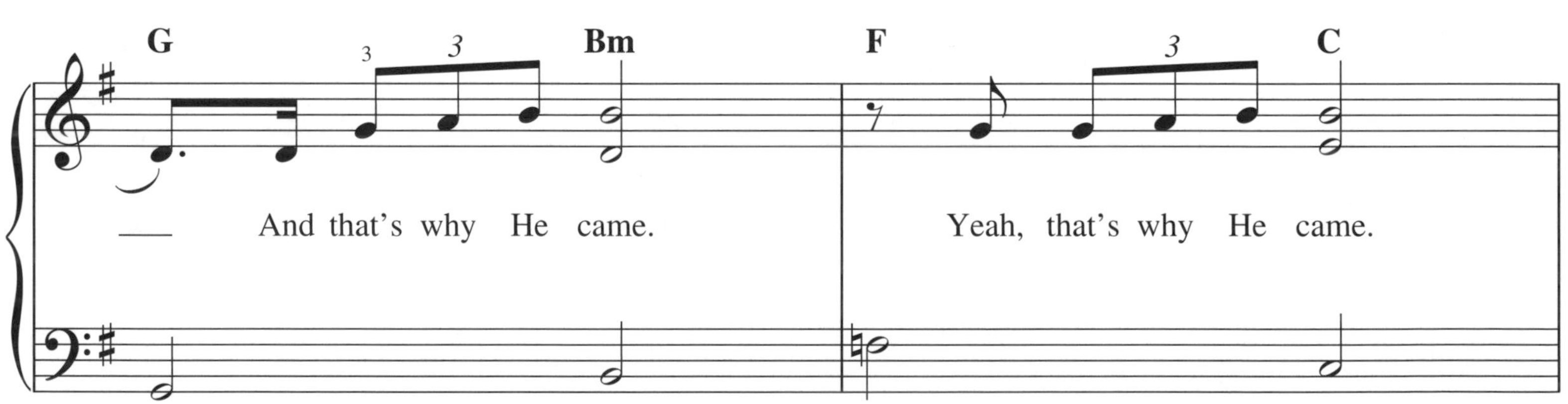
G
Bm
F
C
And that's why He came.
Yeah, that's why He came.

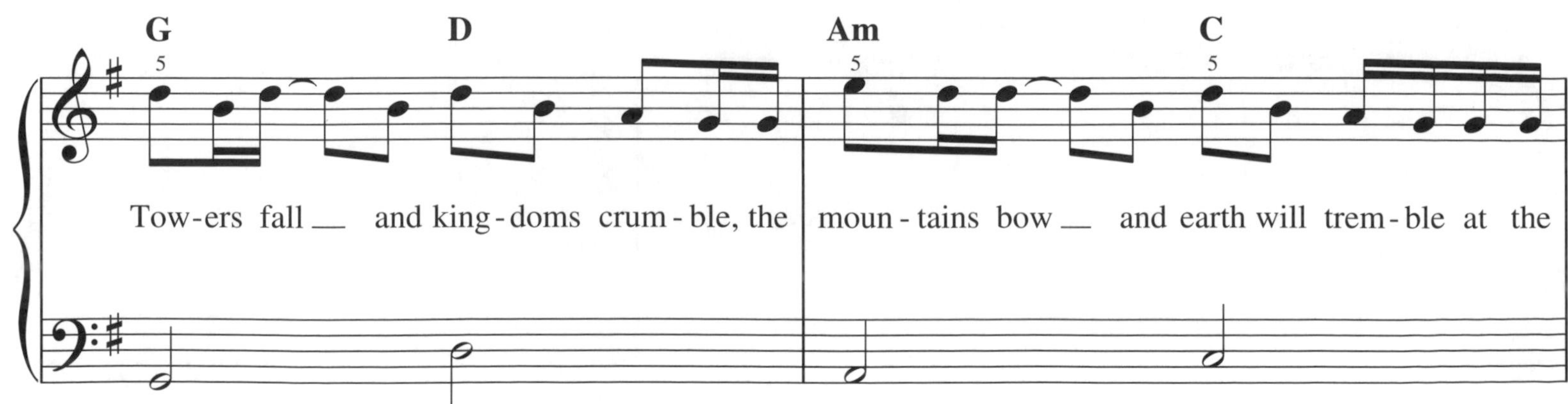
G
D
Am
C
Tow-ers fall and king-doms crum-ble, the
moun-tains bow and earth will trem-ble at the

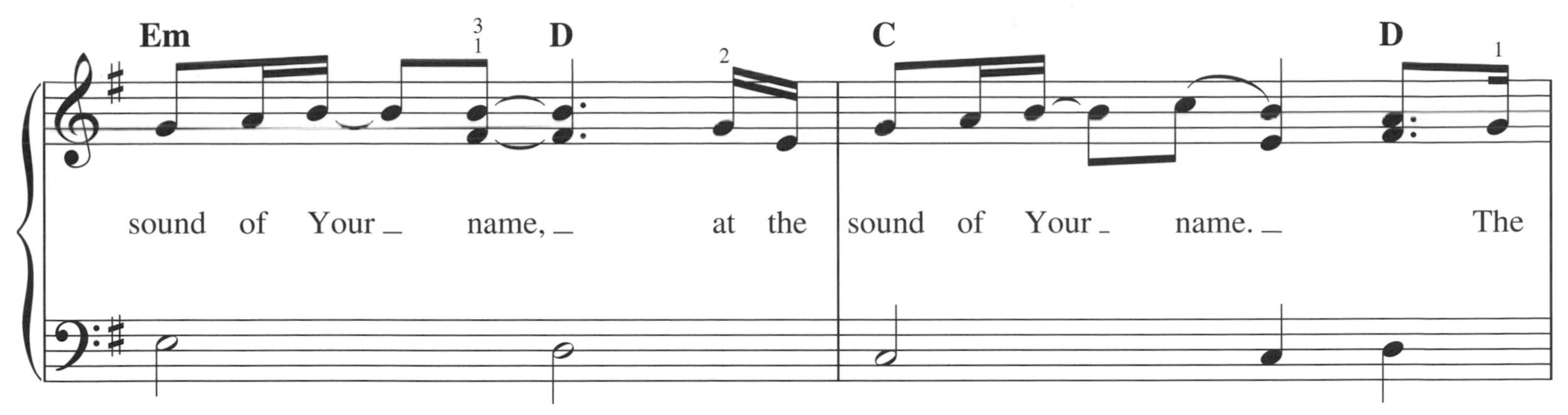
Em D C D
sound of Your name, at the sound of Your name. The

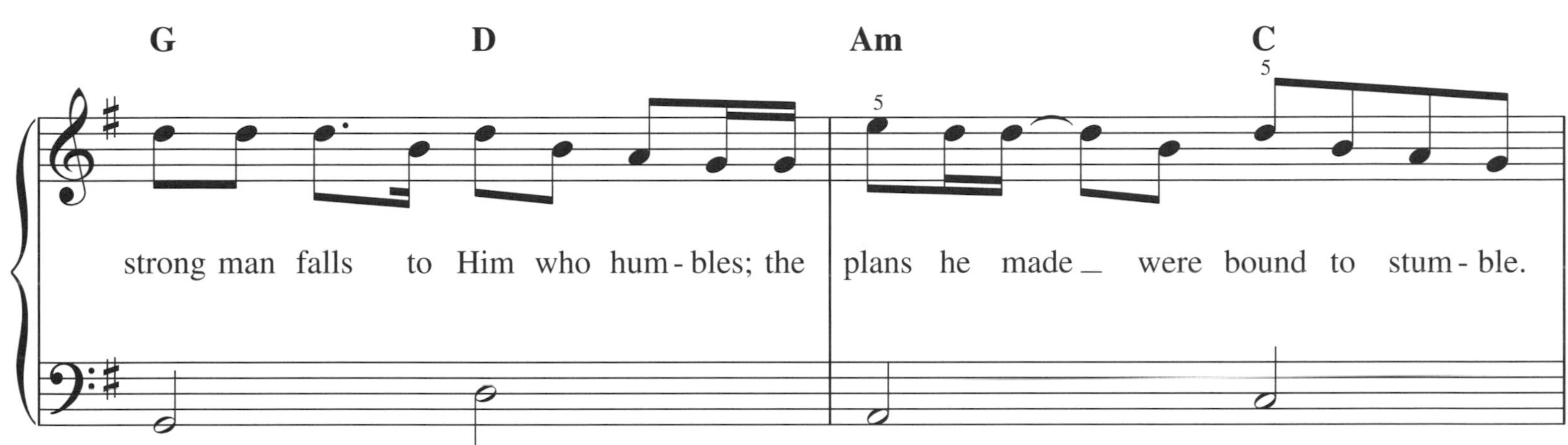
G D Am C
strong man falls to Him who hum-bles; the plans he made were bound to stum-ble.

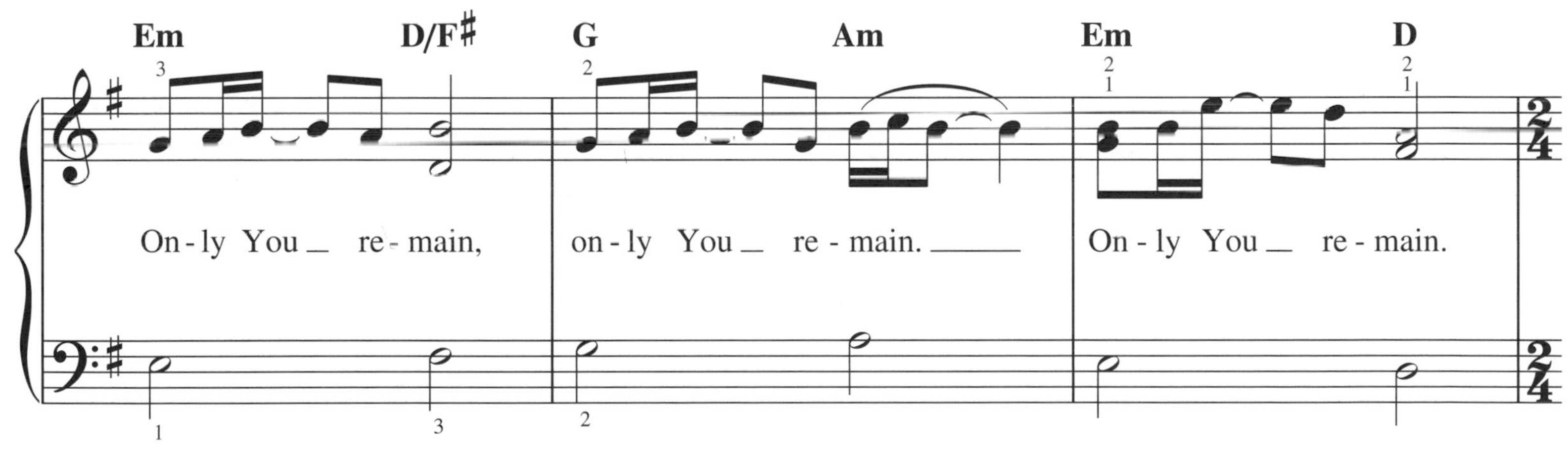
Em D/F# G Am Em D
On-ly You re-main, on-ly You re-main. On-ly You re-main.

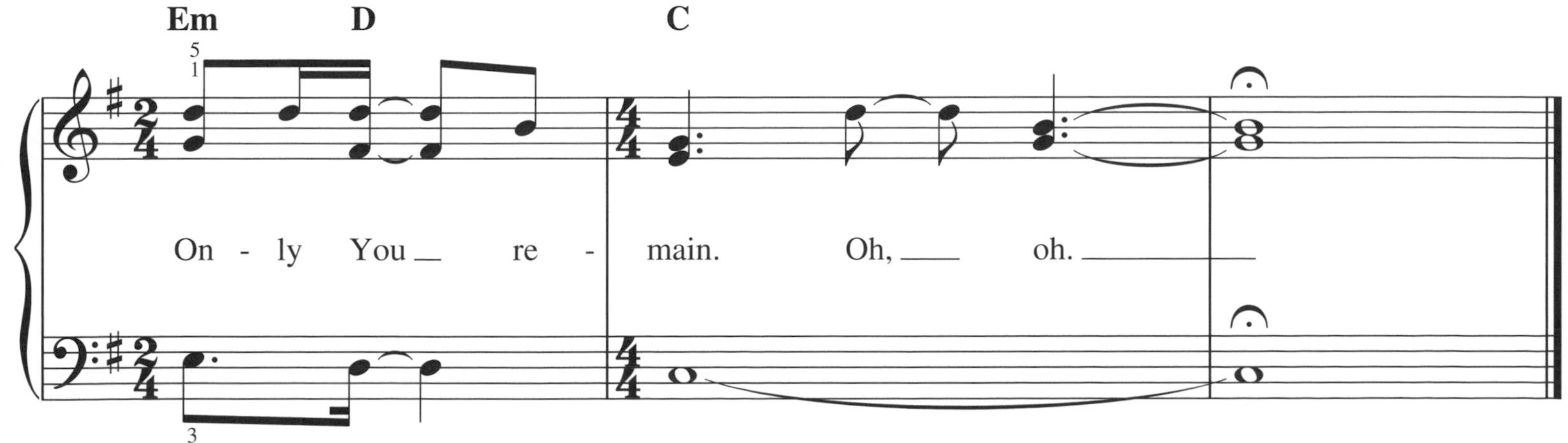
Em D C
On - ly You re - main. Oh, oh.

THERE WILL BE A DAY

Words and Music by
JEREMY CAMP

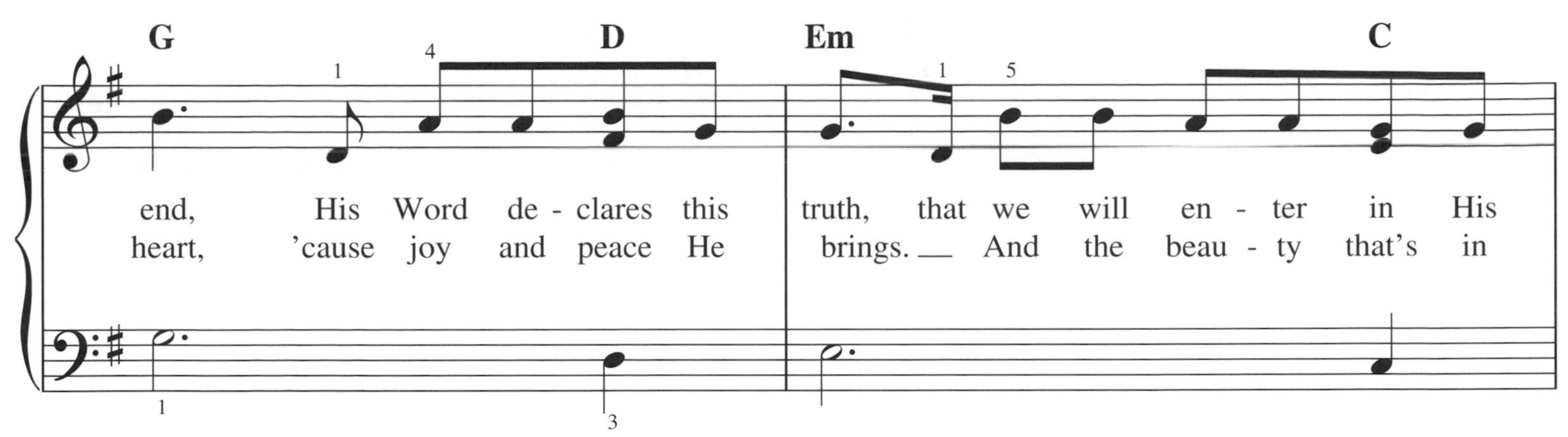
G
D
Em
C
end, His Word de - clares this truth, that we will en - ter in His
heart, 'cause joy and peace He brings. And the beau - ty that's in

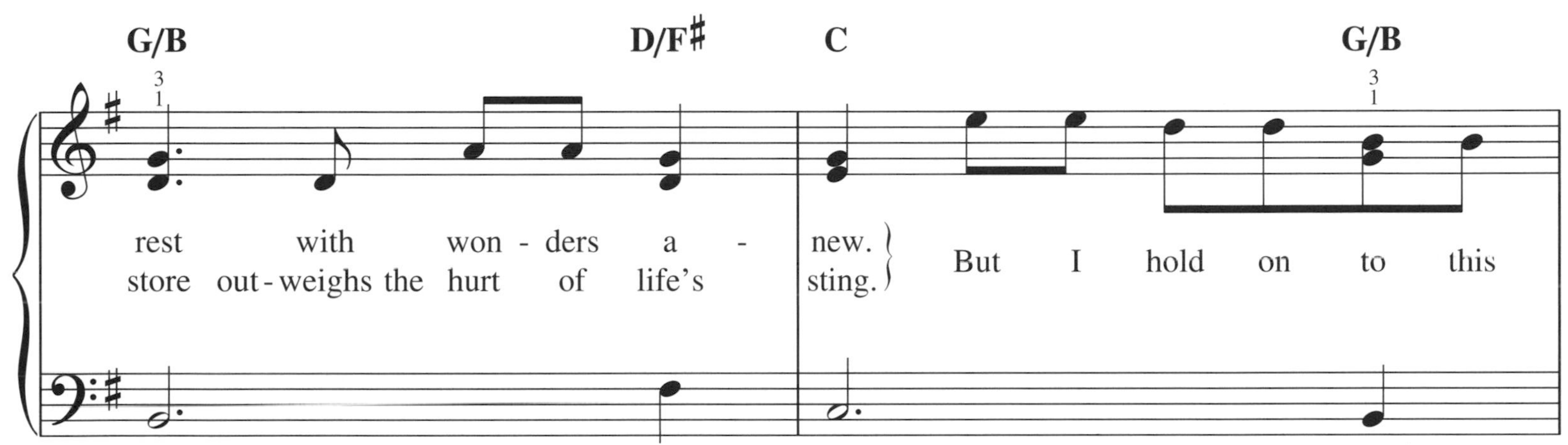
G/B
D/F♯
C
G/B
rest with won - ders a - new.
store out - weighs the hurt of life's sting.
But I hold on to this

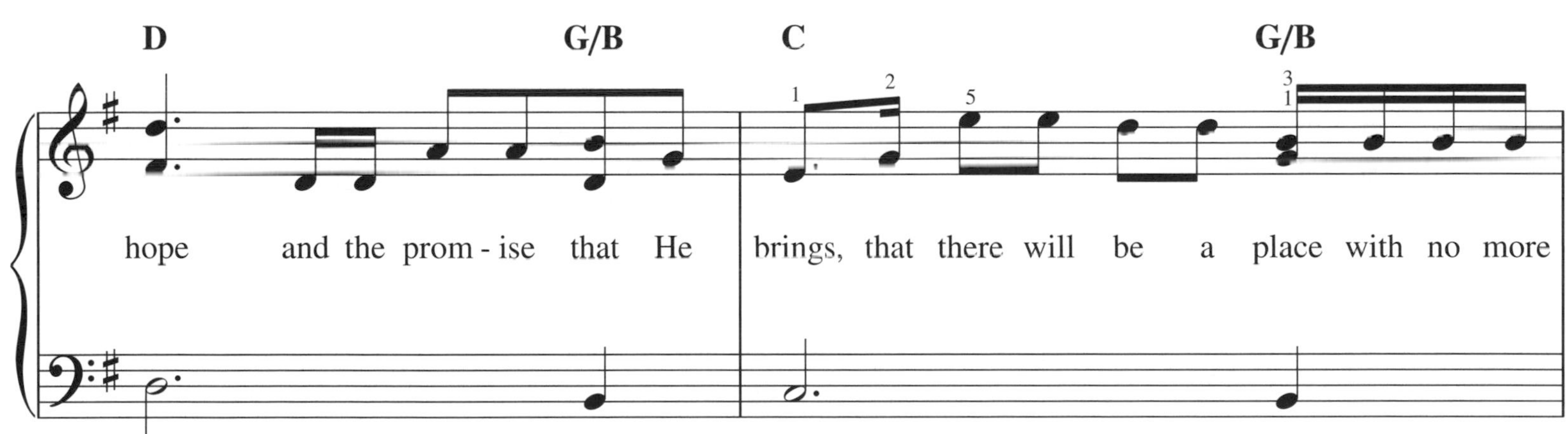
D
G/B
C
G/B
hope and the prom - ise that He brings, that there will be a place with no more

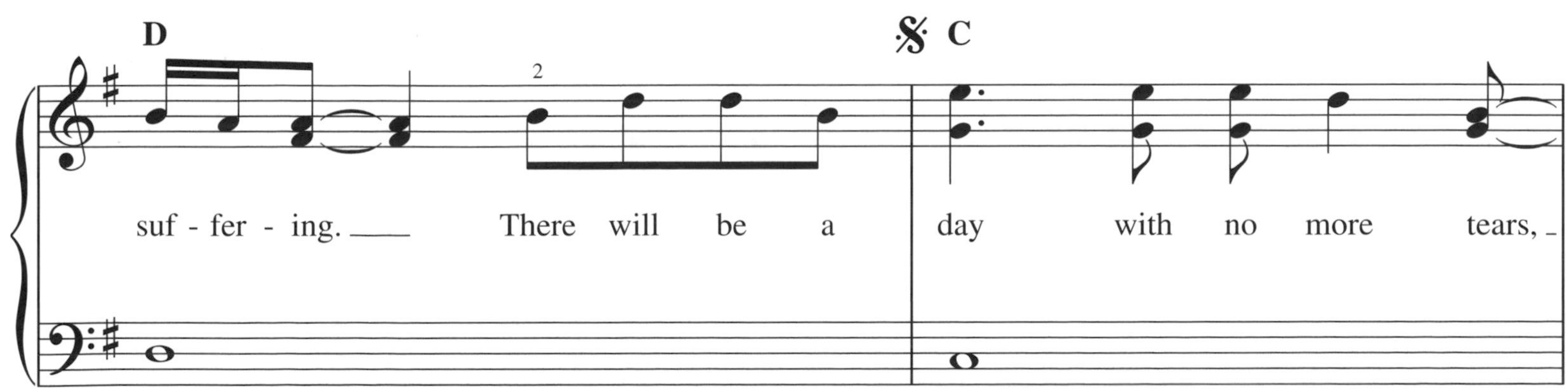
D
C
suf - fer - ing. There will be a day with no more tears,

Em
D
G
no more pain
and no more fears.
There will be a

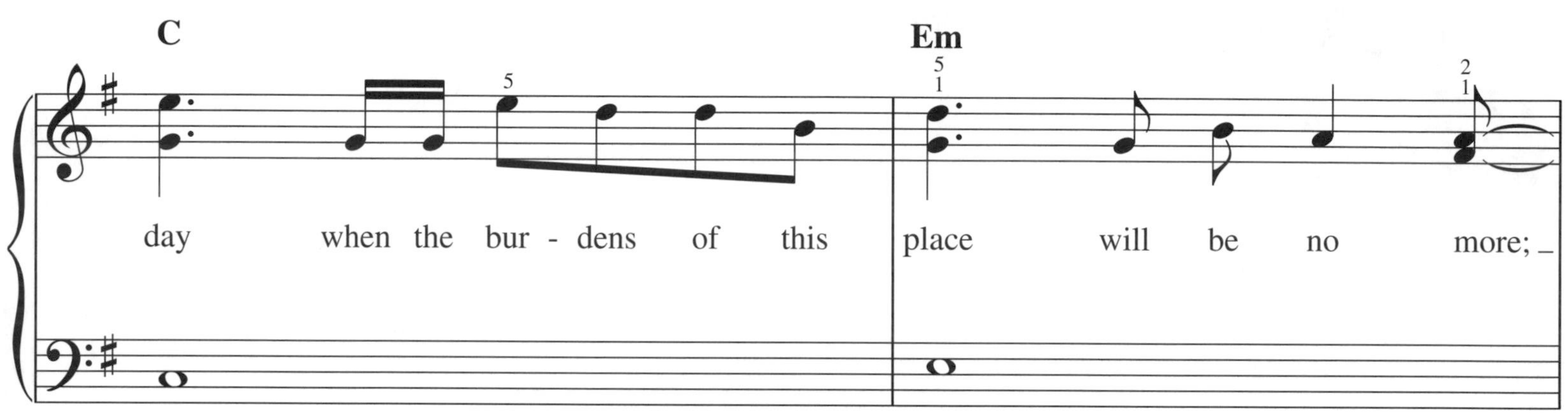
C
Em
day when the bur - dens of this
place will be no more;

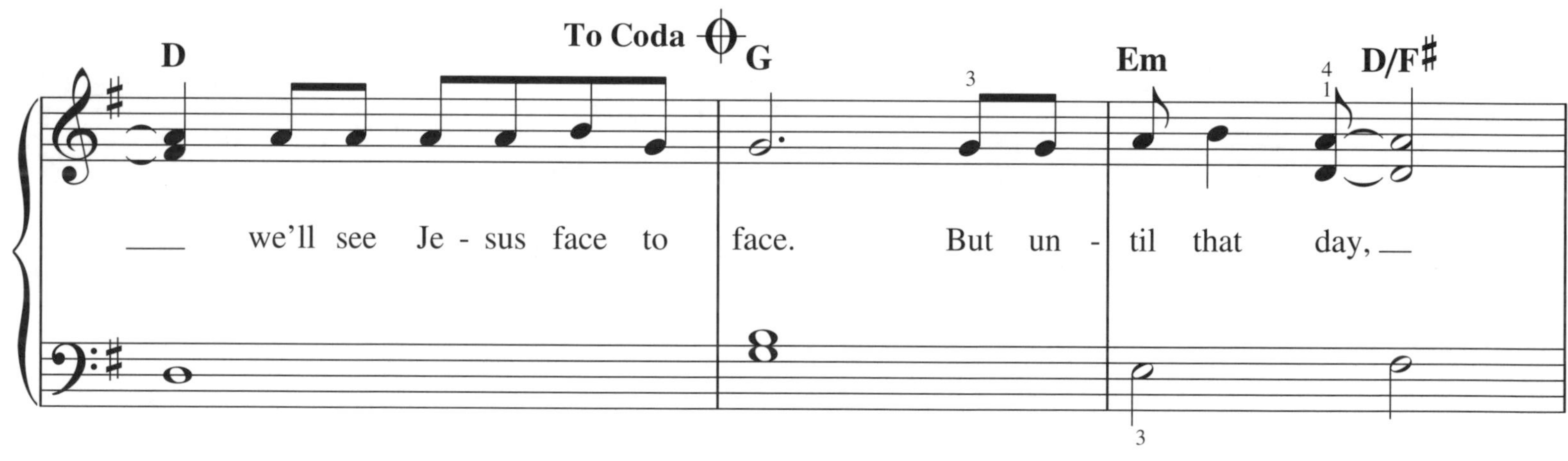
D
To Coda
G
Em
D/F#
we'll see Je - sus face to
face. But un - til that day,

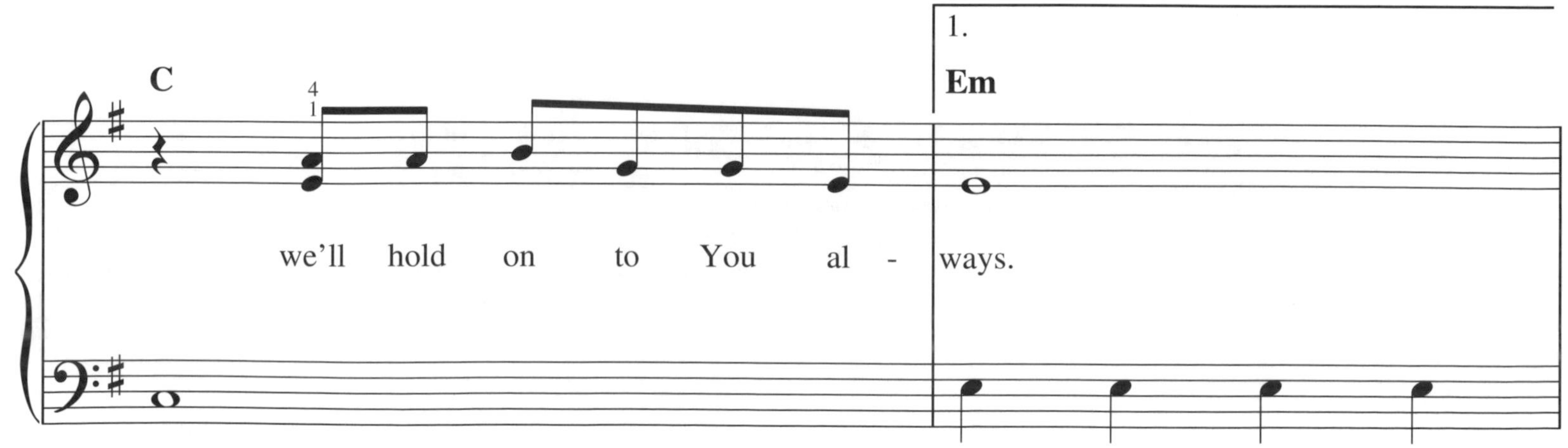
C
1.
Em
we'll hold on to You al - ways.

C
G
D
2

2.
D
Em
ways.
I can't wait un - til that day where the

C/E
G/D
ver - y One I've live for al - ways will
wipe a - way the sor - row that I've

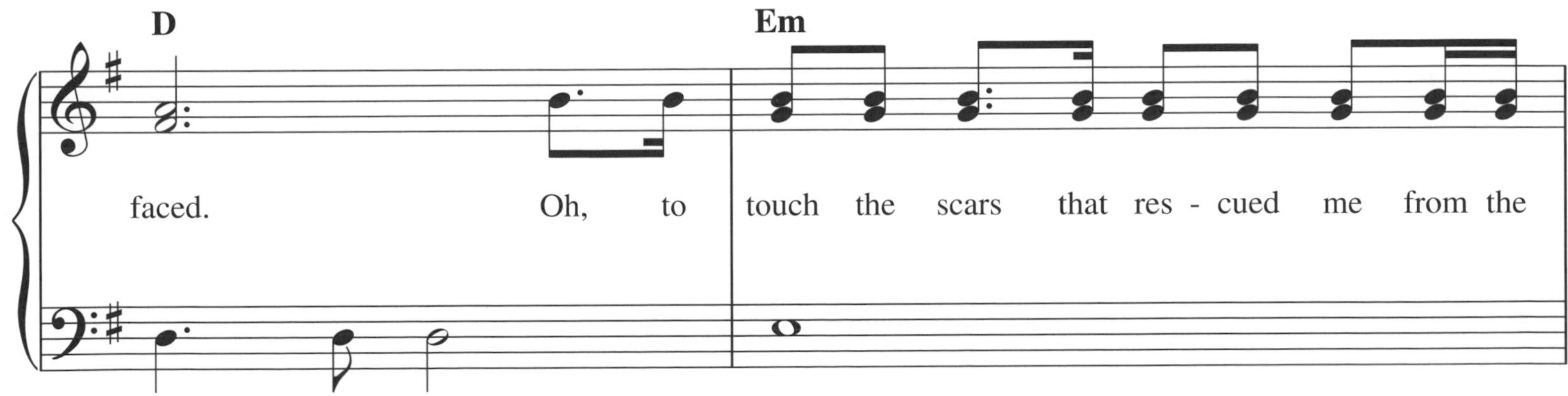
D
Em
faced.
Oh, to
touch the scars that res - cued me from the

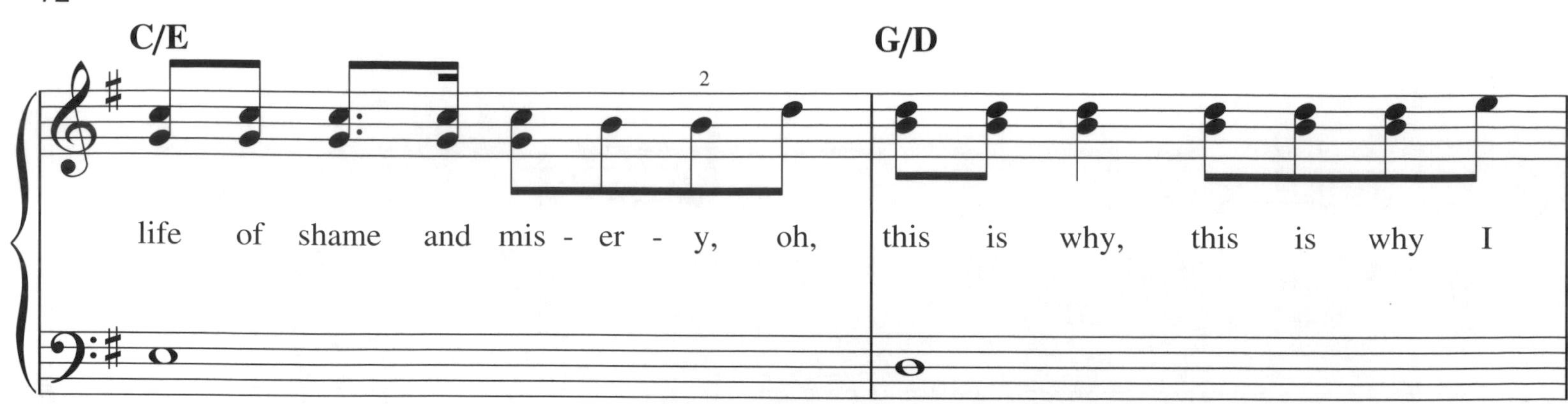
C/E
G/D
2
life of shame and mis - er - y, oh, this is why, this is why I

D
4
1
2
D.S. al Coda
sing. There will be a

CODA
D
2
face. There will be a

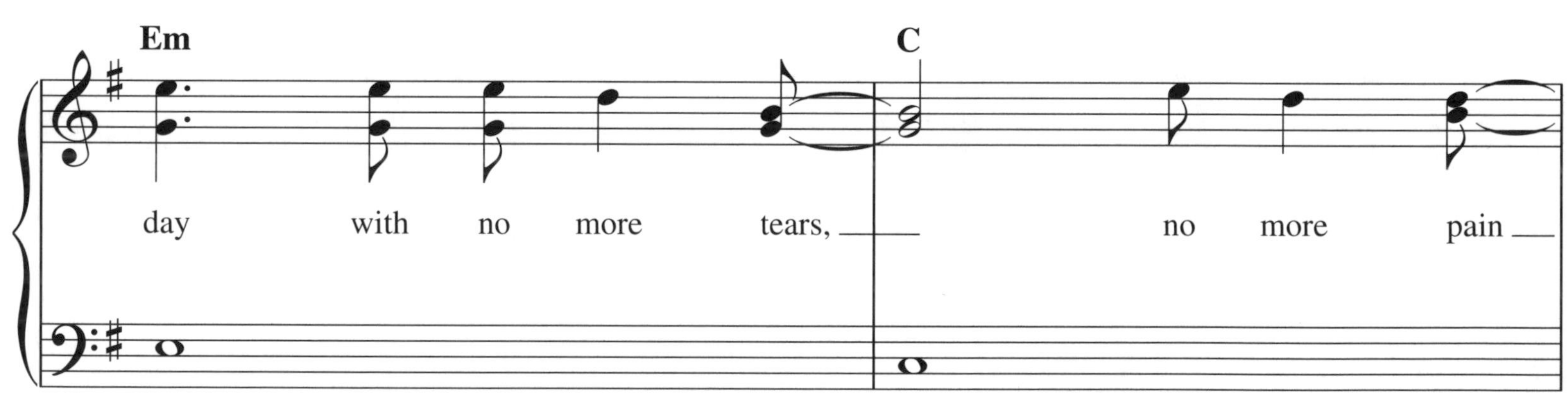
Em
C
day with no more tears, no more pain

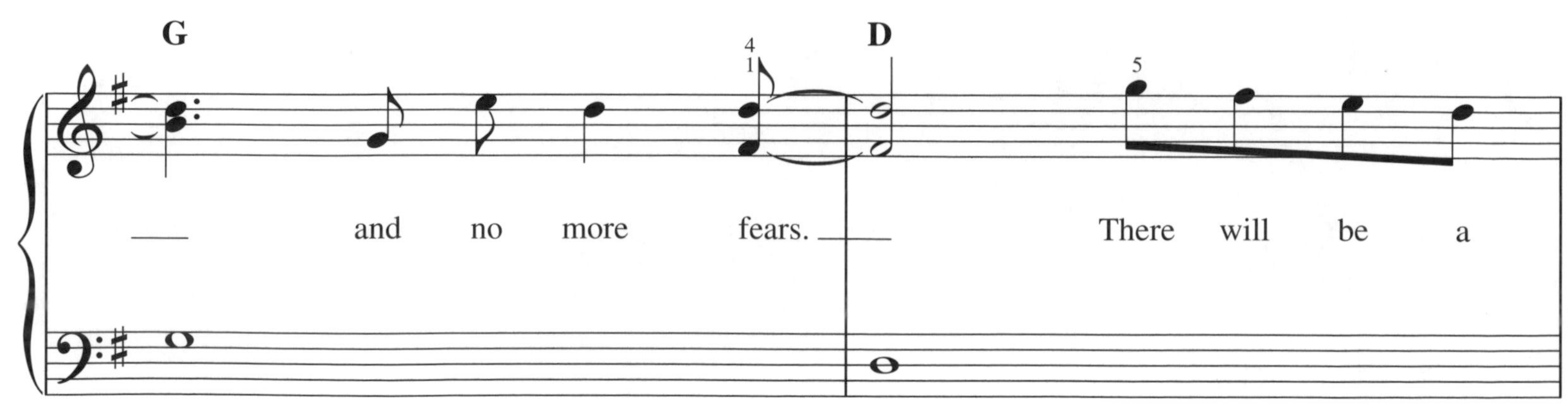
G
4
1
D
5
and no more fears. There will be a

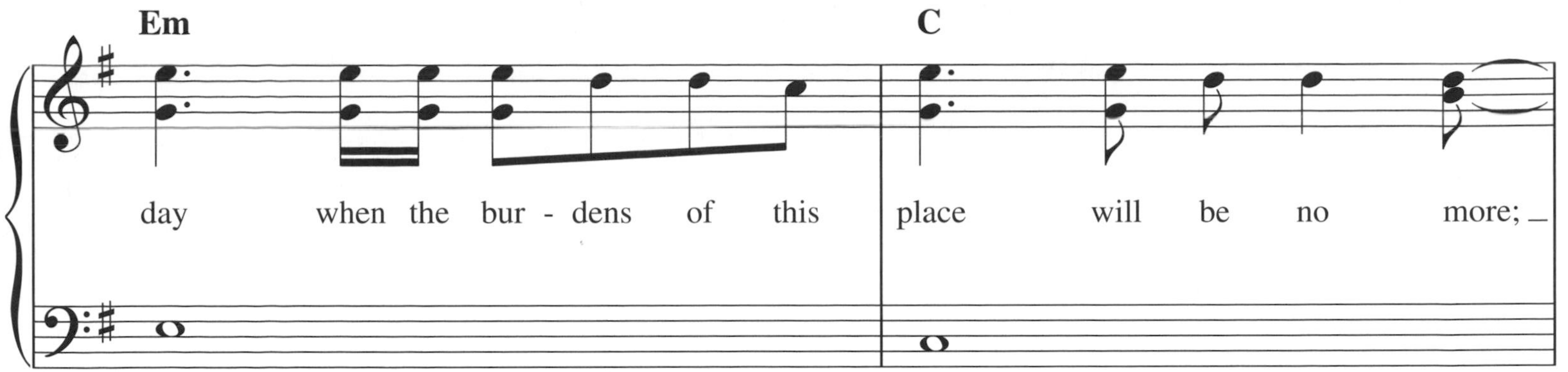
Em
C
day when the bur - dens of this
place will be no more; _

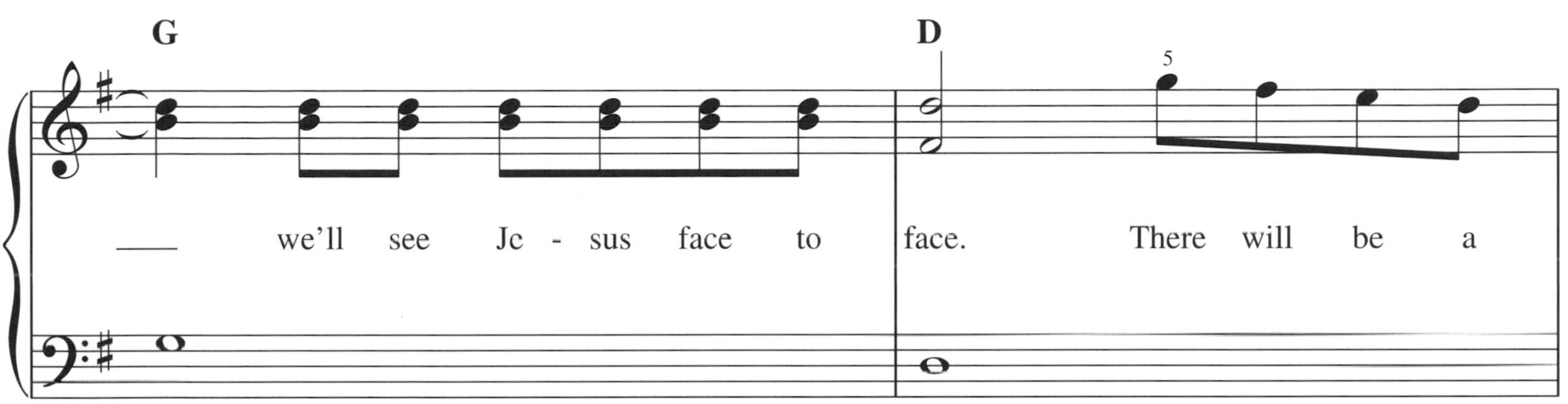
G
D
5
___ we'll see Je - sus face to
face. There will be a

Em
C
3
1
day. He will wipe a - way the
tears, He will wipe a - way the

G
D
C
3
1
2
tears, He will wipe a - way the
tears. There will be a
day.

THIS IS HOME

from Walt Disney Pictures' and Walden Media's
THE CHRONICLES OF NARNIA: PRINCE CASPIAN

Written by JONATHAN FOREMAN,
ANDY DODD and ADAM WATTS

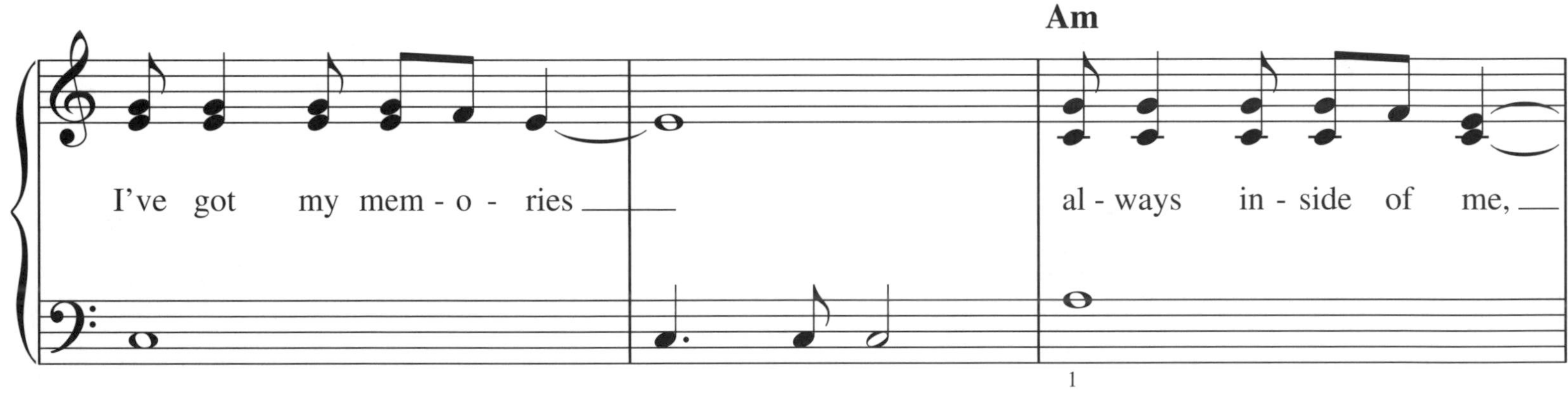

Am
Gsus
C
was.
I be - lieve you now;

Am
I've come too far.
No, I

F
Gsus
Am
can't go back,
back to how it was.

Dm
Am
Cre - at - ed for a place I've nev - er known,

G
C
this is
home. Now I'm

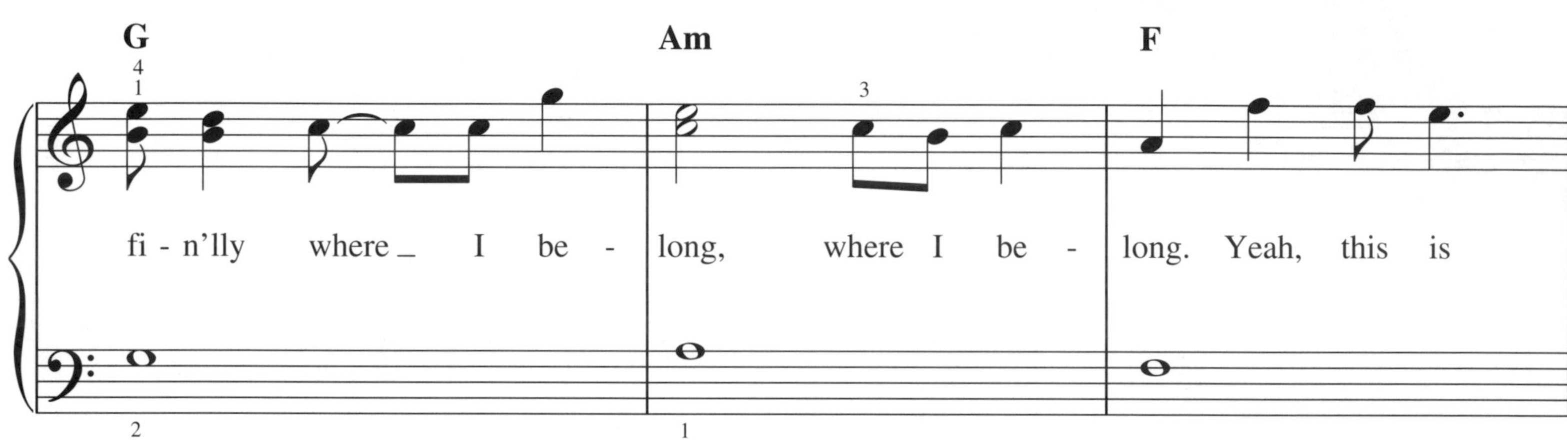
G
Am
F
fi - n'lly where I be - long, where I be - long. Yeah, this is

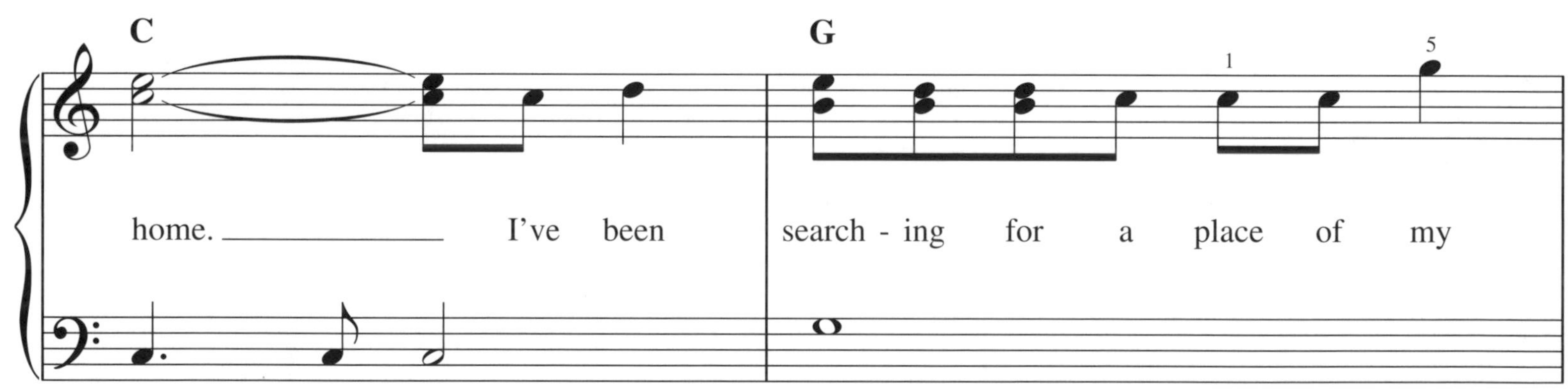
C
G
home. I've been search - ing for a place of my

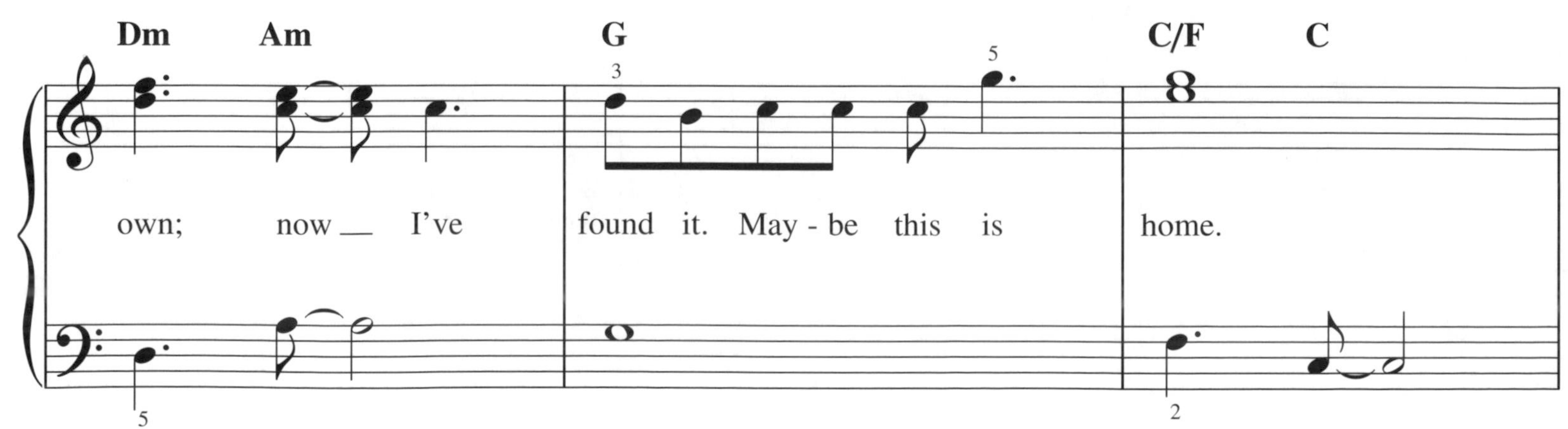
Dm
Am
G
C/F
C
own; now I've found it. May - be this is home.

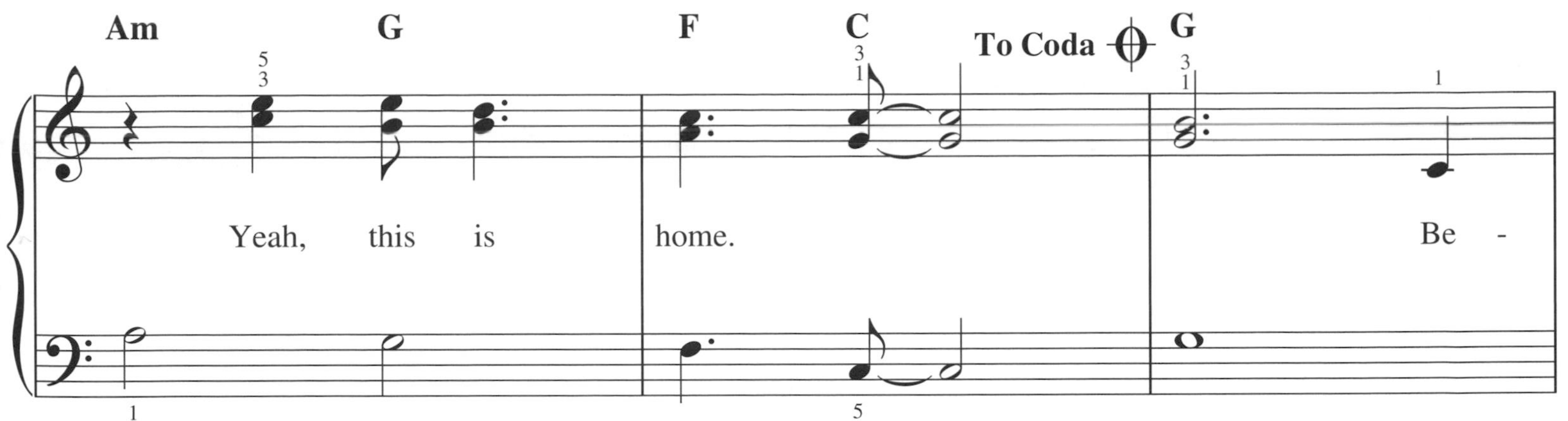
Am
G
F
C
To Coda
G
Yeah, this is home.
Be -

C
Am
lief o - ver mis - er - y,
I've seen the en - e - my,

F
Gsus
and I won't go back,
back to how it

Am
Gsus
C
was.
And I got my heart set on what

G
1
hap - pens next. ___ I
got my eyes wide; it's not

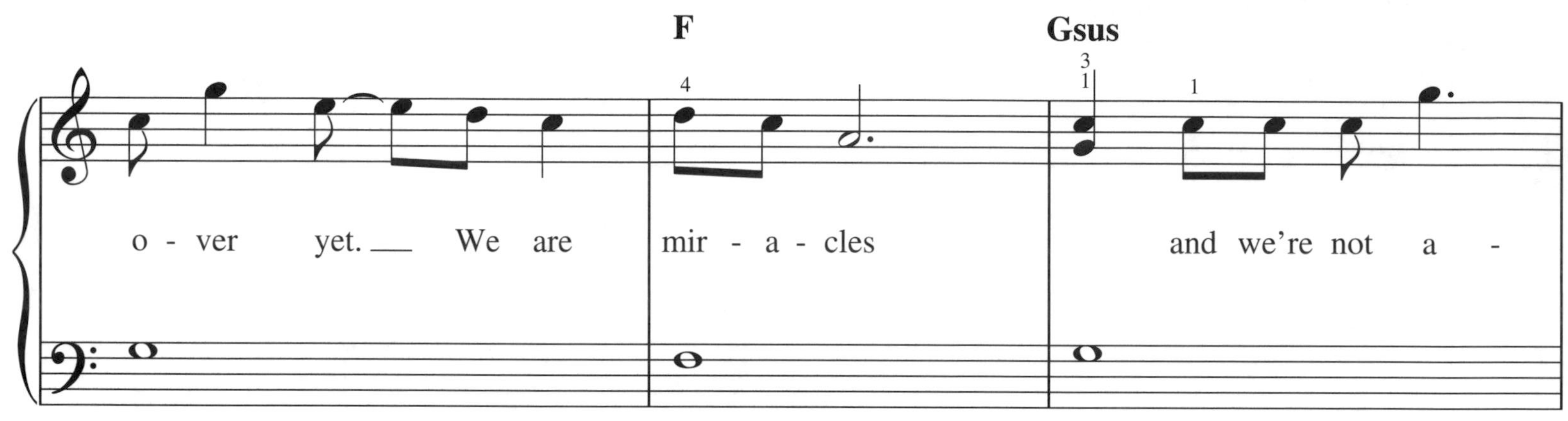
F
Gsus
4
3
1
1
o - ver yet. ___ We are
mir - a - cles
and we're not a -

Am
G
D.S. al Coda
1
lone. ___
Yeah, this is

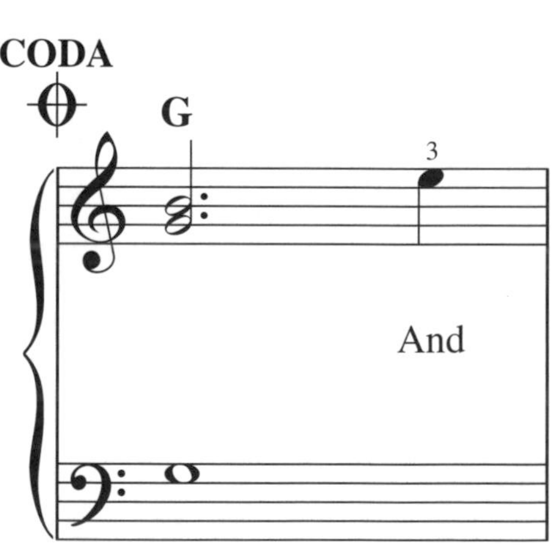
CODA
G
3
And

C
Gm
4
1
2
1
now,
af - ter all ___ my
search - ing, ___

F
af - ter all ___ my ques - tions, _ I'm gon - na call it home. _

C
Gm
___ I've got a brand - new mind - set; ___ I can

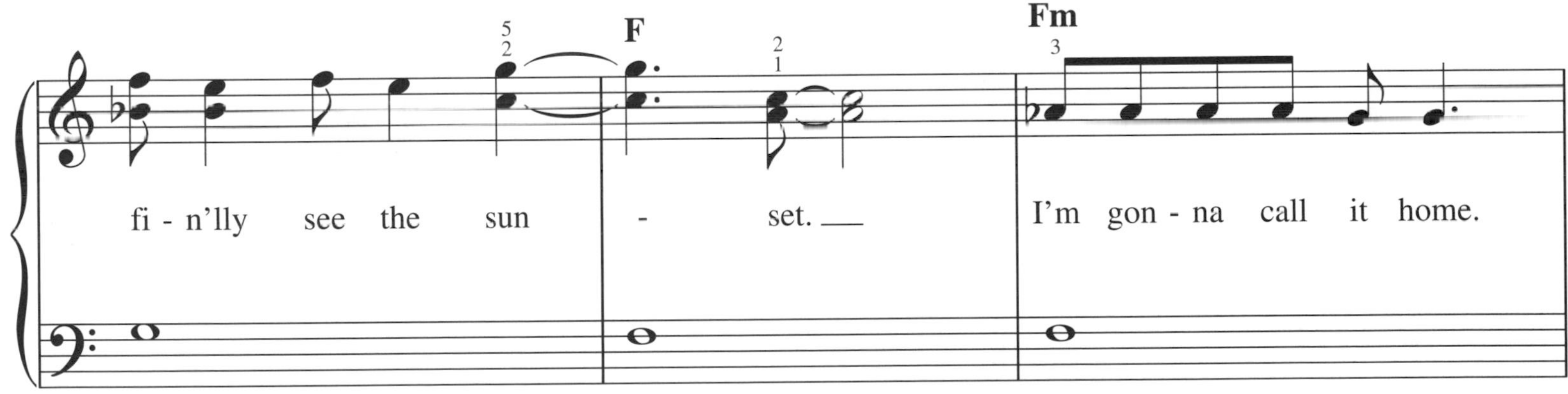
F
Fm
fi - n'lly see the sun - set. ___ I'm gon - na call it home.

C

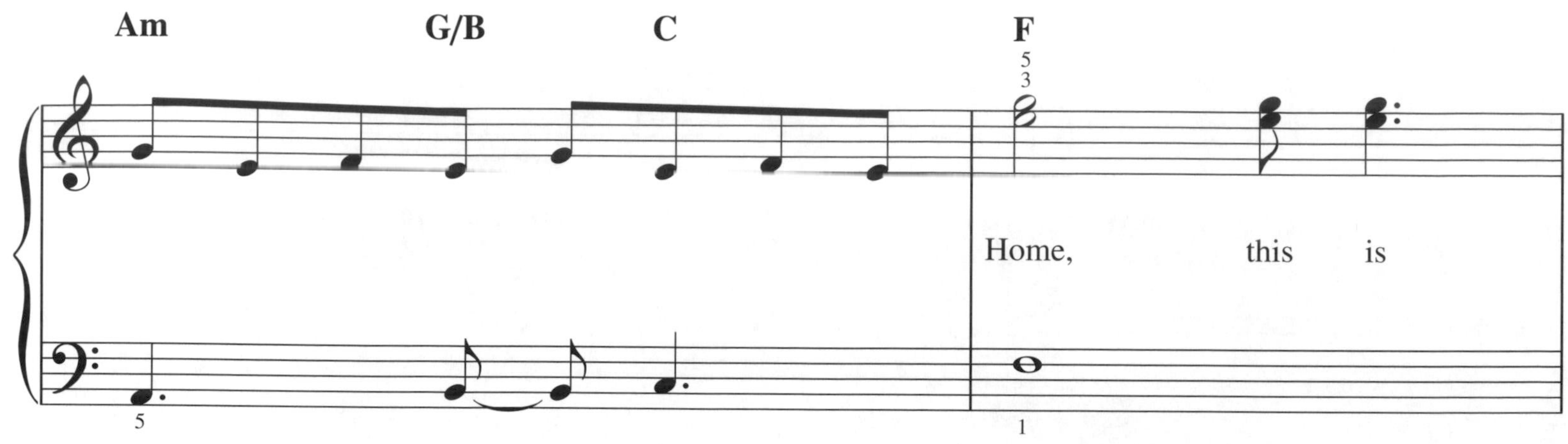
Am
G/B
C
F
Home, this is

C
G
Am
home. ___ Now I'm
fi - n'lly where _ I be -
long, where I be -

F
C
G
long. Yeah, this is
home. ___ I've been
search-ing for a place of my

Dm
Am
G
C/F
C
own; now _ I've
found it. May - be this is
home.

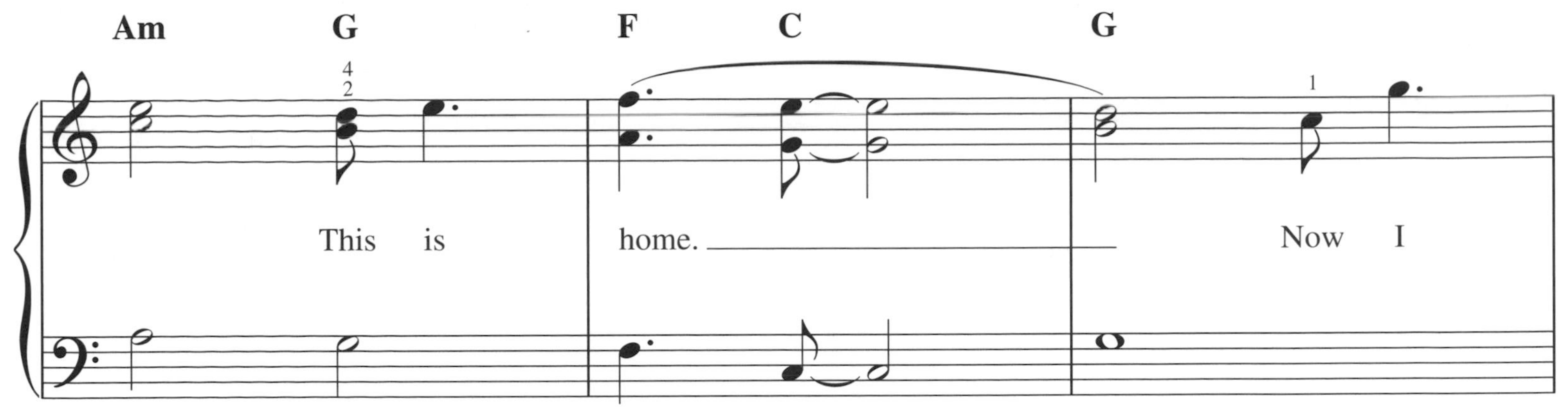
Am
G
F
C
G
This is
home.
Now I

Dm
Am
C
G
F
C
know,
yeah, this is
home.

G
C
I've
come too far,
and I

Am
F
C
won't go back.
Yeah, this is
home.

TODAY IS THE DAY

Words and Music by LINCOLN BREWSTER
and PAUL BALOCHE

D/A G Em G
1
You, Je - sus. I'm reach - ing my
You, Je - sus. I'm reach - ing my

D Bm D/A G D Bm
hand to Yours,
hands to Yours,
be - liev - ing there's so much more,

D/A G D Bm D/A G
know - ing that all You have in store for me is

Em G D
5 5 1 2
good, is good. To - day is the day You have

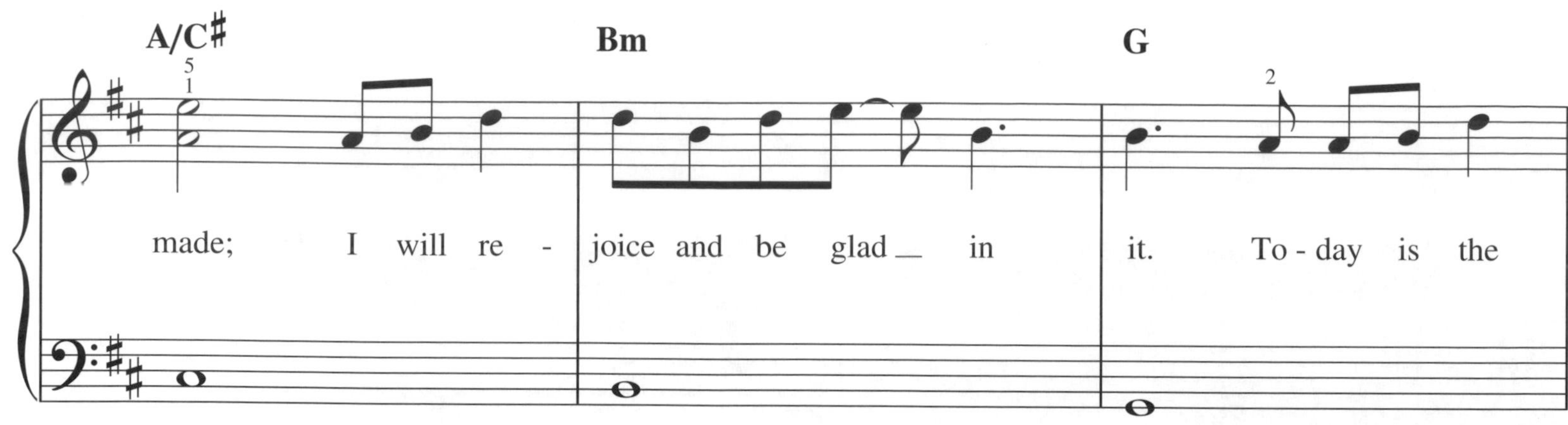
A/C♯
Bm
G
made; I will re - joice and be glad __ in it. To - day is the

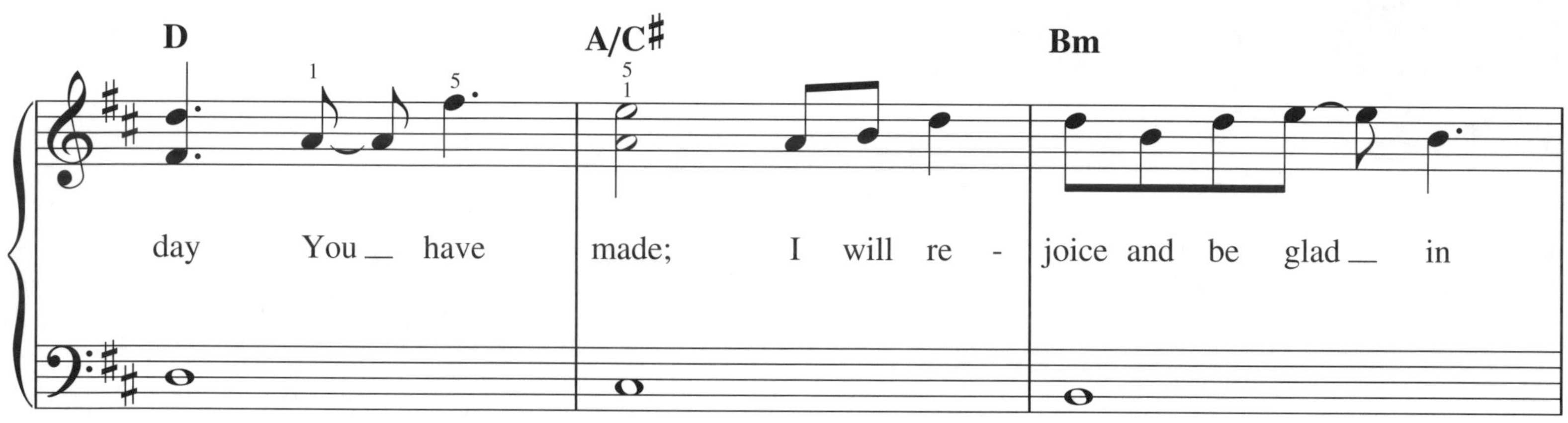
D
A/C♯
Bm
day You __ have made; I will re - joice and be glad __ in

G
Em
D/F♯
it. And I won't wor - ry 'bout to - mor - row, I'm

G
A
D
Bm
trust - ing in what __ You say. To - day is the day.

1.
D/A G D Bm D/A G
To - day is the day. I'm put - ting my
2.
D/A G D G
I will stand up - on Your truth. (I
D G D
will stand up - on Your truth.) And all my days I'll live
1.
G D G
for You. (All my days I'll live for You.) I

2.
D
G
my days I'll live. To - day is the

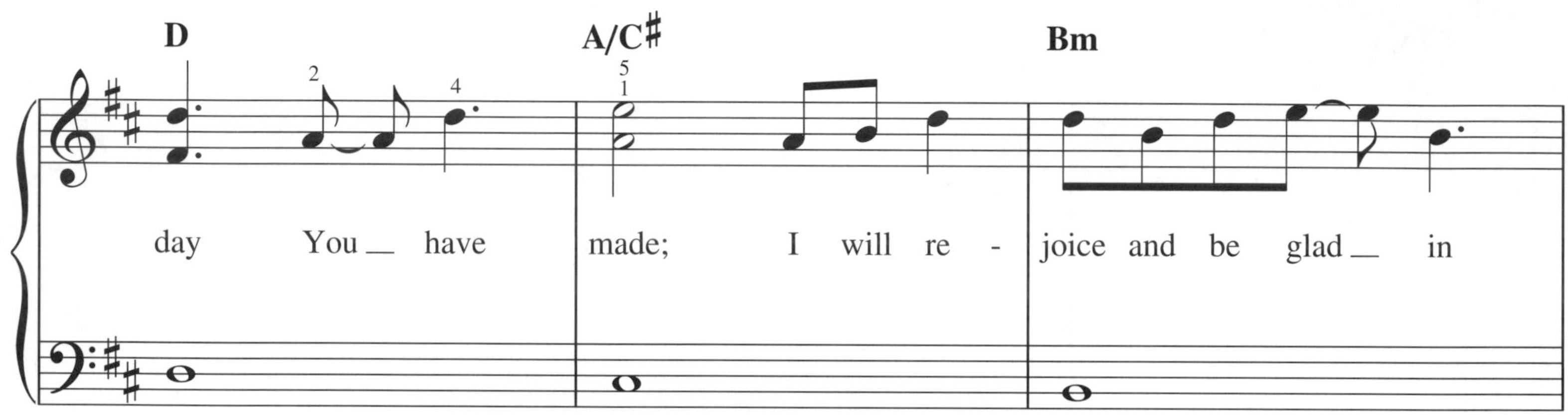
D
A/C♯
Bm
day You have made; I will re - joice and be glad in

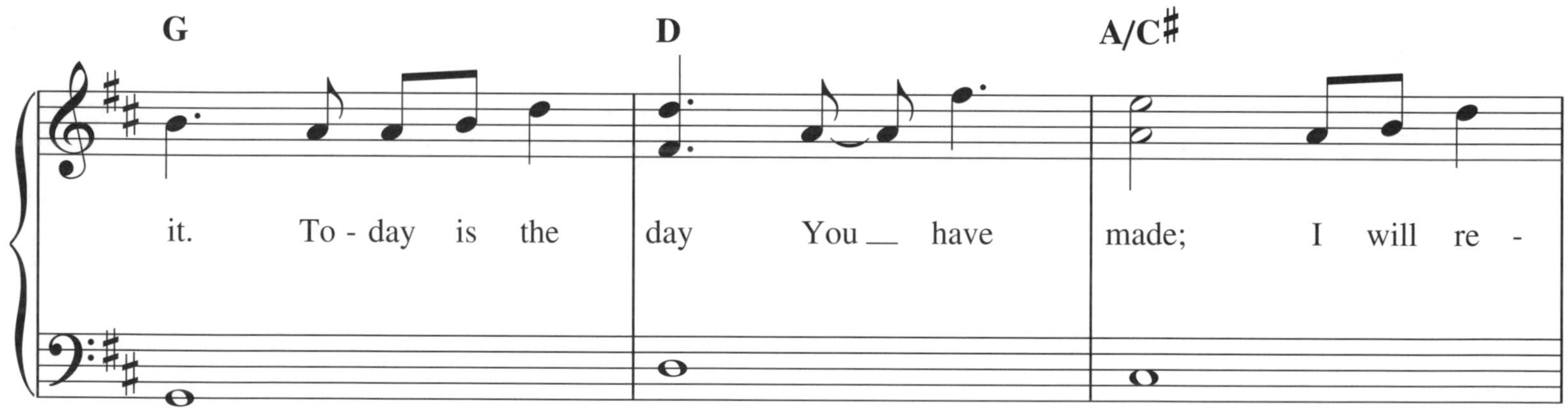
G
D
A/C♯
it. To - day is the day You have made; I will re -

D/F♯
G
Em
joice and be glad in it. And I won't wor - ry

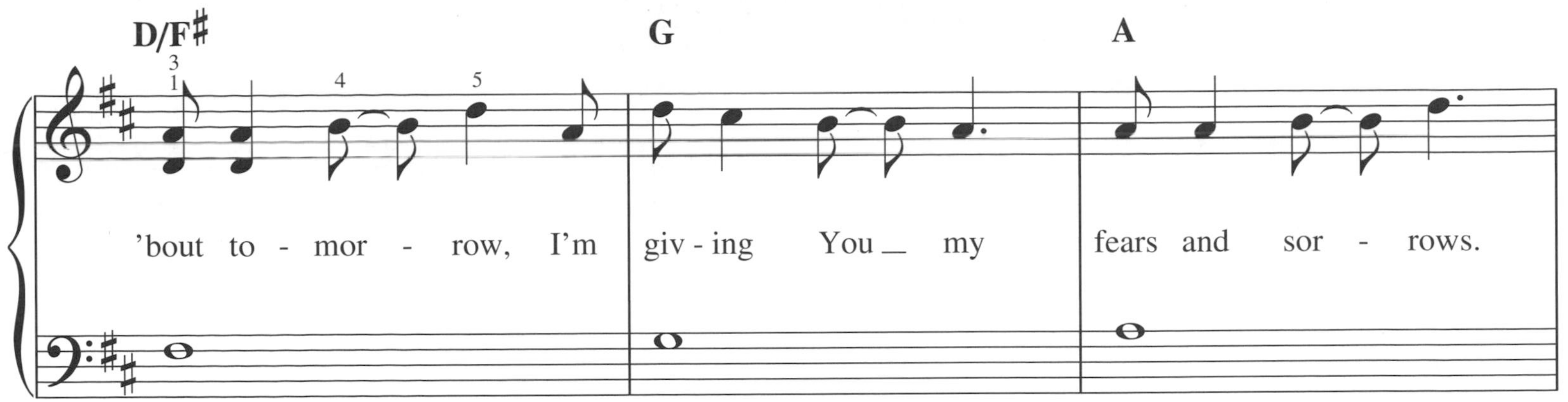
D/F#
G
A
'bout to - mor - row, I'm giv - ing You my fears and sor - rows.

Em
D/F#
Where You lead me, I will fol - low. I'm

G
A
D
Bm
trust - ing in what You say. To - day is the day.

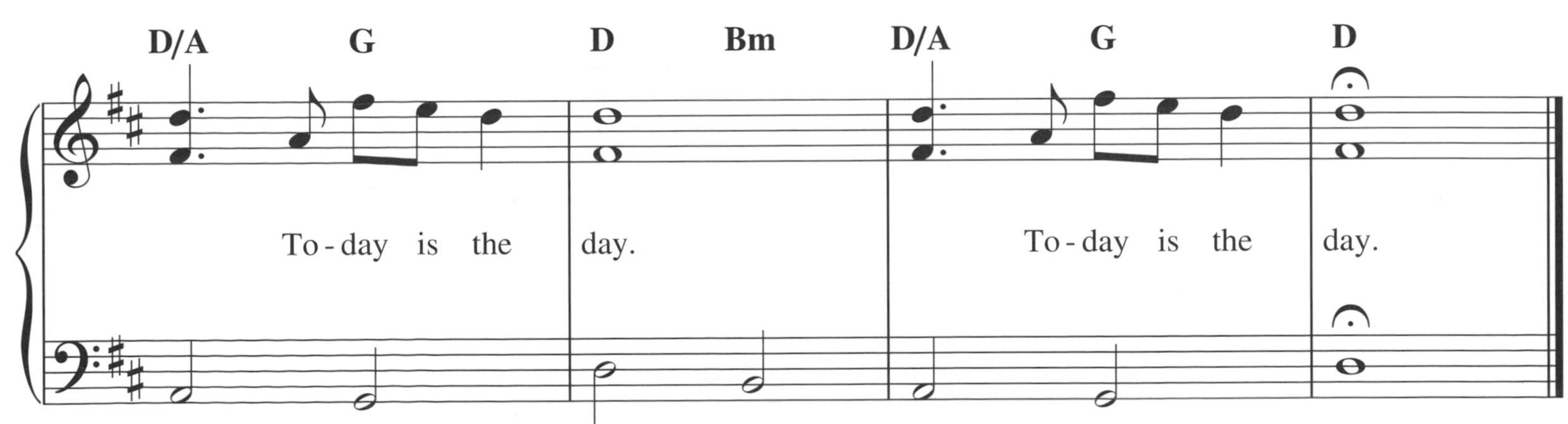
D/A
G
D
Bm
D/A
G
D
To - day is the day. To - day is the day.

UNBREAKABLE

Words and Music by ROB HAWKINS,
WENDY DRENNEN, GLENN DRENNEN,
JUSTIN COX, DAWN RICHARDSON
and PHILLIP "PHEE" SHORB

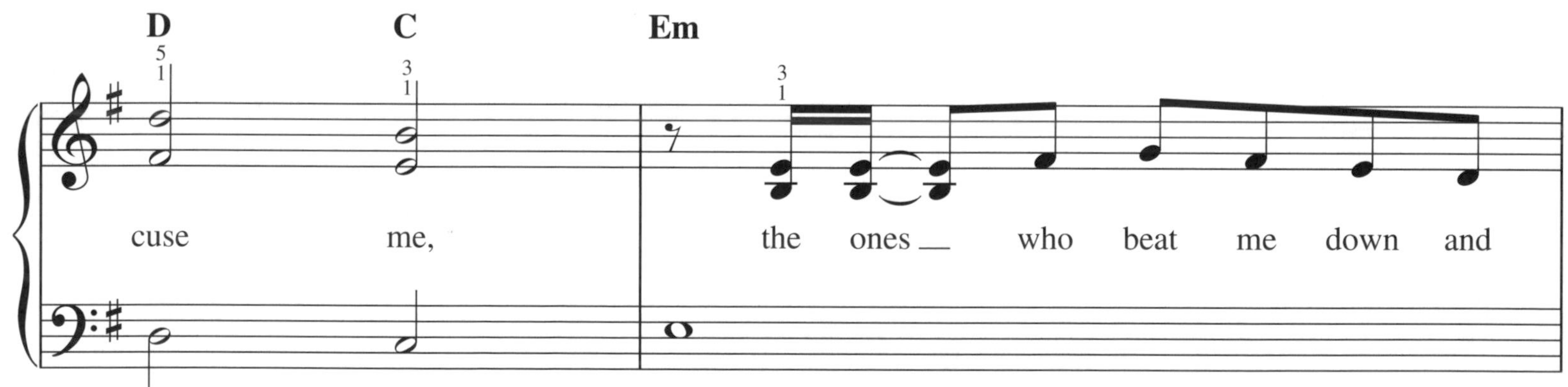

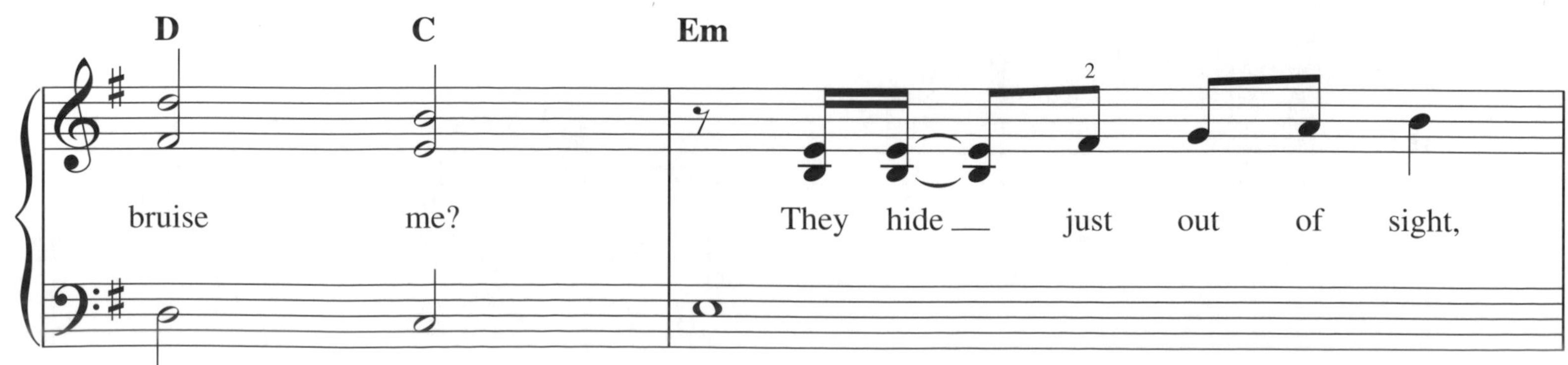

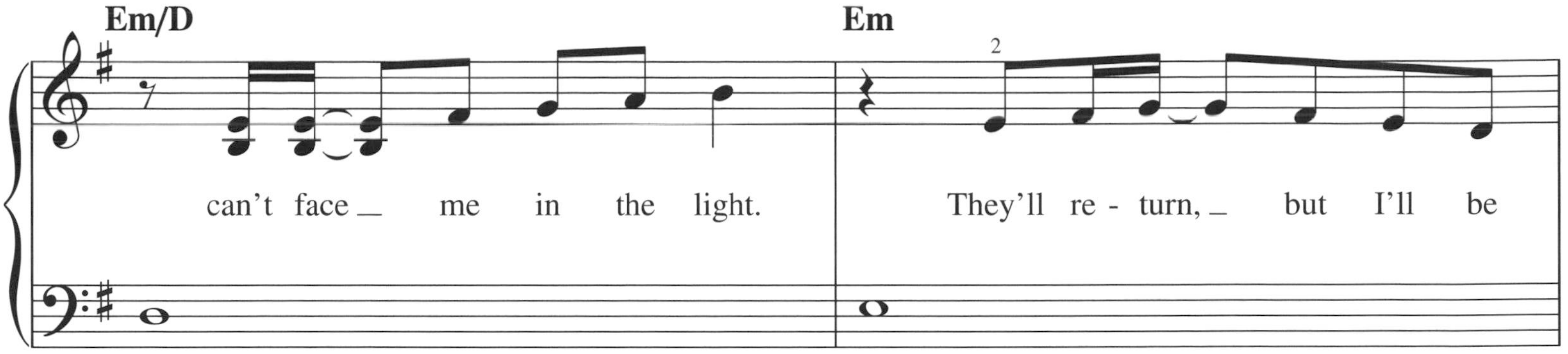
Em/D
Em
can't face me in the light.
They'll re - turn, but I'll be

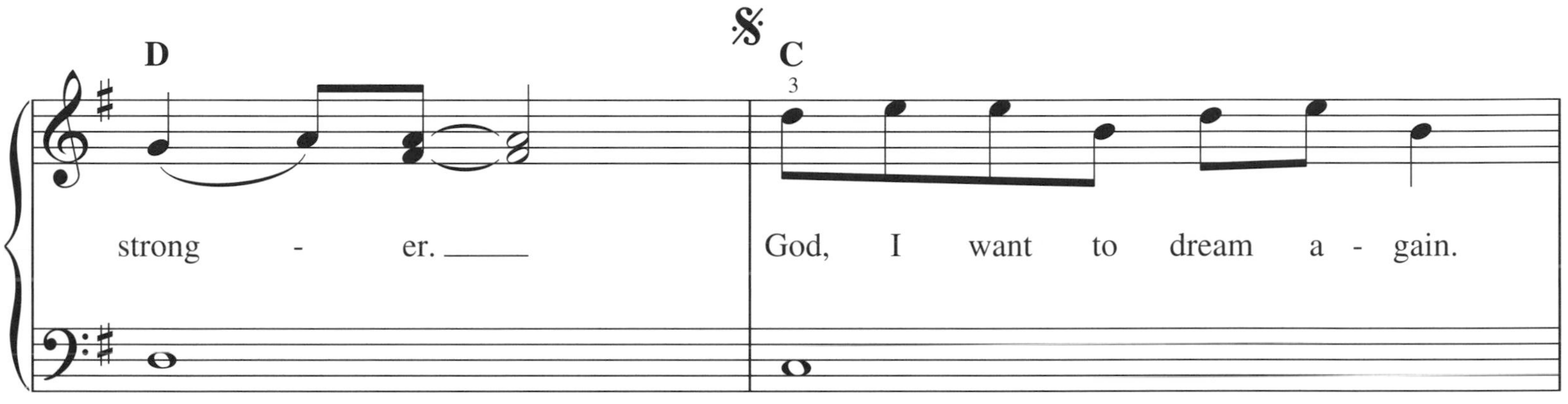
D
C
strong - er.
God, I want to dream a - gain.

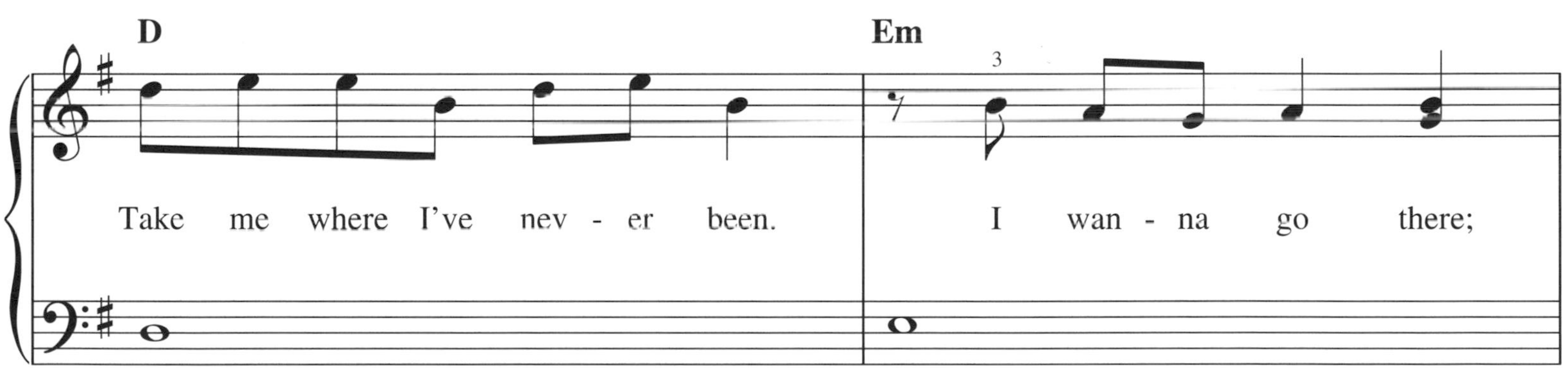
D
Em
Take me where I've nev - er been.
I wan - na go there;

C
this time I'm not scared.
Now I am un - break - a - ble,

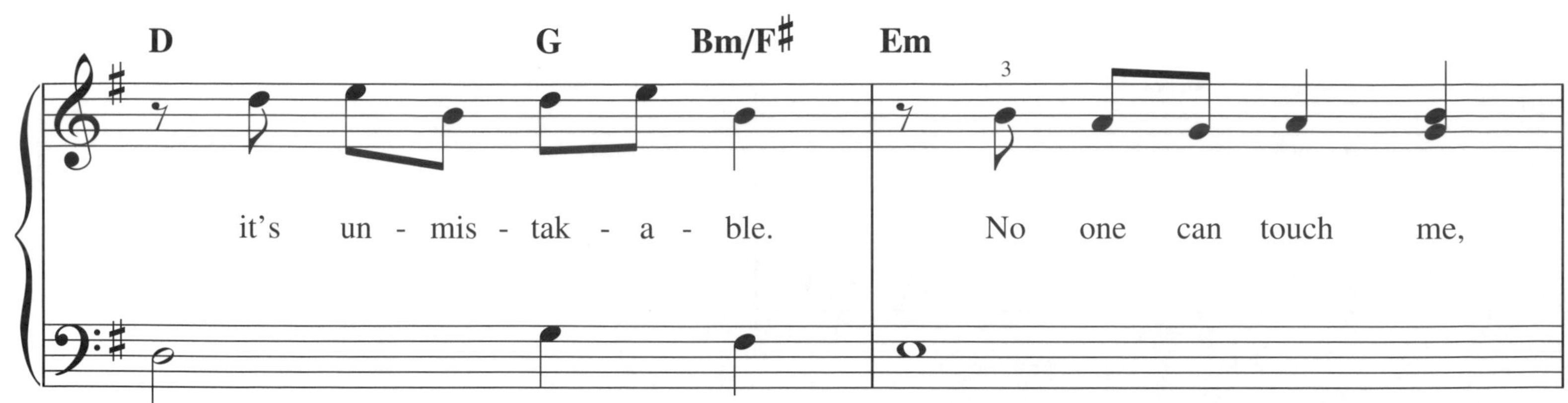
D
G
Bm/F♯
Em
it's un - mis - tak - a - ble.
No one can touch me,

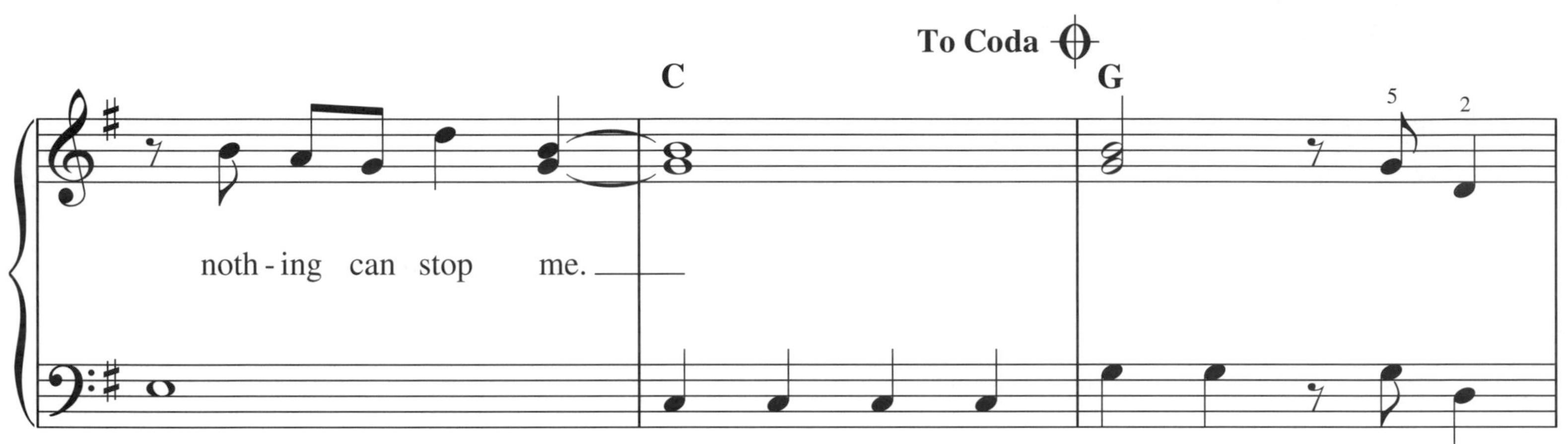
To Coda
C
G
noth - ing can stop me.

Em
D
C
Some - times it's hard to just keep go - ing,

Em
D
C
but faith is mov - ing with - out know - ing.

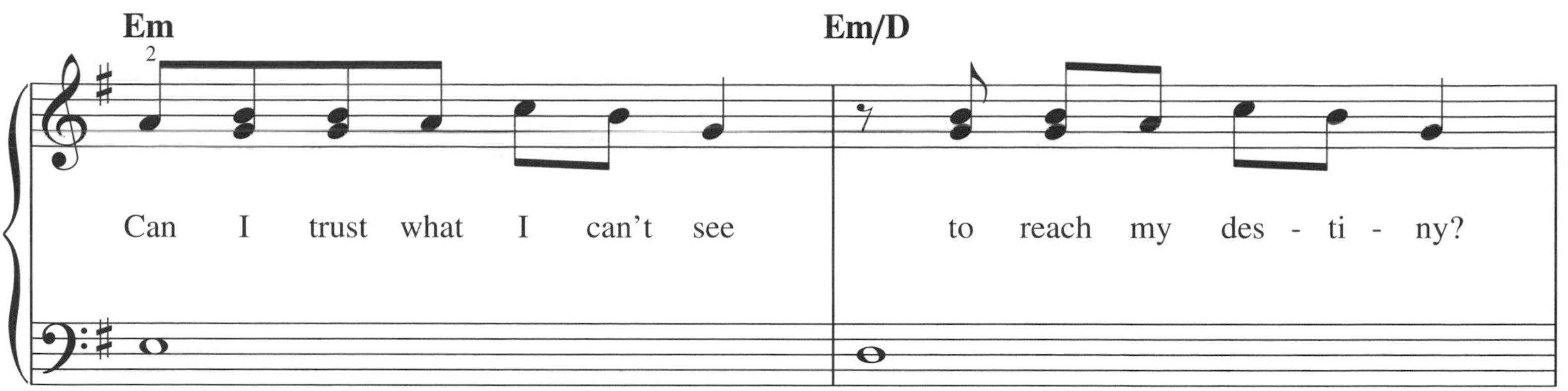
Em
Em/D
Can I trust what I can't see
to reach my des - ti - ny?

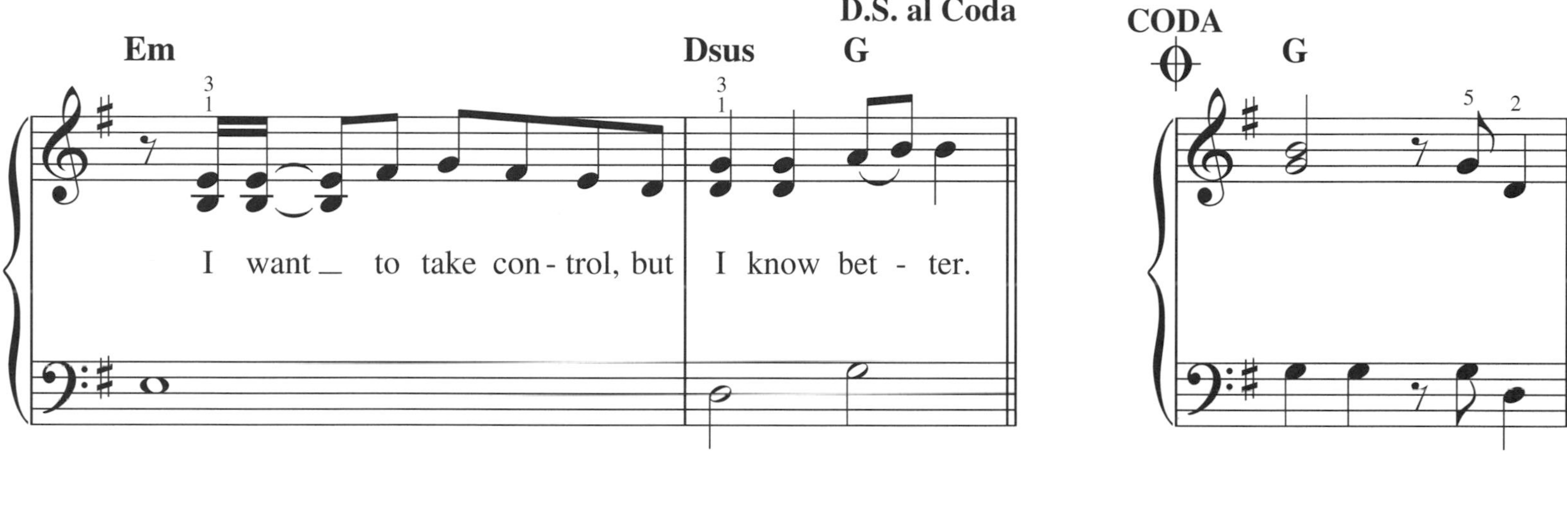
Em
Dsus
D.S. al Coda
G
CODA
G
I want _ to take con - trol, but
I know bet - ter.

Em
For - get the fear; _ it's just a crutch that tries to hold _

Bm/D
C
Em
___ you back and turn your dreams to dust. _
All you need _ to do ___ is just ___

4
5
try.

N.C.
C
3
God, I want to dream a - gain.

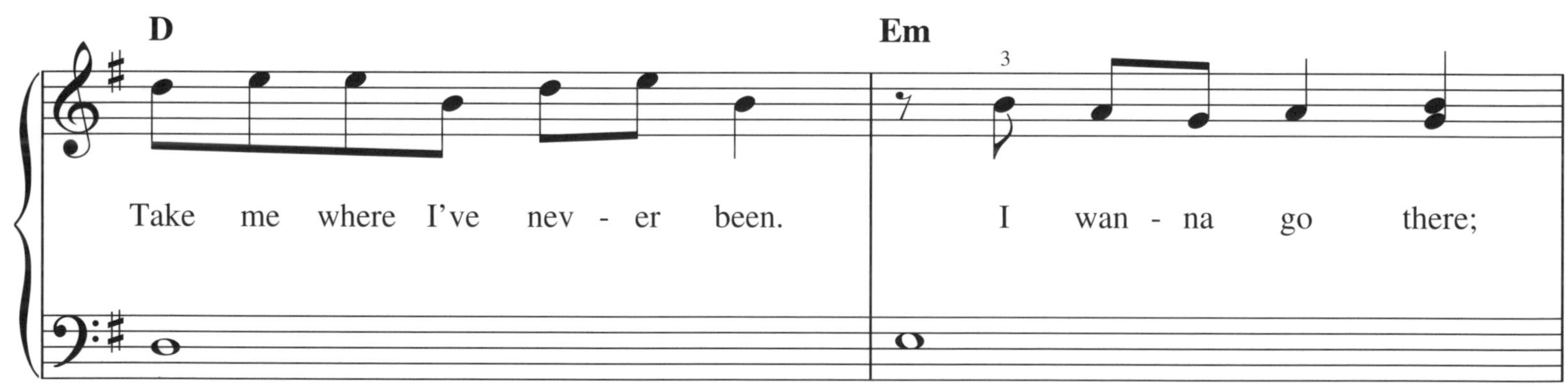

D
Em
3
Take me where I've nev - er been.
I wan - na go there;

C
3
this time I'm not scared.
Now I am un - break - a - ble,

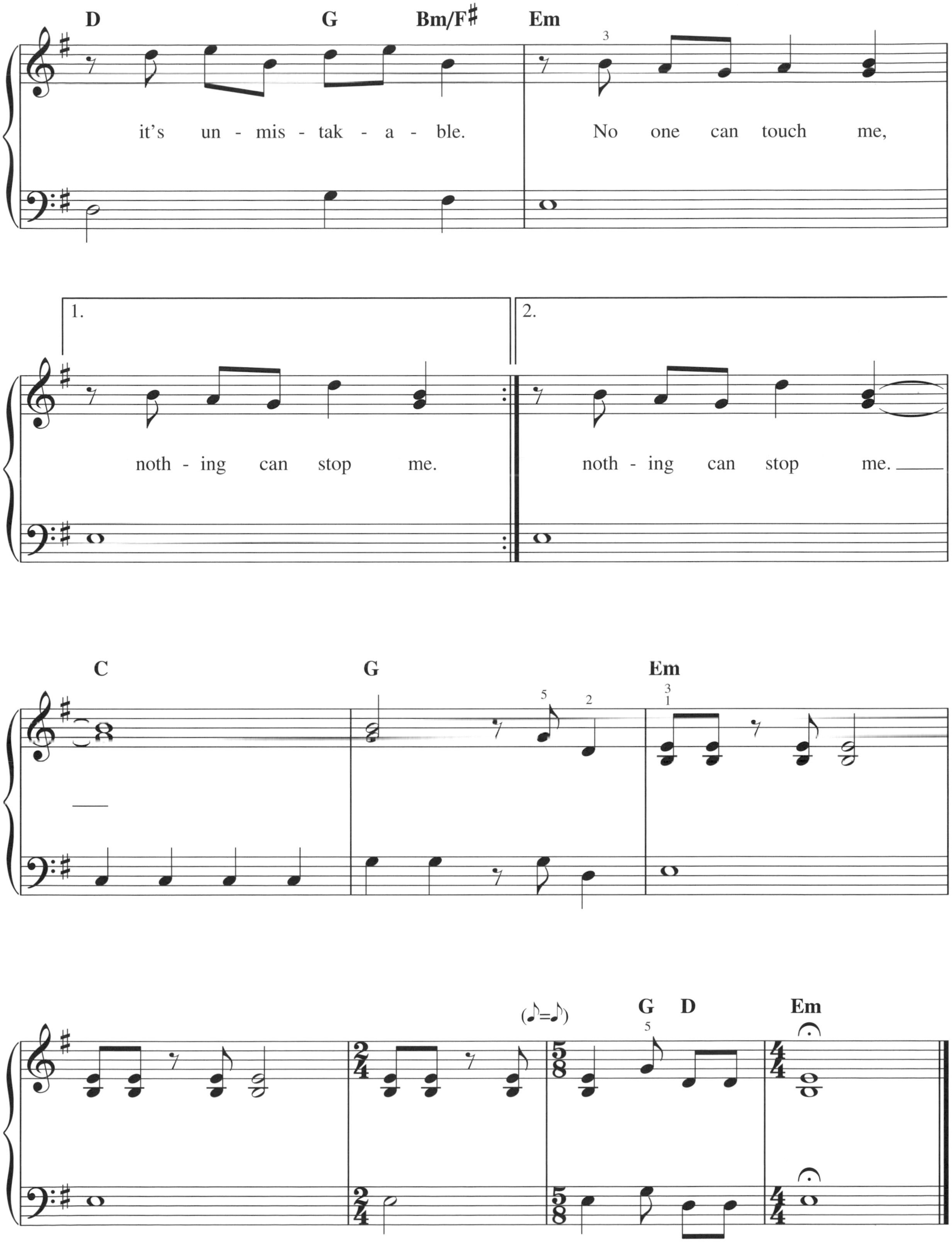

D G Bm/F♯ Em

it's un - mis - tak - a - ble. No one can touch me,

1. noth - ing can stop me.

2. noth - ing can stop me.

C G Em

WHATEVER YOU'RE DOING
(Something Heavenly)

Words and Music by MATT HAMMITT, CHRIS ROHMAN, MARK GRAALMAN, DAN GARTLEY and PETER PROVOST

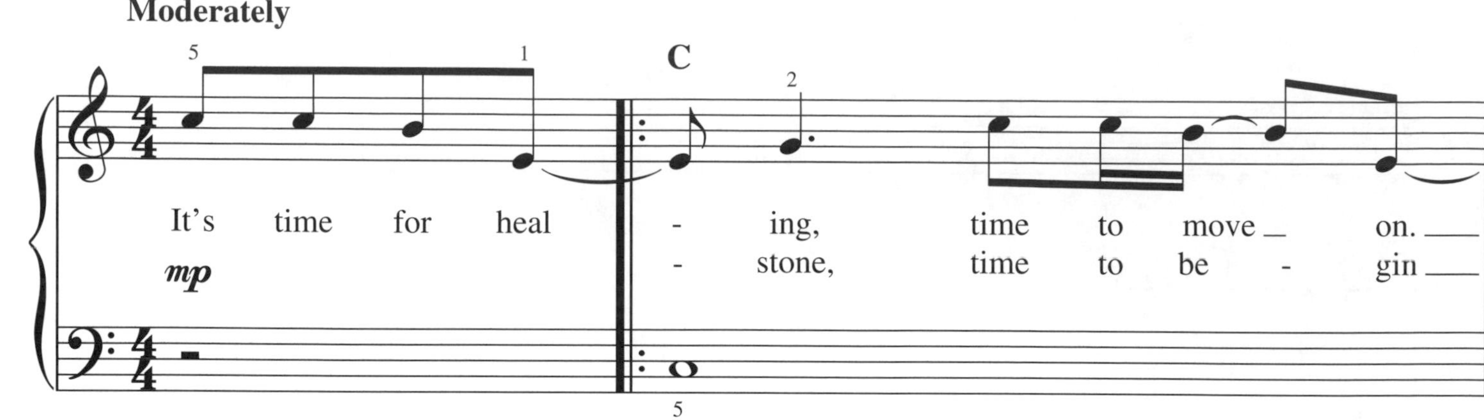

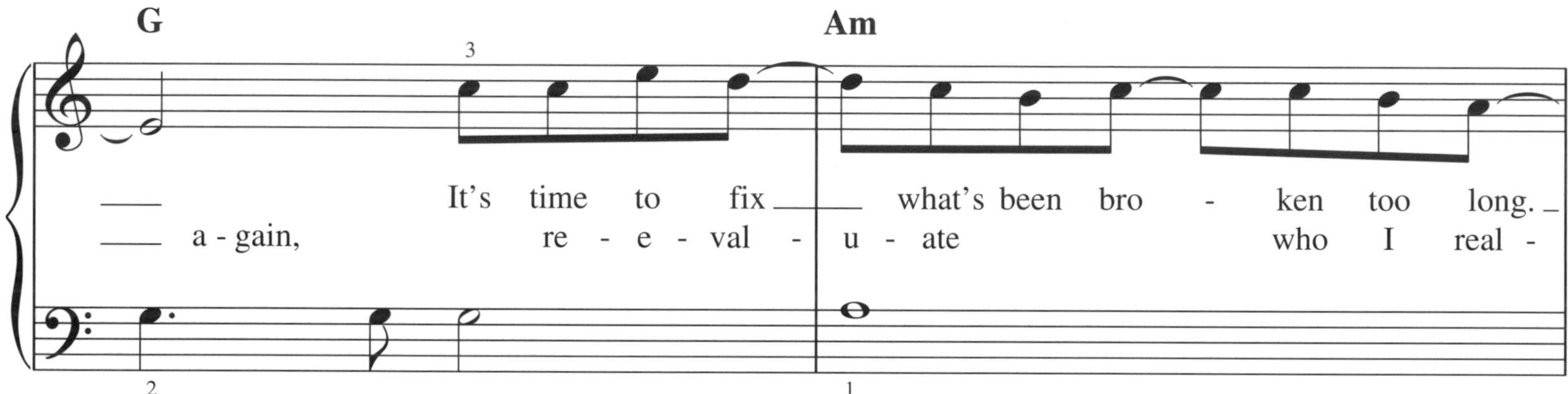

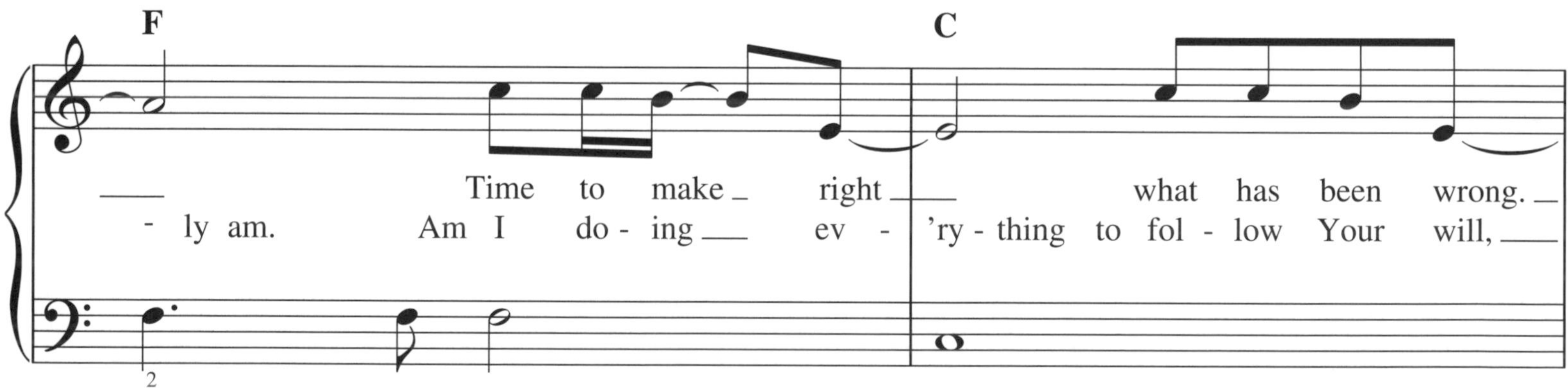

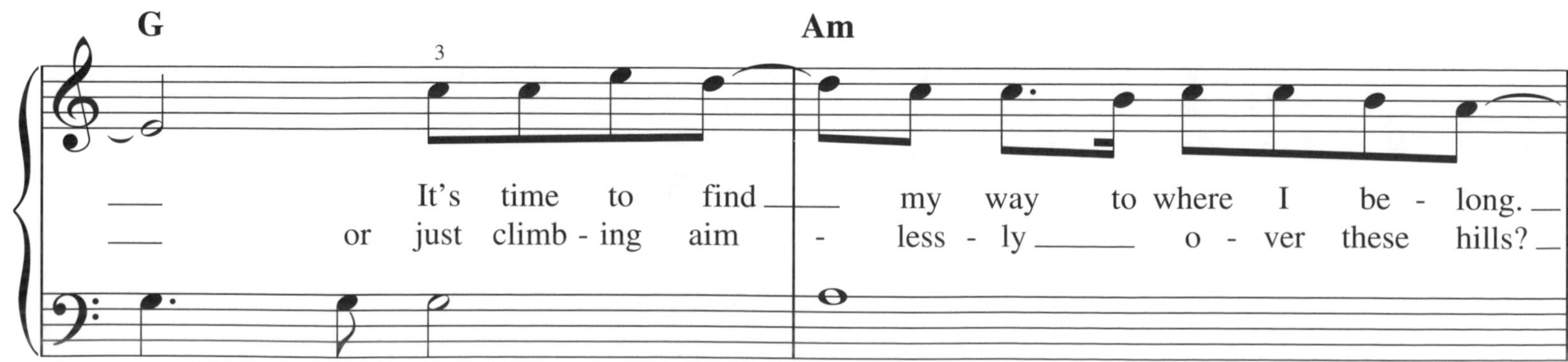

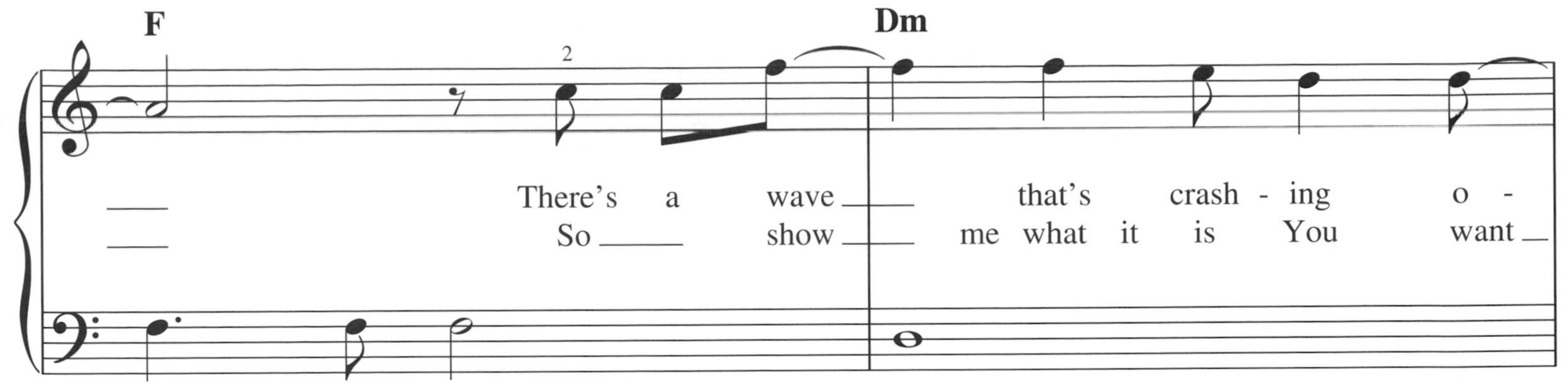
F
Dm
2
There's a wave that's crash - ing o -
So show me what it is You want

Am
C
3
- ver me, and all I can do is sur - ren -
from me. I give You ev - 'ry - thing, I sur - ren -

F
C
2
5
2
1
4
2
- der.
- der.
What - ev - er You're do - ing in - side of me,

G
Em
1
4
it feels like cha - os, but some - how there's peace.

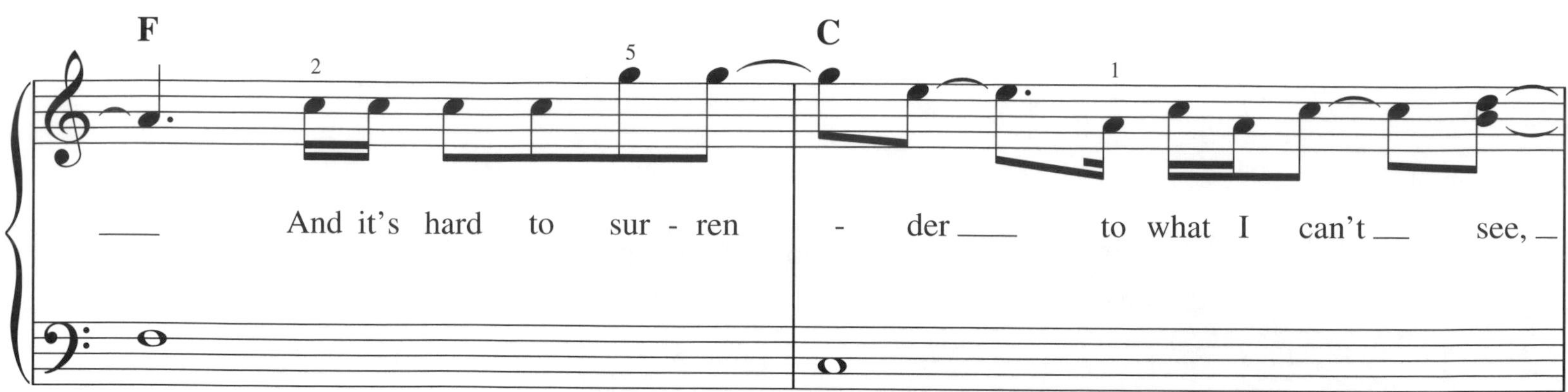
F
C
And it's hard to sur - ren - der to what I can't see,

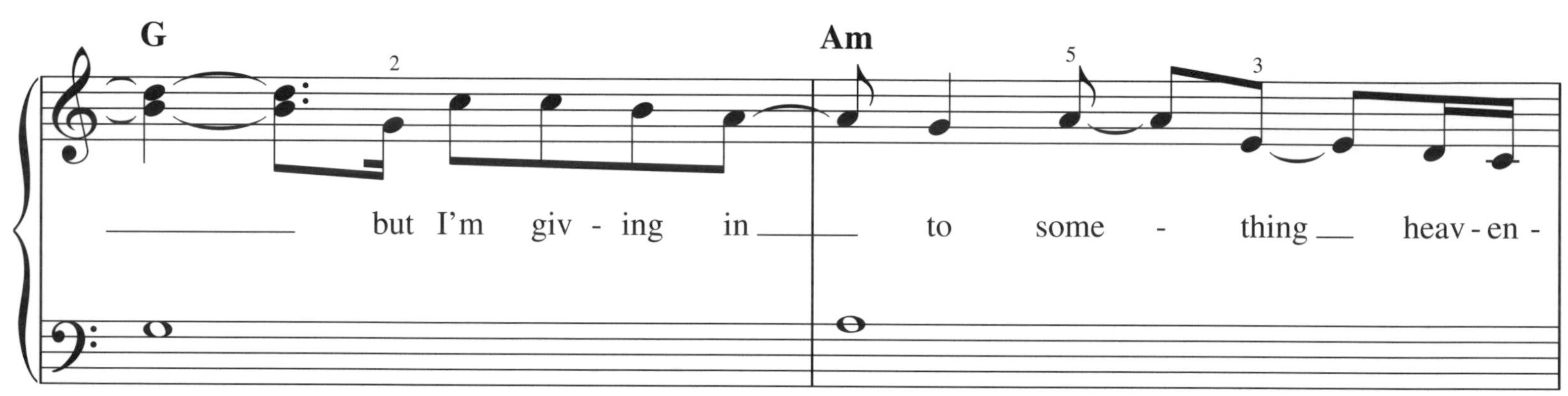
G
Am
but I'm giv - ing in to some - thing heav - en -

1.
2.
F
F
ly.
Time for a mile -
ly,
some - thing heav - en -

C
G
Am
ly.

F
C
4
1
2
1
Time to face up, clean this old

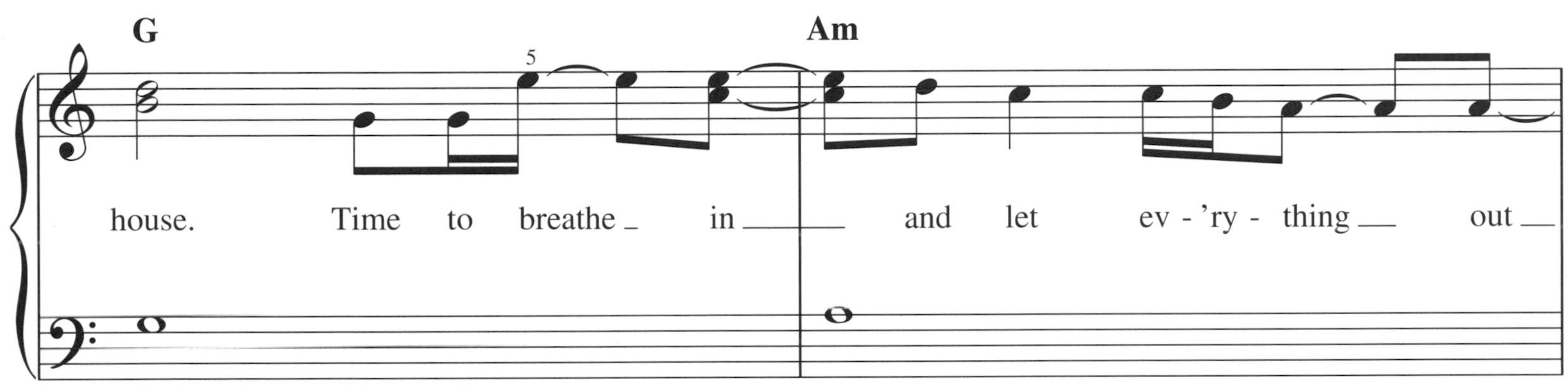
G
Am
5
house. Time to breathe in and let ev - 'ry - thing out

F
C
2
1
that I've want - ed to say for so man - y years.

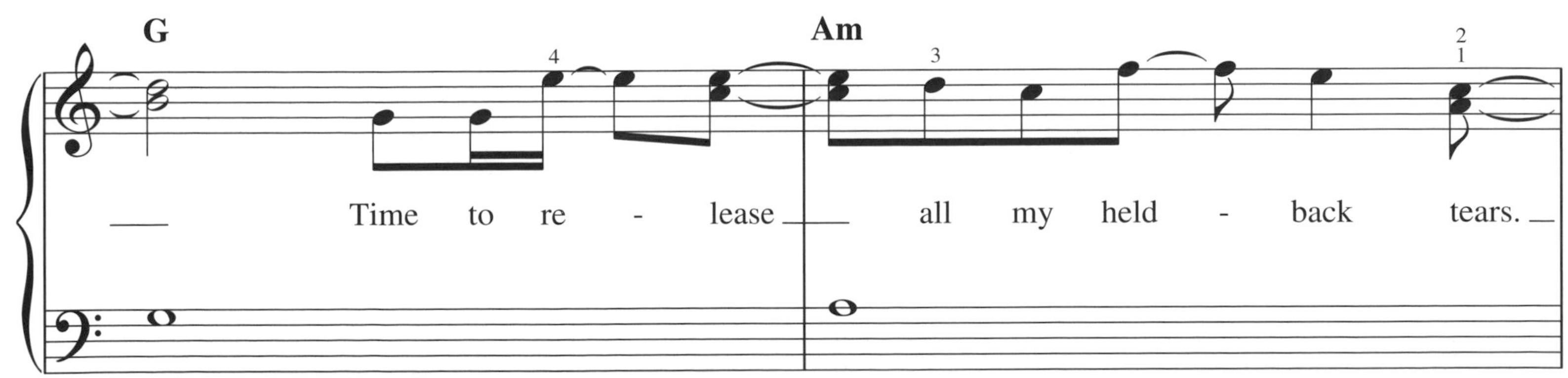
G
Am
4
3
2
1
Time to re - lease all my held - back tears.

F
C
1
2
1
4
2
What - ev - er You're do - ing in - side of me,

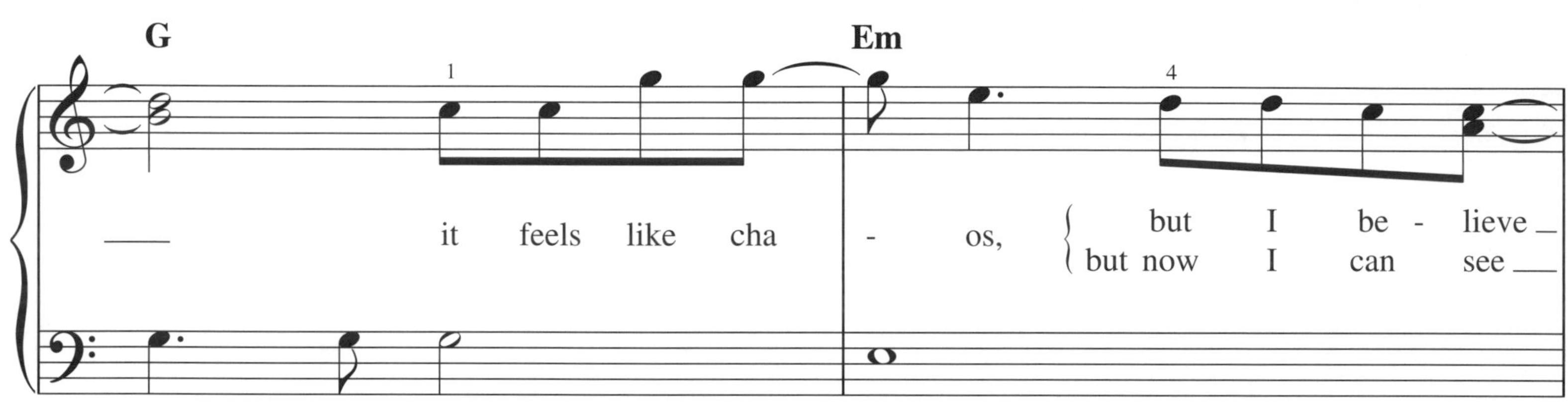
G
Em
1
4
it feels like cha - os,
but I be - lieve
but now I can see

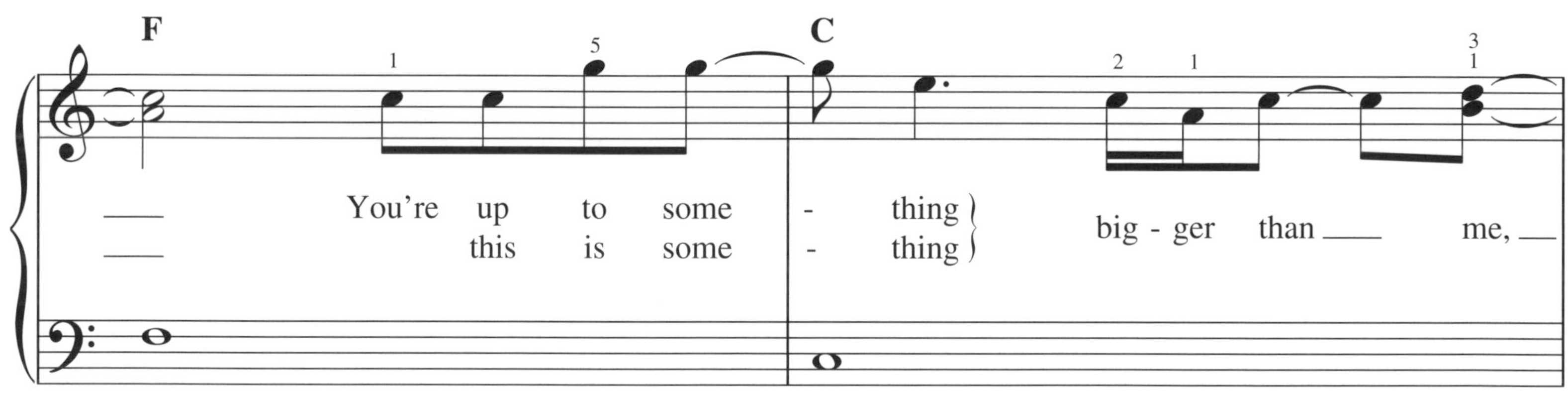
F
C
1
5
2
1
3
1
You're up to some - thing
this is some - thing
big - ger than me,

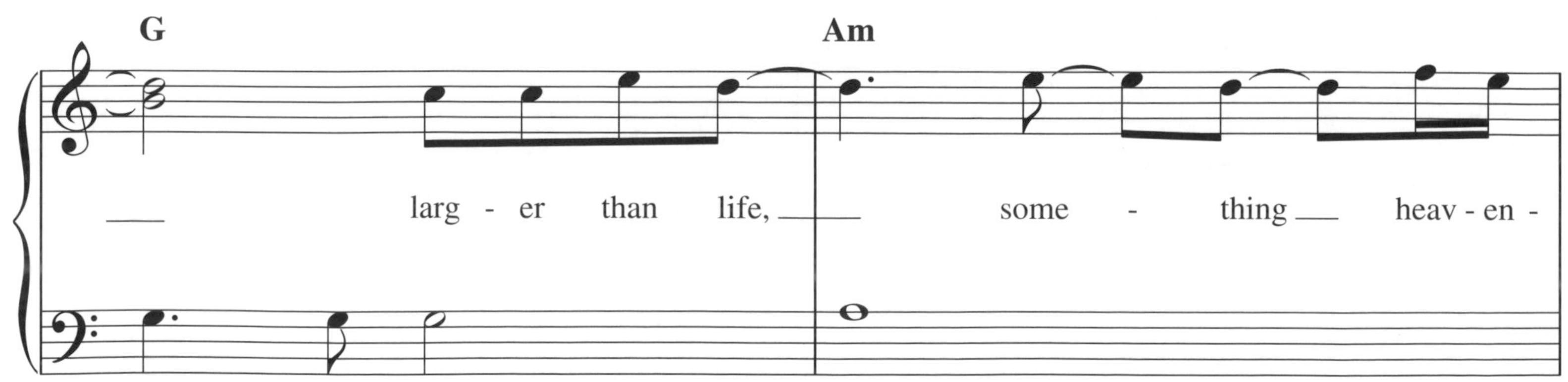
G
Am
larg - er than life, some - thing heav - en -

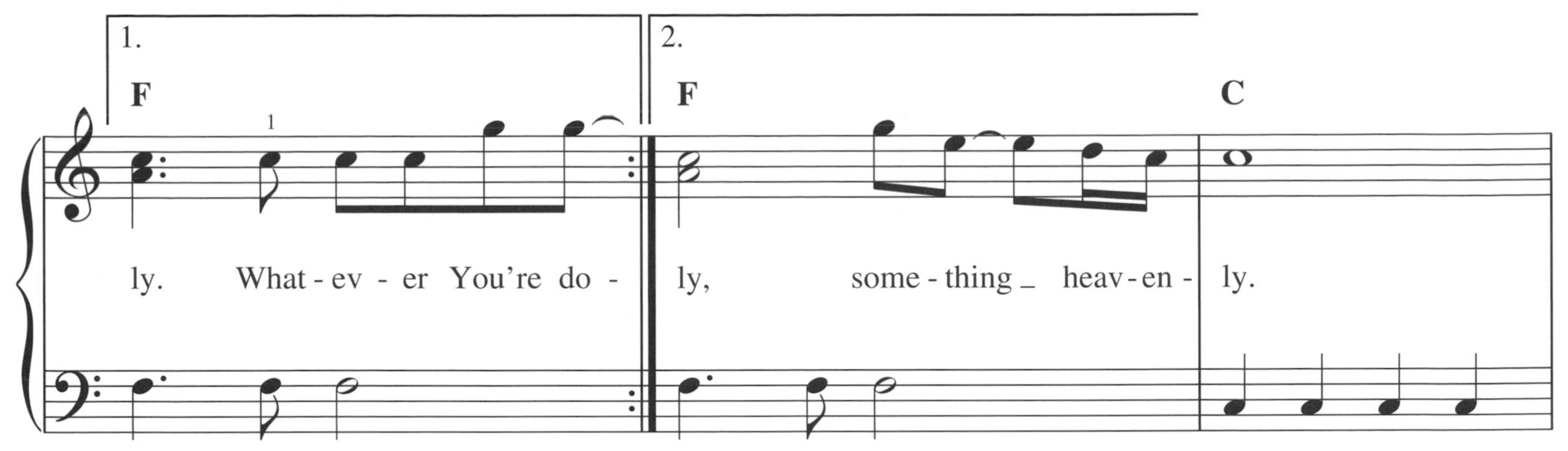
1.
2.
F
F
C
ly. What - ev - er You're do -
ly, some - thing heav - en -
ly.

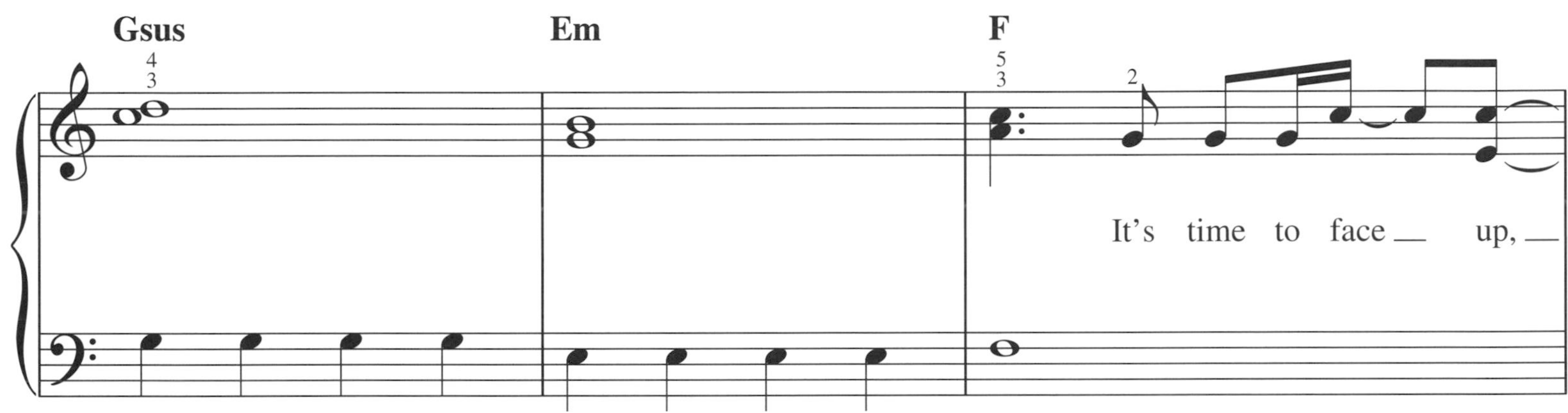
Gsus
Em
F
It's time to face up,

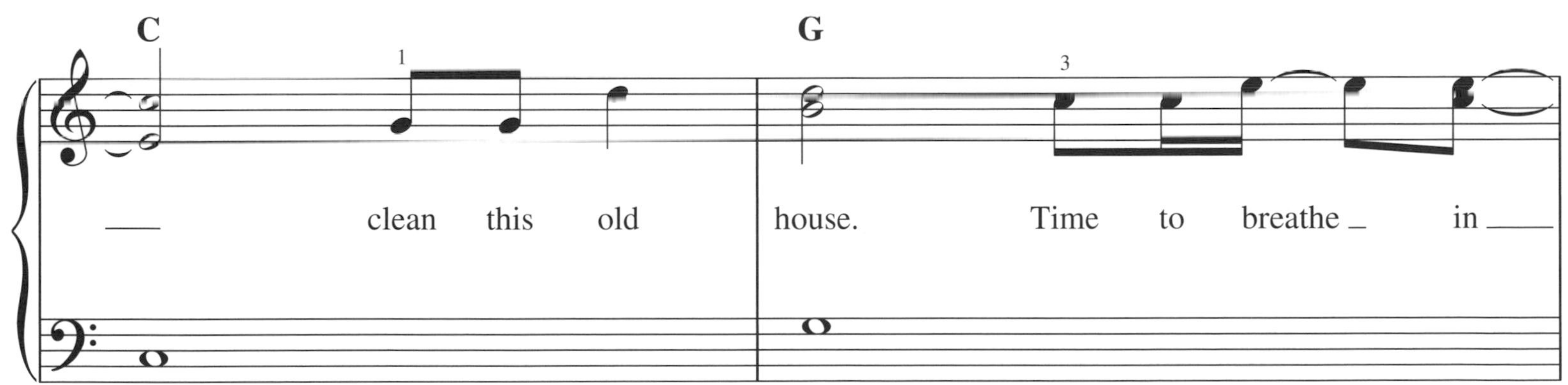
C
G
clean this old
house. Time to breathe in

Am
F
C
and let ev - 'ry - thing out.

WHEN OUR HEARTS SING

Words and Music by MATT BRONLEEWE,
JASON INGRAM, KEVIN HUGULEY
and WES WILLIS

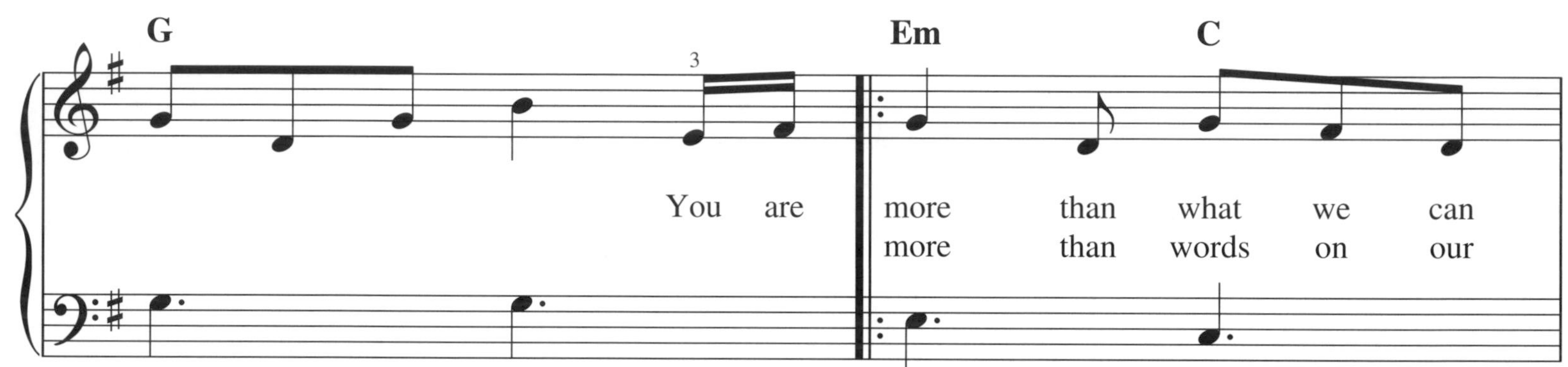

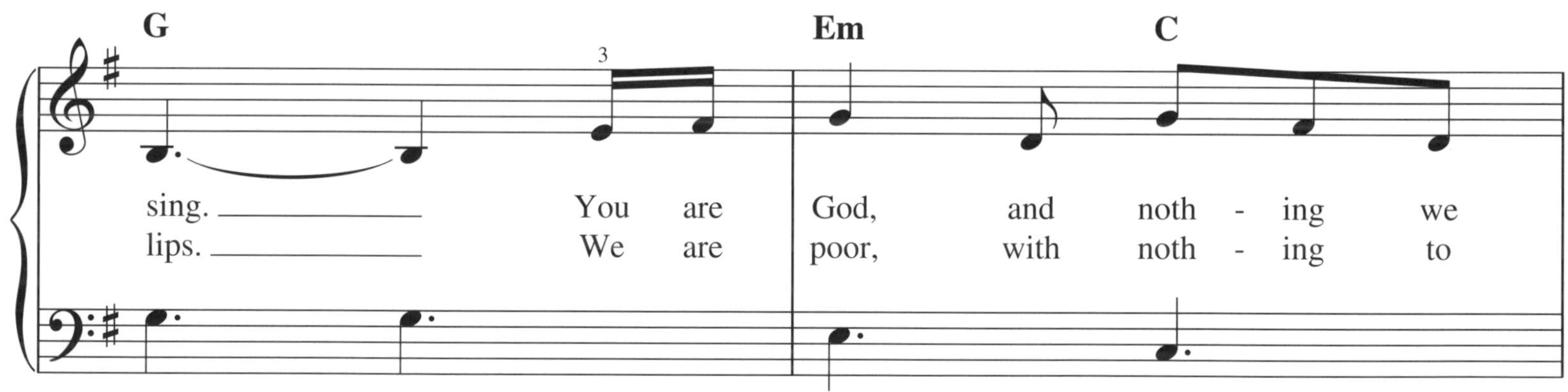

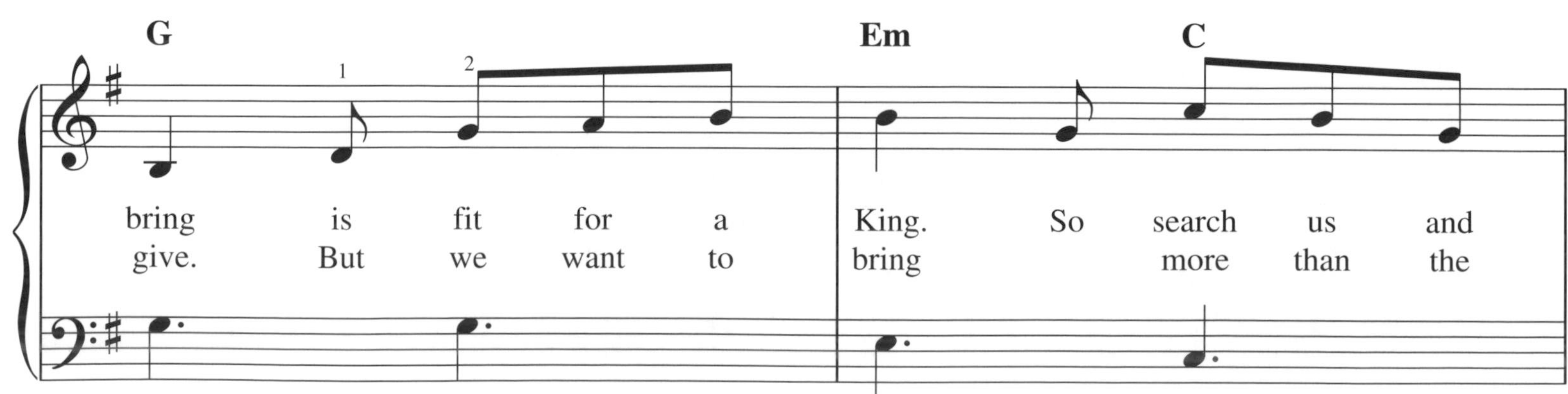

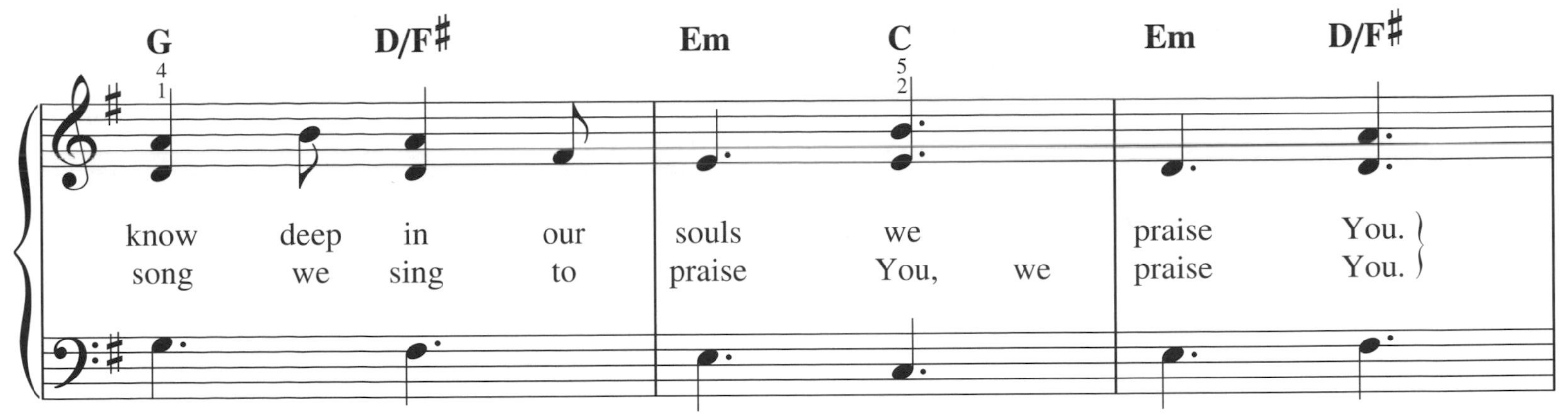
G D/F♯ Em C Em D/F♯
know deep in our souls we praise You.
song we sing to praise You, we praise You.

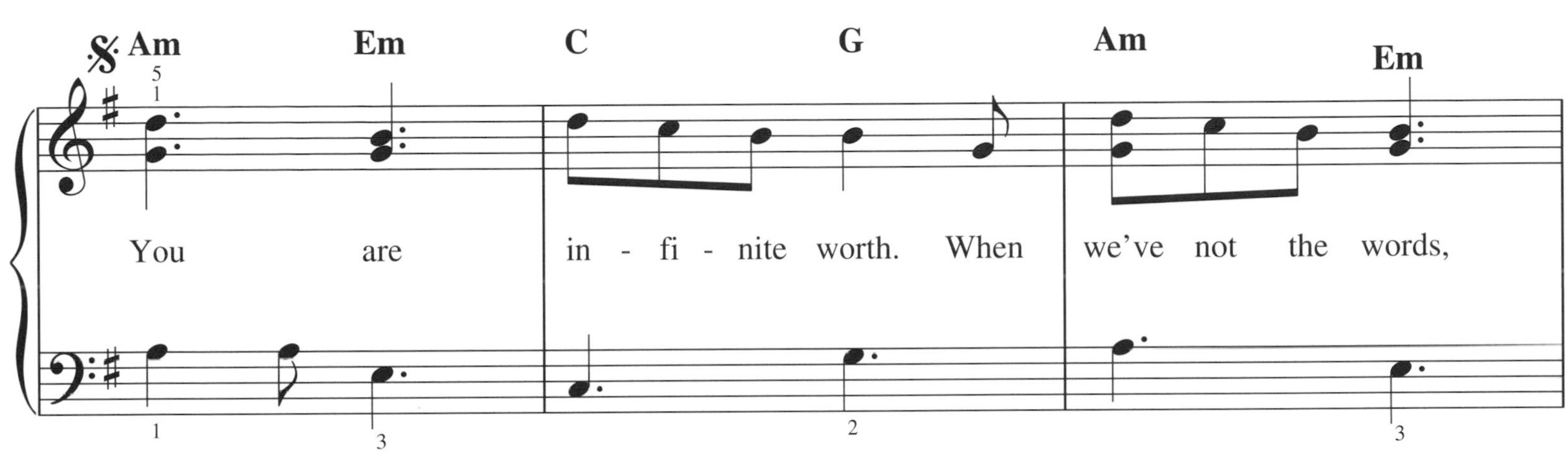
Am Em C G Am Em
You are in - fi - nite worth. When we've not the words,

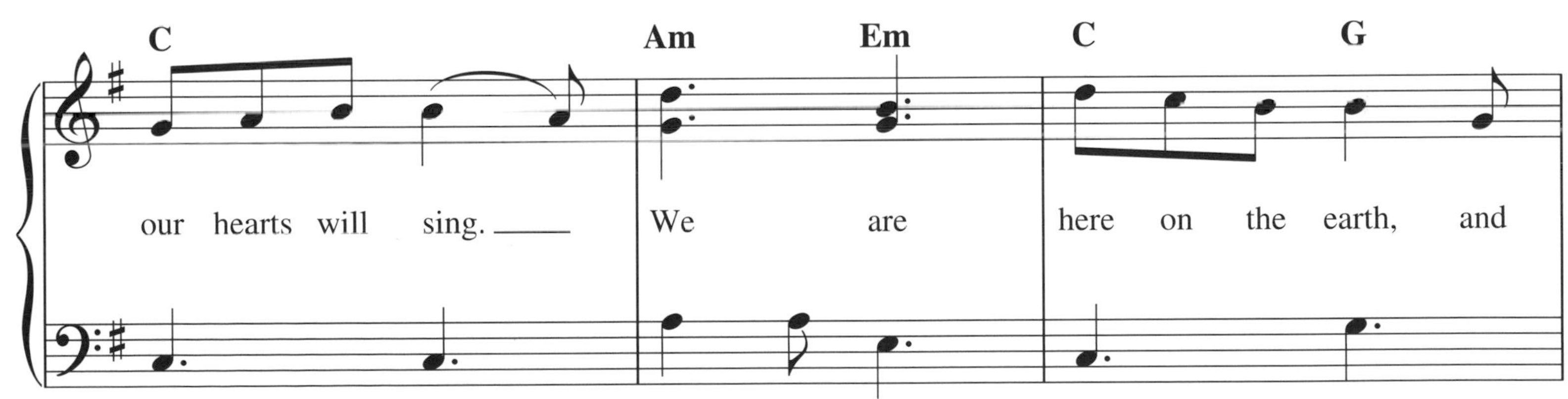
C Am Em C G
our hearts will sing. We are here on the earth, and

To Coda
1.
Am Em C Em C
some - how we're heard when our hearts sing to You.

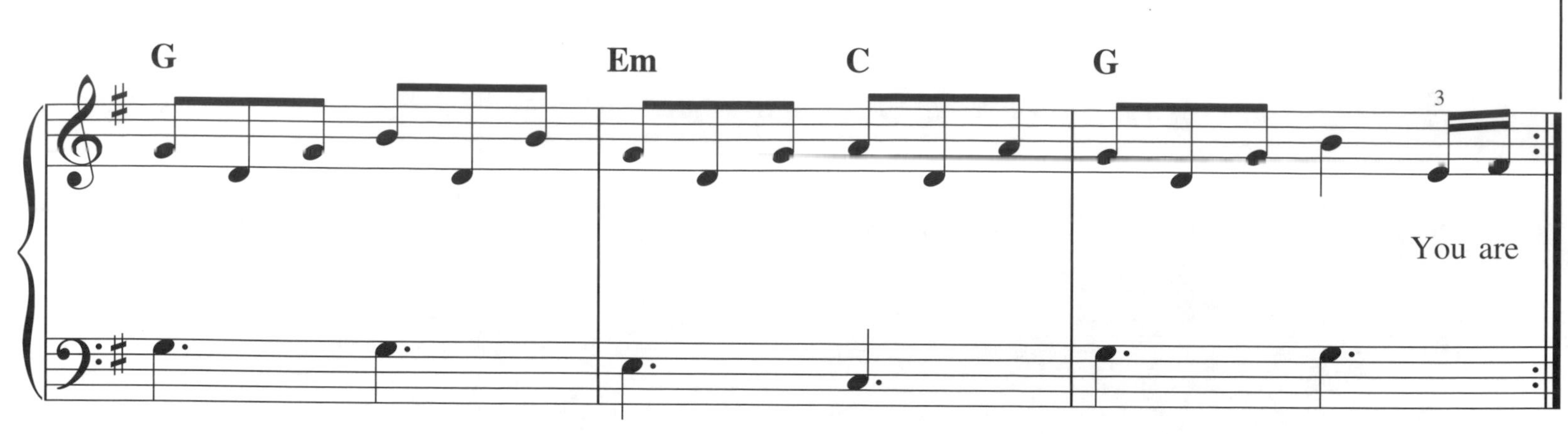
G
Em
C
G
3
You are

2.
C
1
G/B
when our hearts sing — to You.
It's You we en -
5

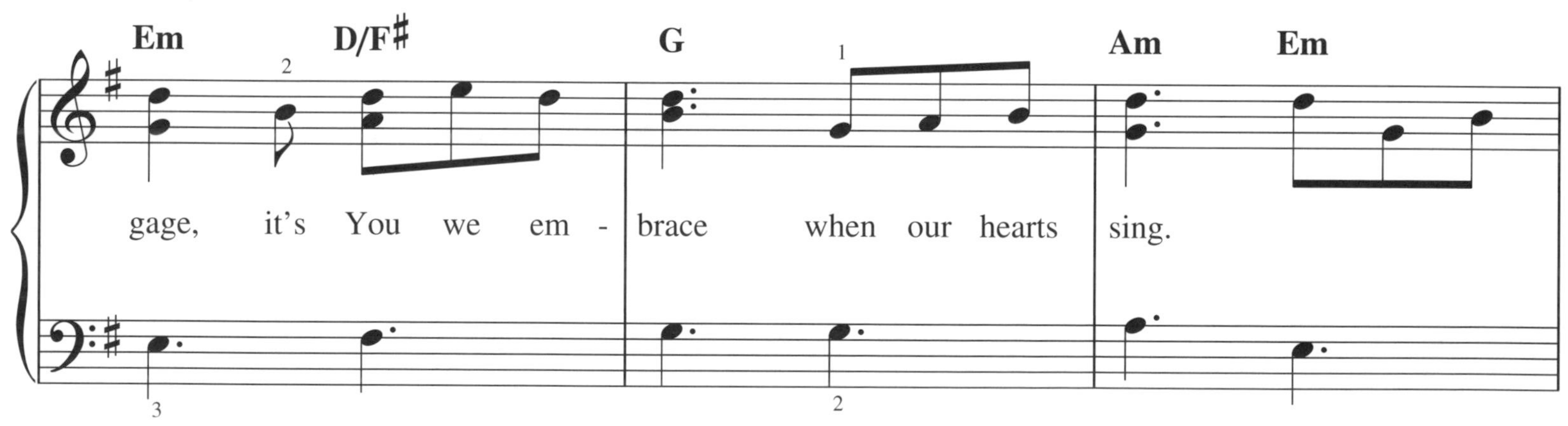
Em
D/F♯
2
G
1
Am
Em
gage, it's You we em - brace when our hearts sing.
3
2

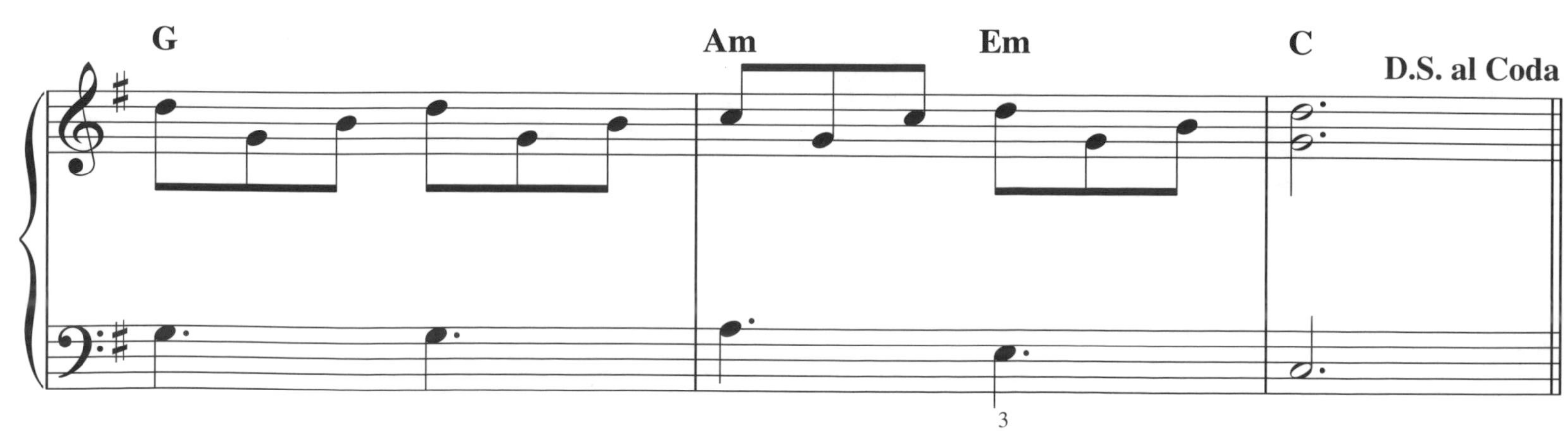
G
Am
Em
C
D.S. al Coda
3

CODA

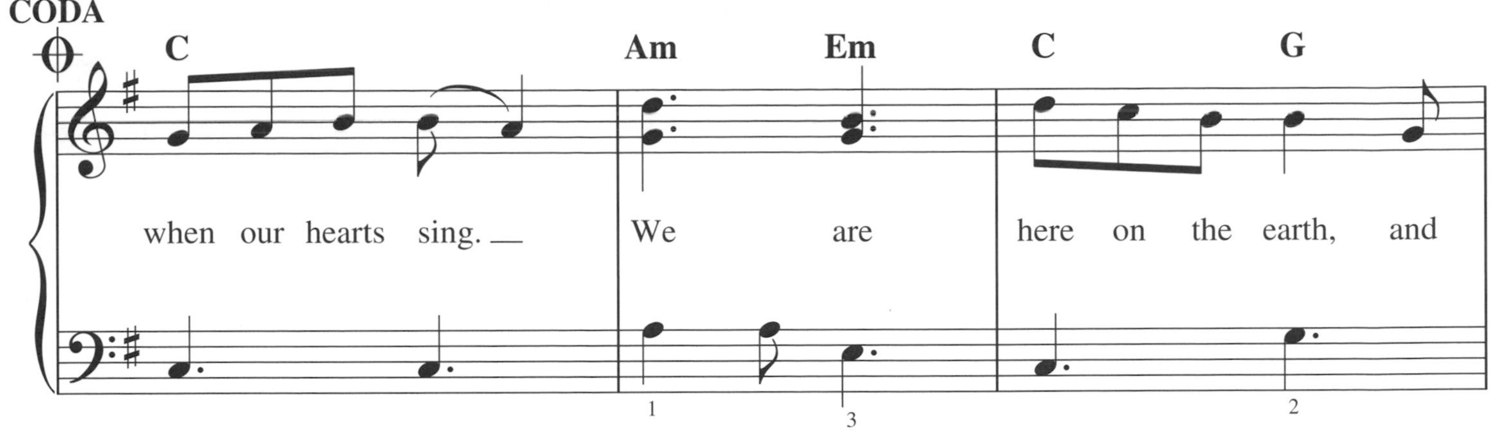
CODA
C
Am
Em
C
G
when our hearts sing. __
We are
here on the earth, and

Am
Em
C
Em
C
some - how we're heard
when our hearts sing __ to
You.

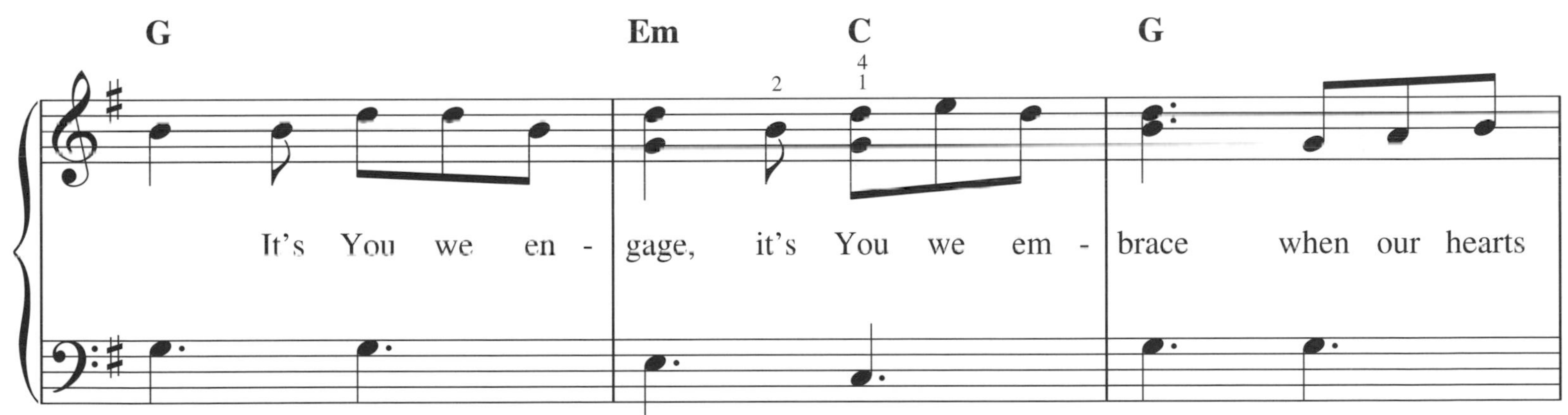
G
Em
C
G
It's You we en -
gage, it's You we em -
brace when our hearts

Em
C
G
Em
C
Em9
sing.

YOU REIGN

Words and Music by STEVEN CURTIS CHAPMAN,
BART MILLARD and BARRY GRAUL

G
Am
F
e - ven be - fore the world was put in mo - tion,
e - ven be - fore we had to be for - giv - en,

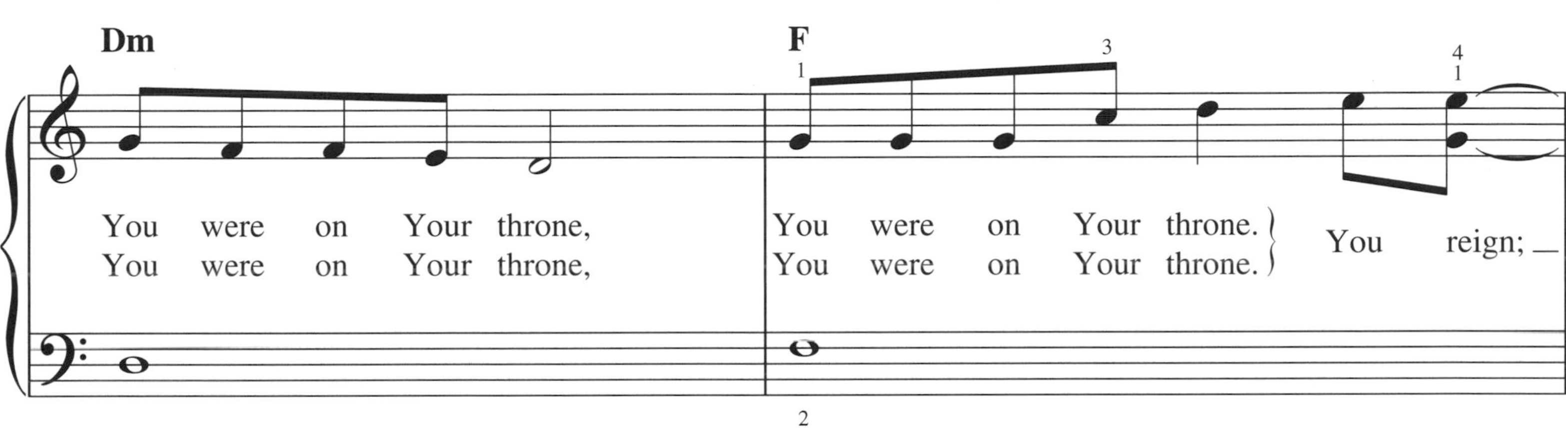
Dm
F
You were on Your throne, You were on Your throne.
You were on Your throne, You were on Your throne.
You reign;

C
glo - ry in the high - est, You reign.

F
Let cre - a - tion tes - ti - fy: by Your name,

C
ev - 'ry knee will bow and ev - 'ry

To Coda
F G Am
C/E F
1.
tongue pro - claim that Je - sus reigns.

Am F
2.
G Dm
reigns. Yes - ter - day, to - day and for -

Am C F G F G Am
ev - er, You are God who was and is

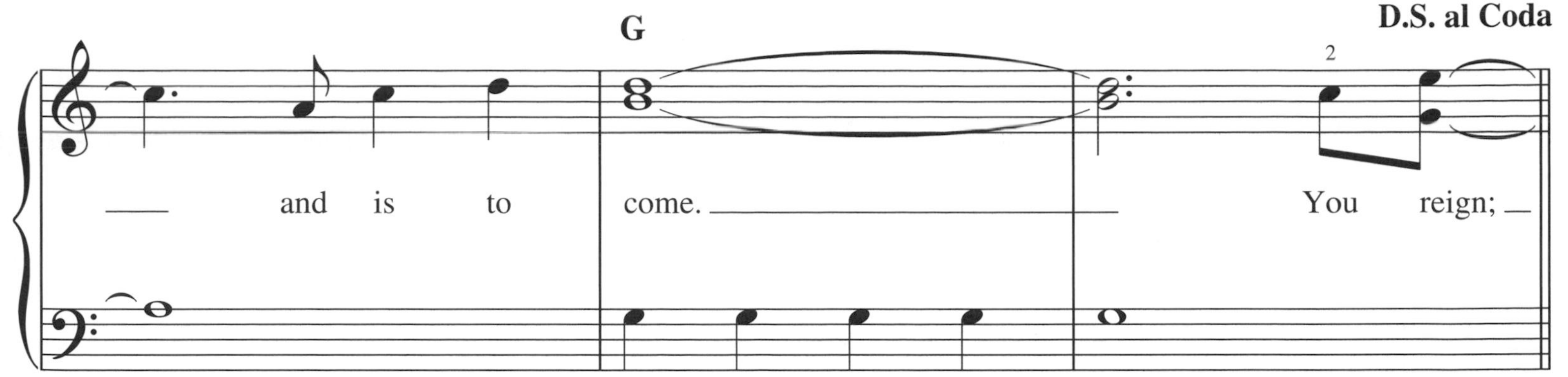
G
D.S. al Coda
and is to
come.
You reign;

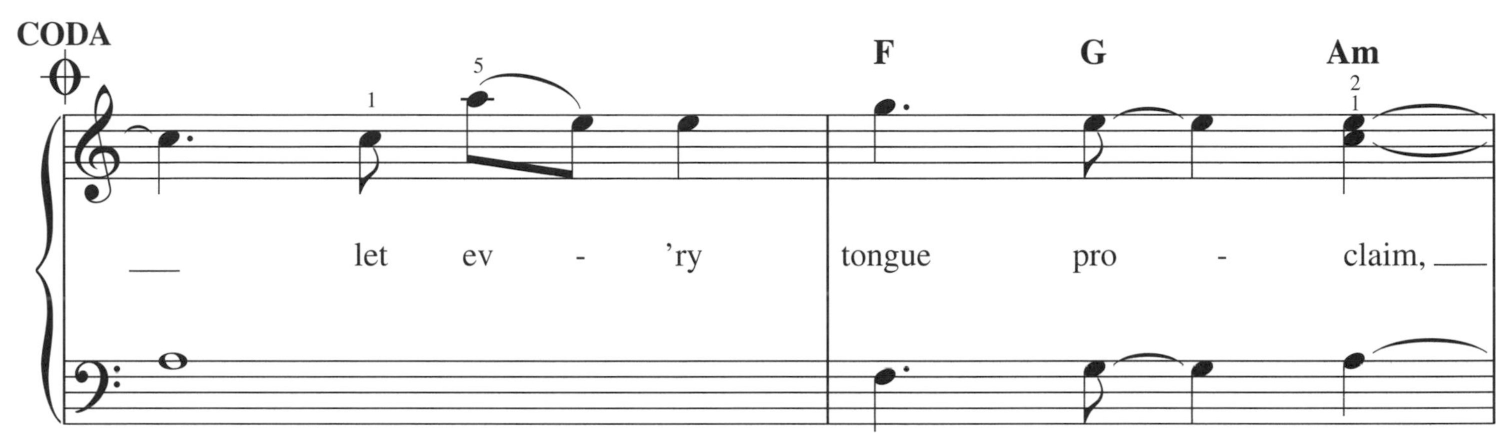
CODA
F G Am
let ev - 'ry
tongue pro - claim,

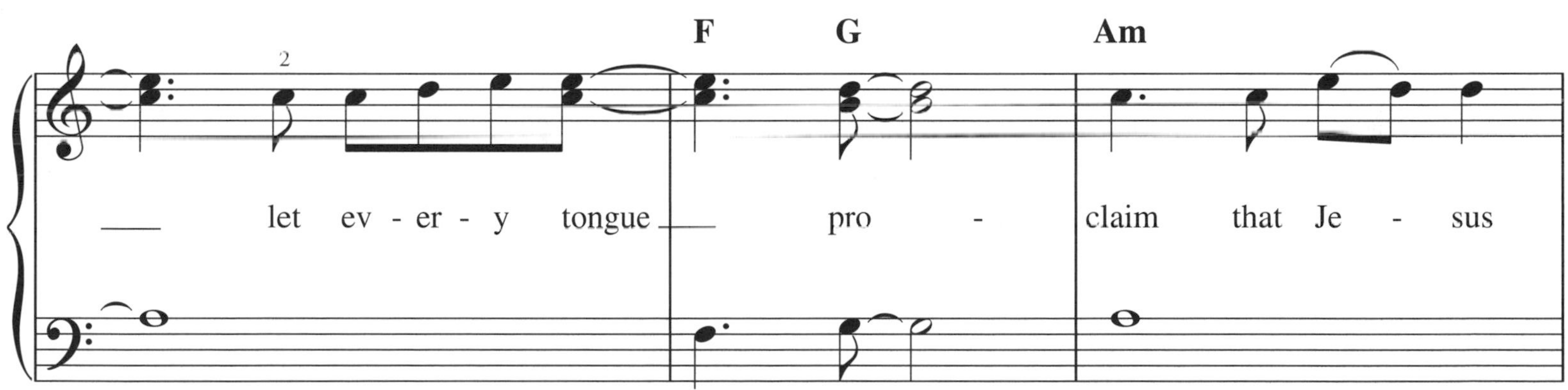
F G Am
let ev - er - y tongue
pro -
claim that Je - sus

Fm C
reigns.

YOUR GRACE IS ENOUGH

Words and Music by
MATT MAHER

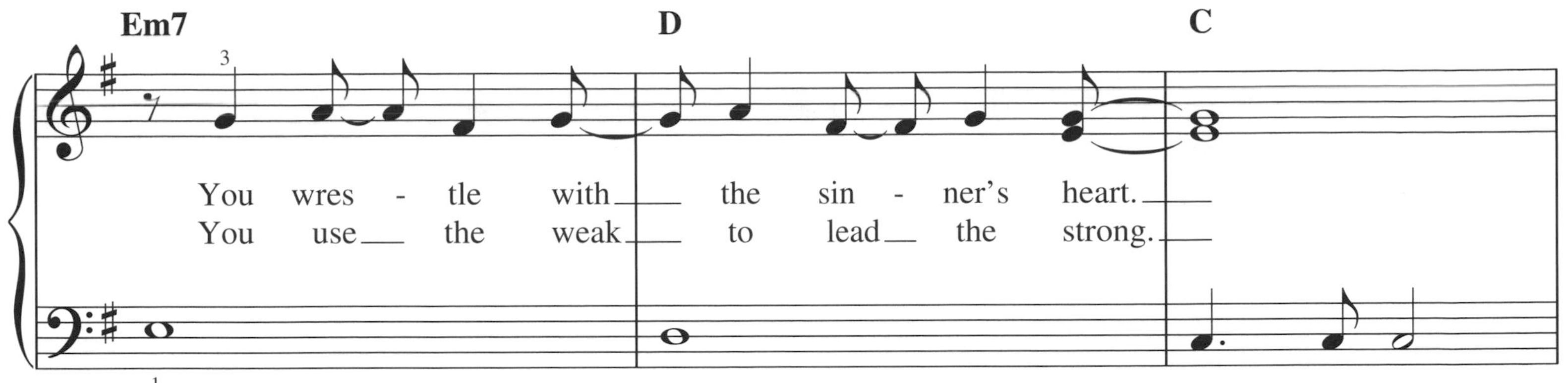
Em7
D
C
You wres - tle with the sin - ner's heart.
You use the weak to lead the strong.

G
G/B
You lead us by still wa - ters in -
You lead us in the song of Your

C
Em7
- to mer - cy, and noth - ing can
sal - va - tion, and all Your peo -

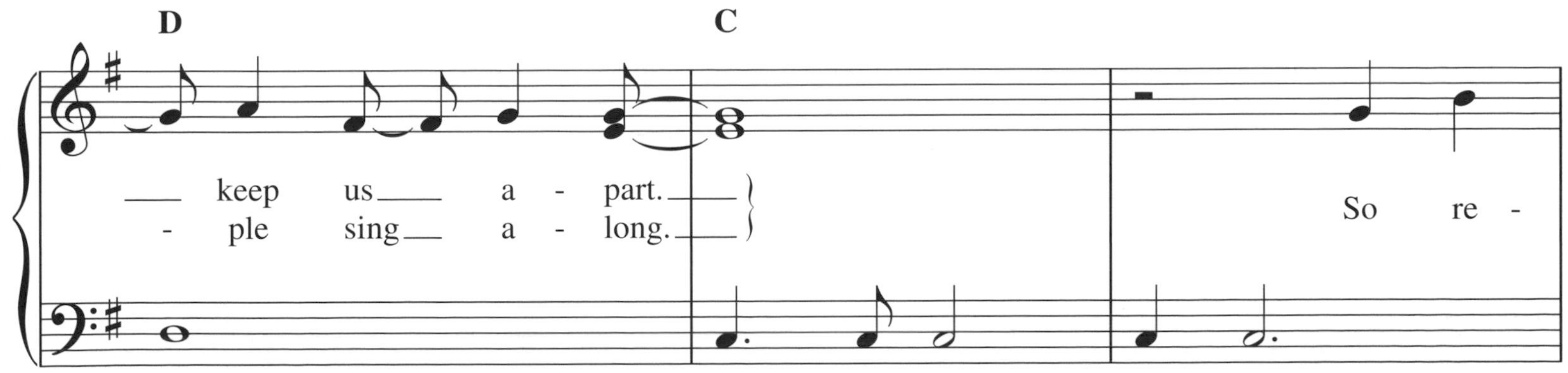
D
C
keep us a - part.
- ple sing a - long.
So re -

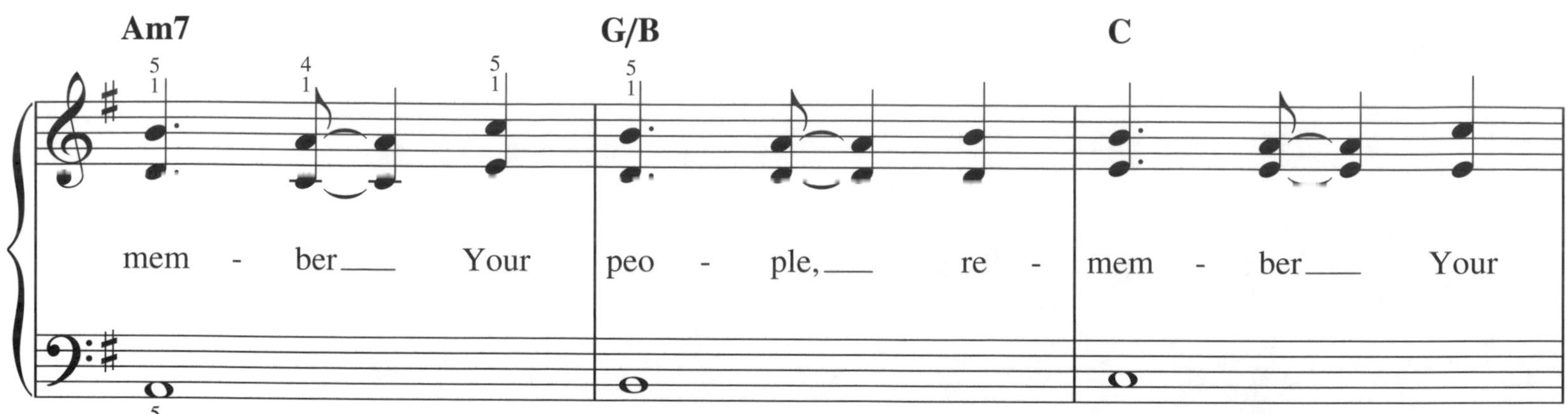
Am7
G/B
C
mem - ber Your
peo - ple, re -
mem - ber Your

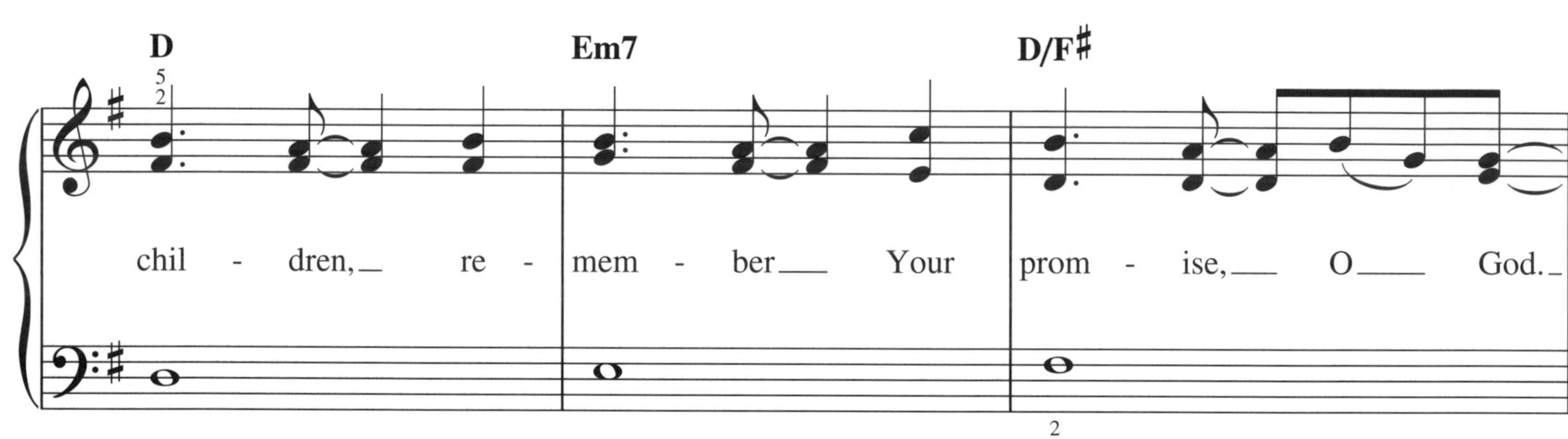
D
Em7
D/F♯
chil - dren, re -
mem - ber Your
prom - ise, O God.

C
G
D
Your
grace is e - nough,
Your

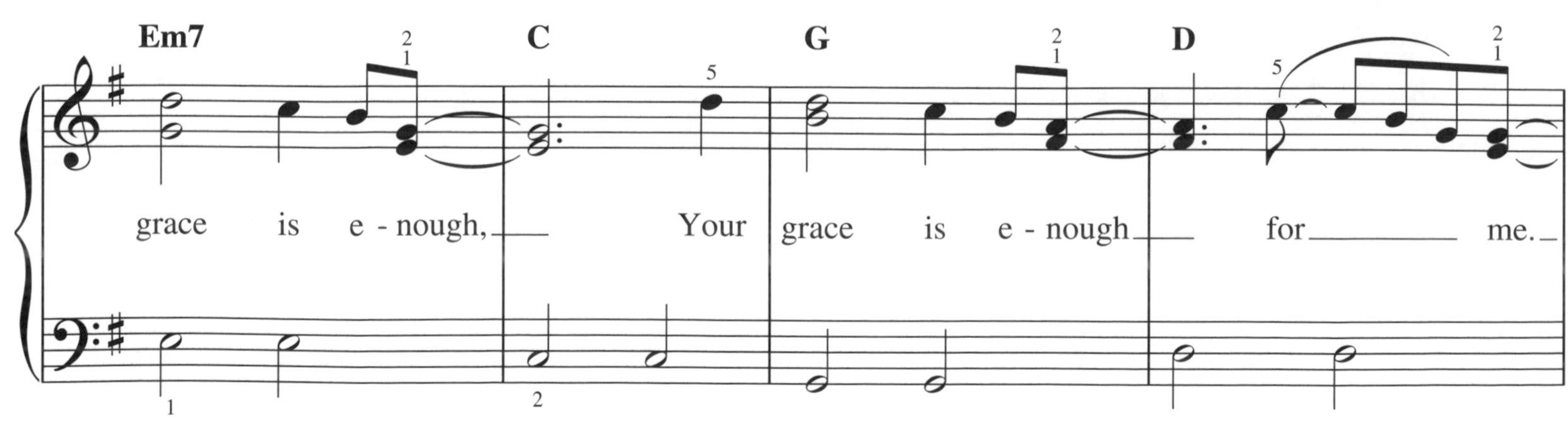
Em7
C
G
D
grace is e - nough,
Your
grace is e - nough
for me.

To Coda
1.
2.
D.S. al Coda
C
Yeah, Your

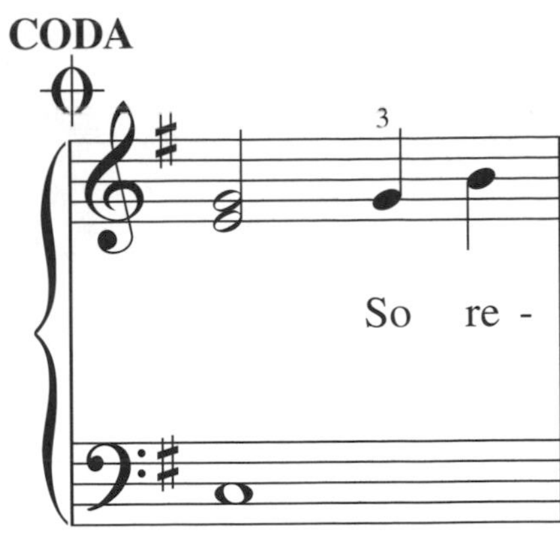

CODA
So re -

Am7
G/B
C
D
mem - ber Your peo - ple, re - mem - ber Your chil - dren, re -

Em7
D/F#
C
mem - ber Your prom - ise, O God.
Your

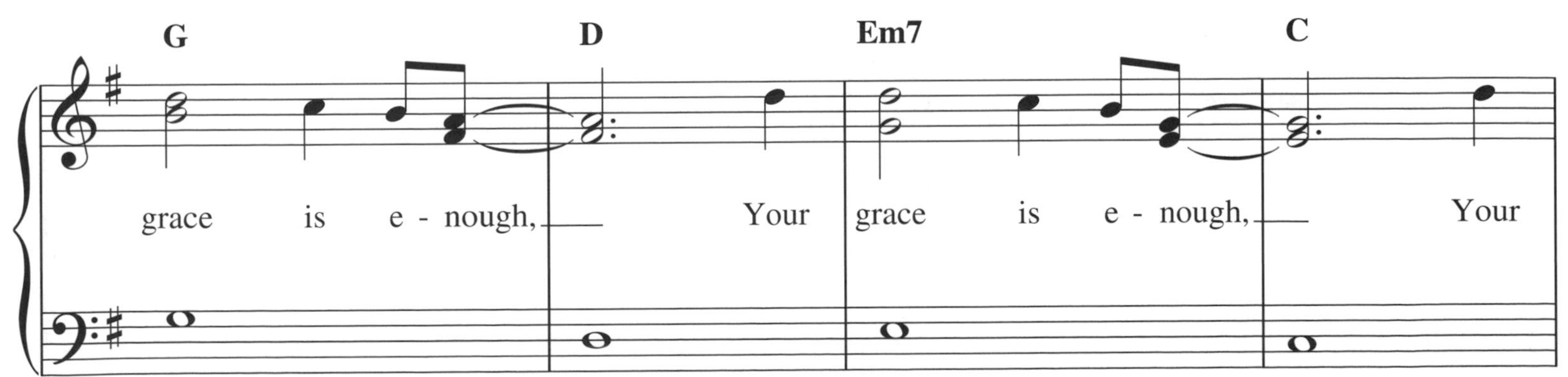

G
D
Em7
C
grace is e - nough, Your grace is e - nough, Your

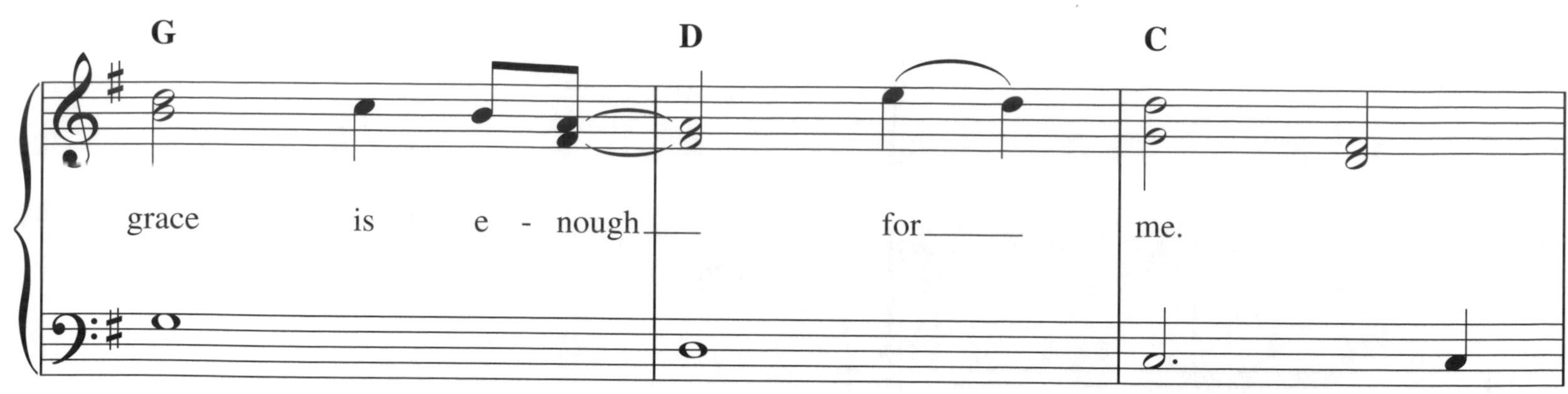
G
D
C
grace is e - nough for me.

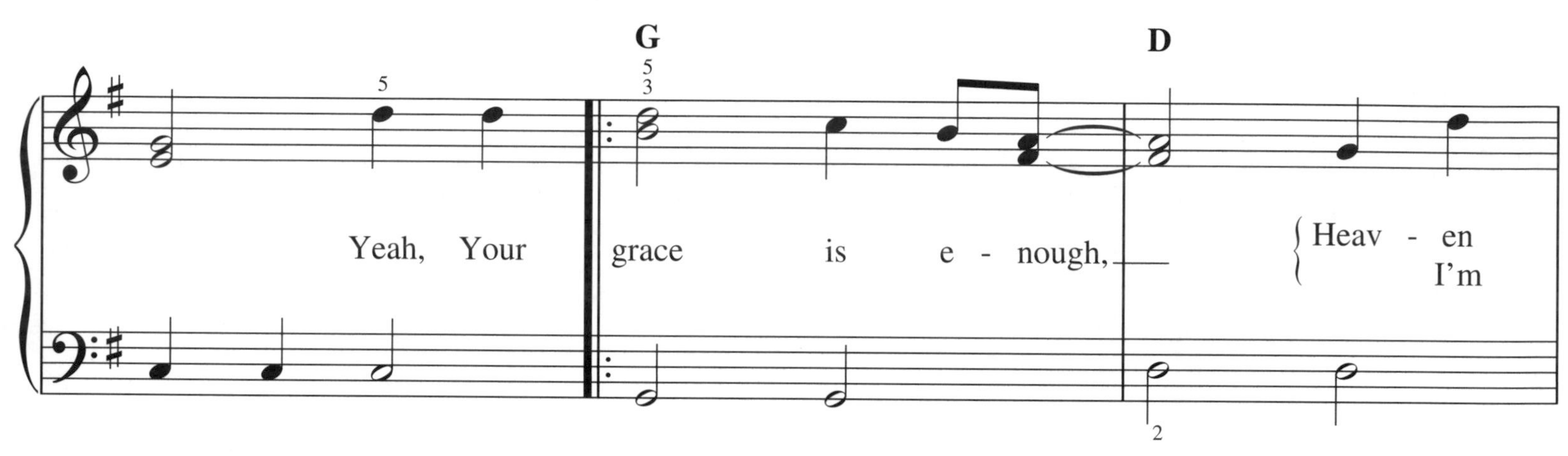
G
D
5
5
3
2
Yeah, Your grace is e - nough,
Heav - en
I'm

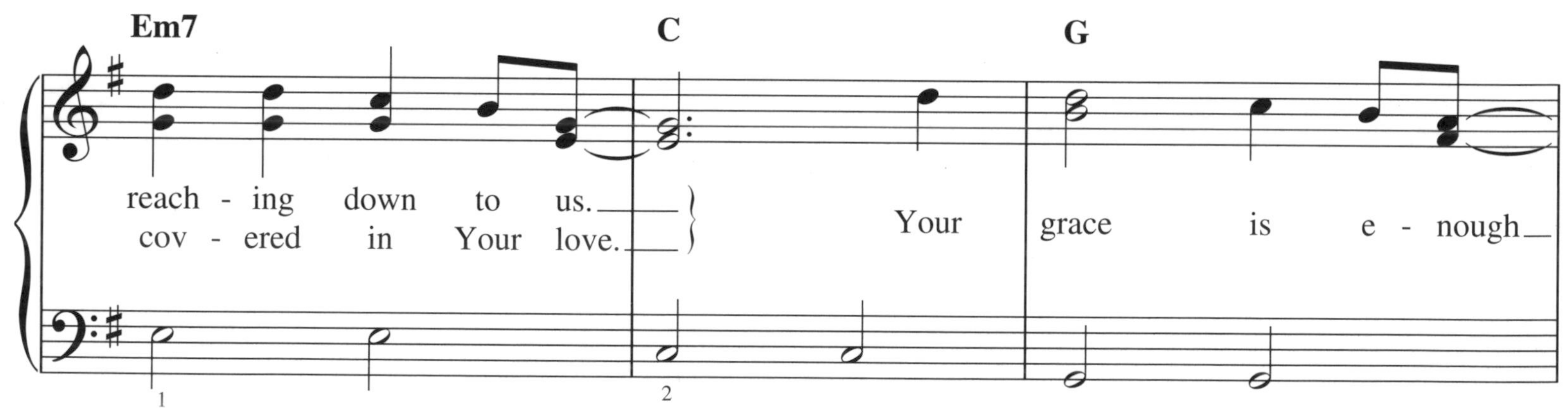
Em7
C
G
reach - ing down to us.
cov - ered in Your love.
Your grace is e - nough
1
2

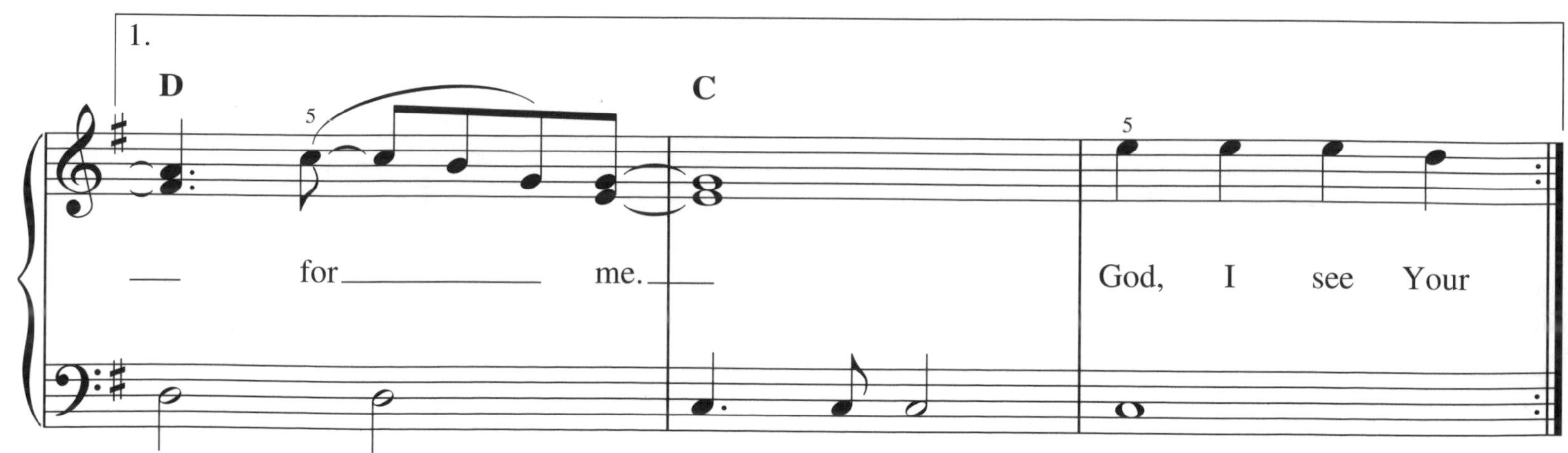
1.
D
C
5
5
for me.
God, I see Your

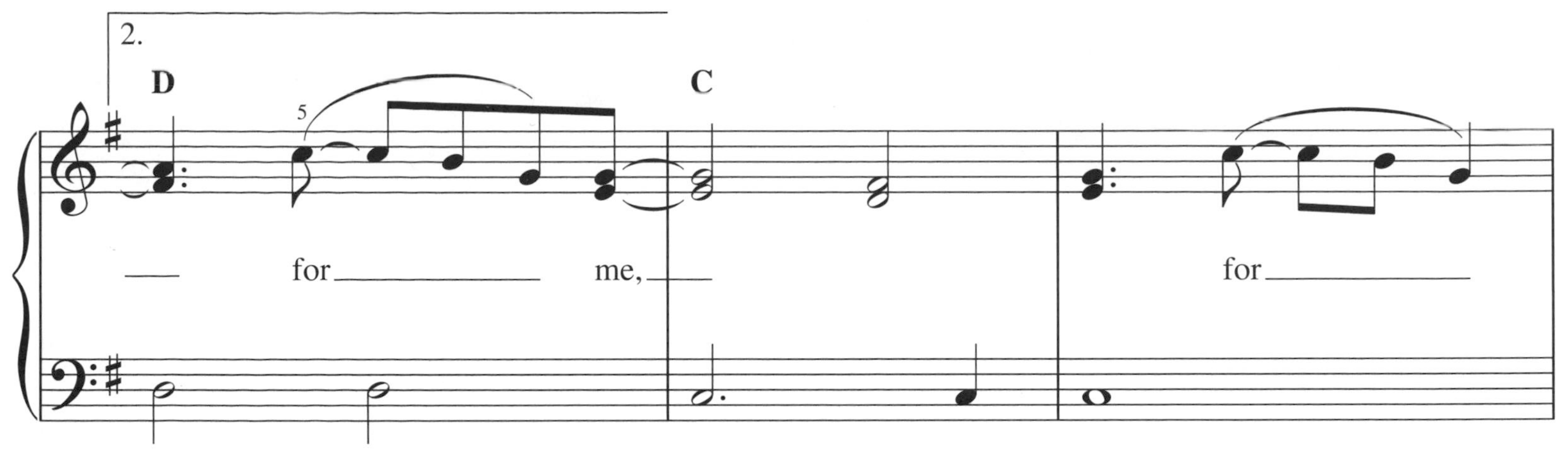
2.
D
C
for
me,
for

G
G/B
C
me.

Em
D
G
G/B

Cmaj7
Em
D
G

YOURS

Words and Music by STEVEN CURTIS CHAPMAN
and JONAS MYRIN

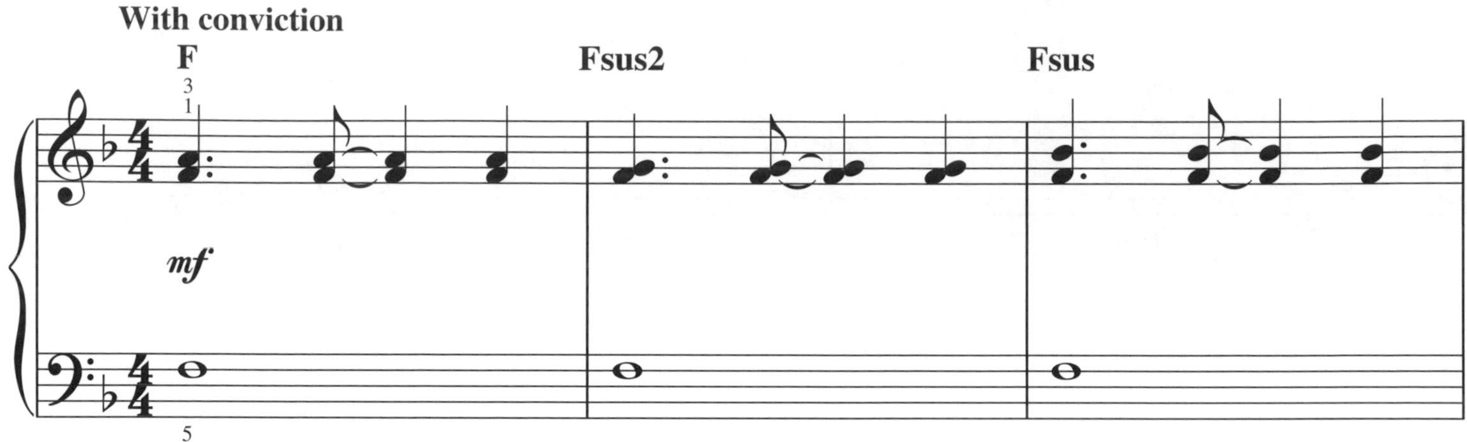

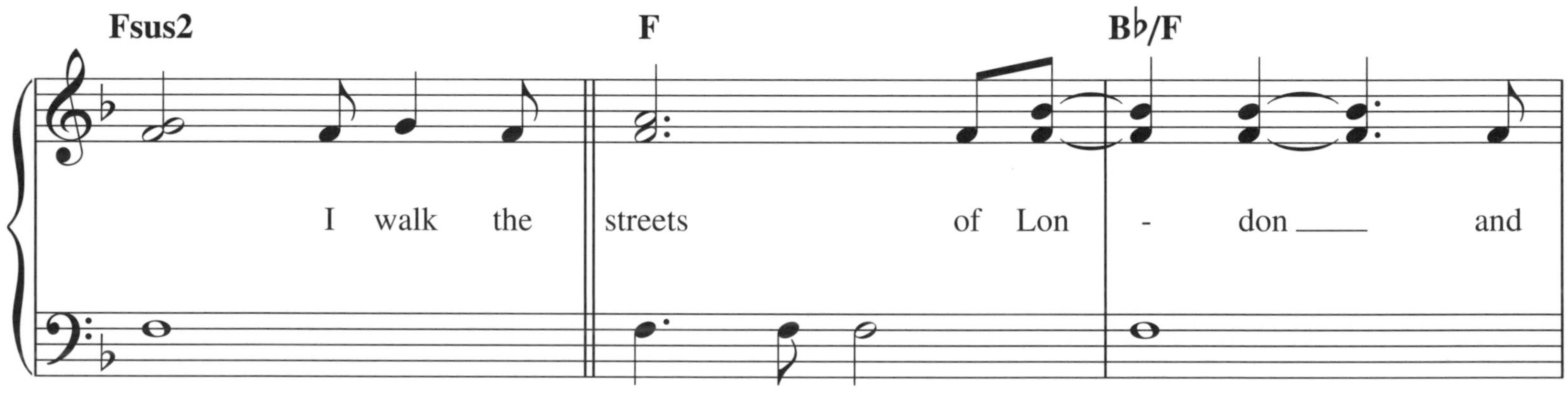

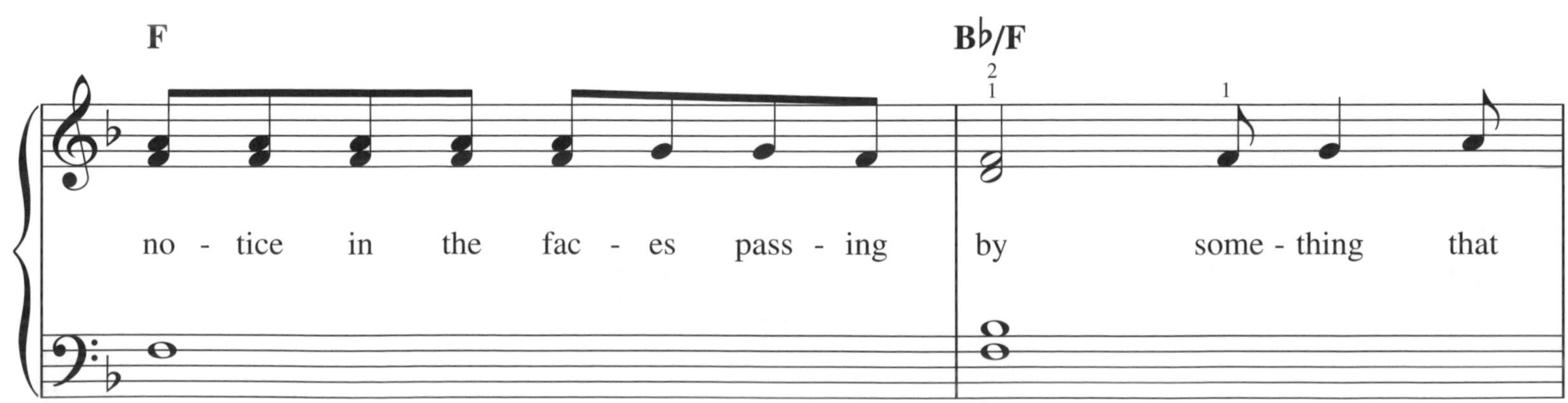

F
B♭/F
F
makes me stop and lis - ten. My heart grows heav - y with the

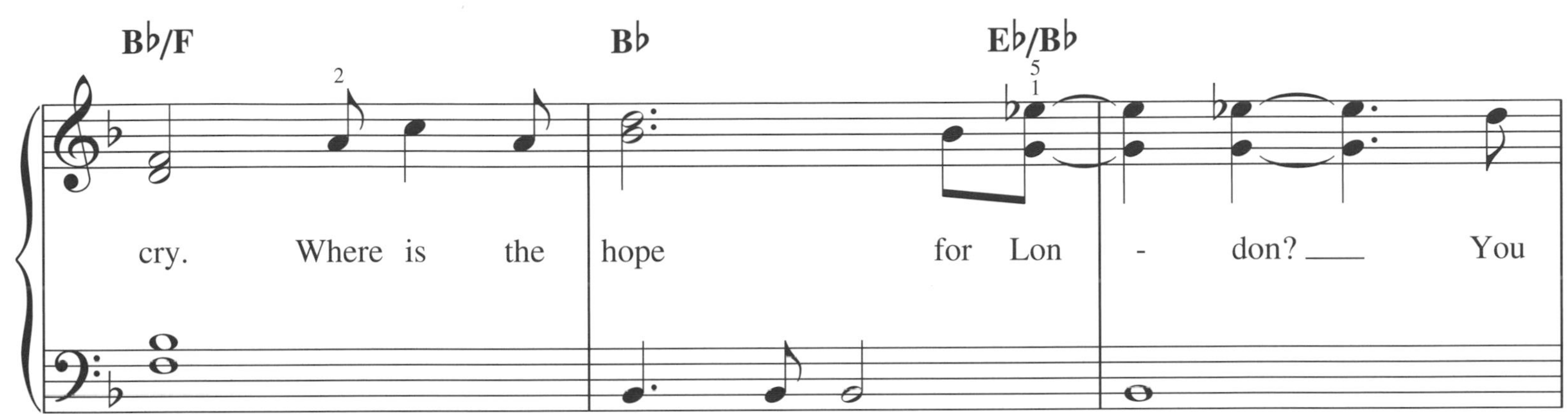
B♭/F
B♭
E♭/B♭
cry. Where is the hope for Lon - don? You

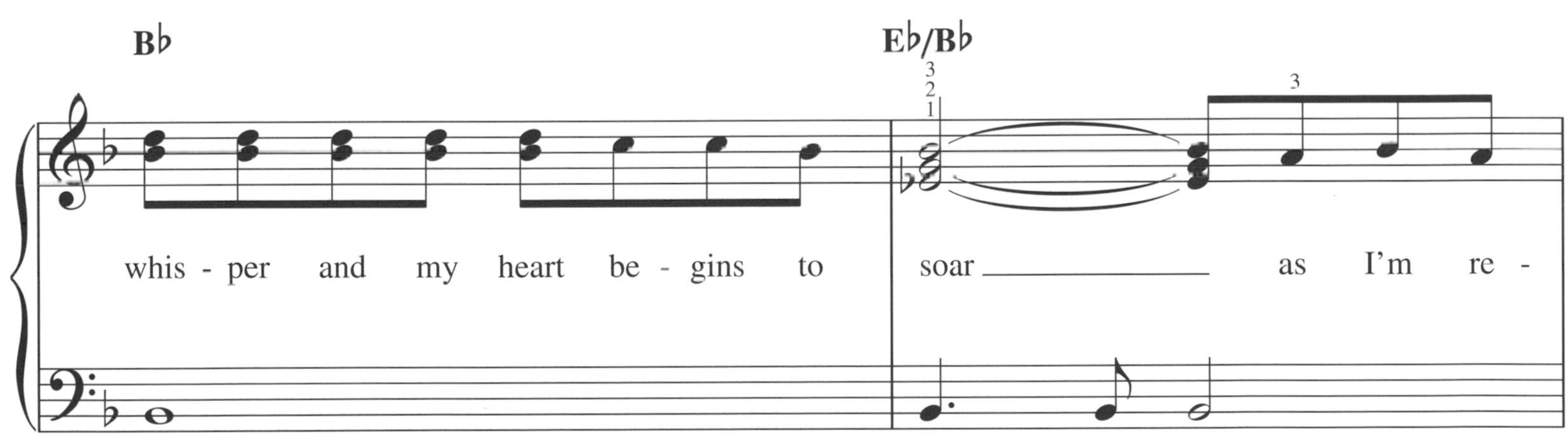
B♭
E♭/B♭
whis - per and my heart be - gins to soar as I'm re -

Dm
C
F
mind - ed: ev - 'ry street in Lon - don is Yours.

B♭/F
F
B♭/F
Oh, yes it is.
I walk the

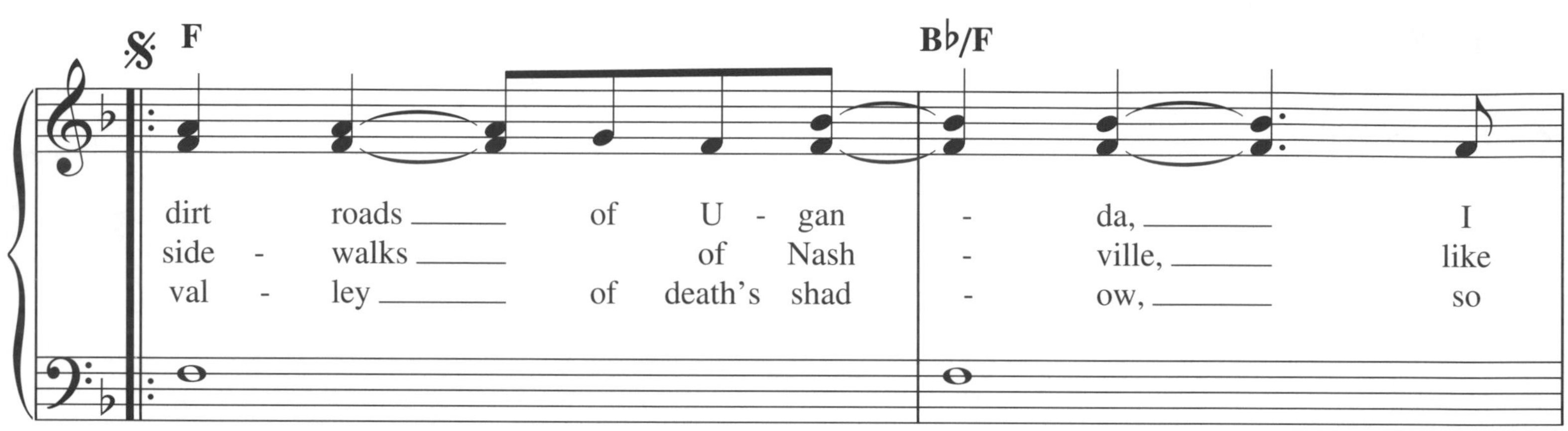
F
B♭/F
dirt roads of U - gan - da, I
side - walks of Nash - ville, like
val - ley of death's shad - ow, so

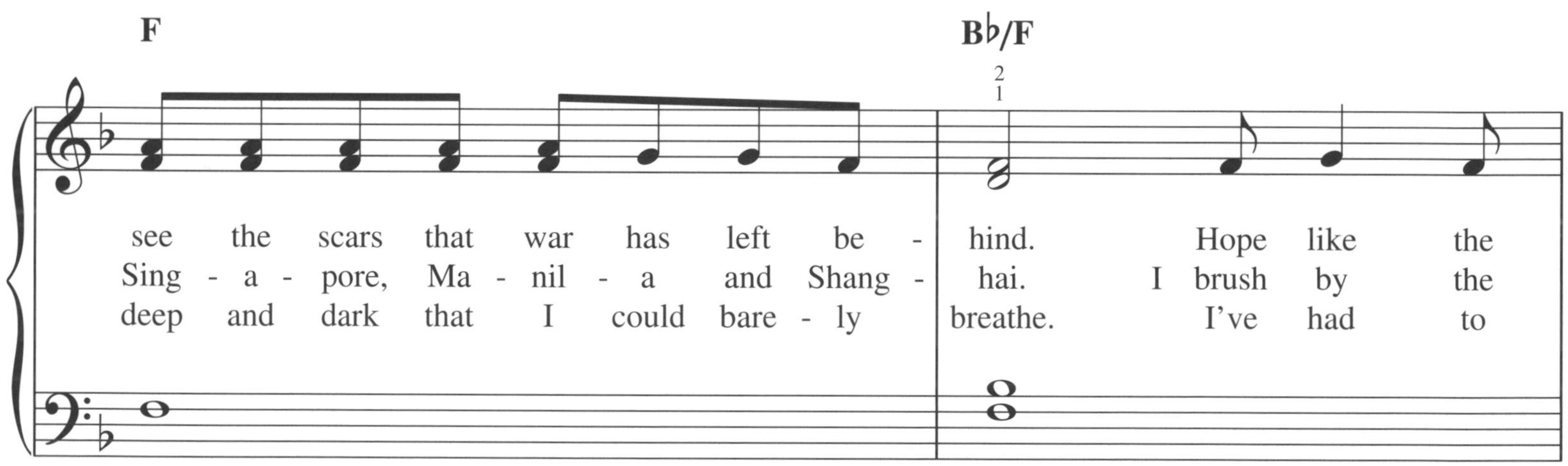
F
B♭/F
see the scars that war has left be - hind. Hope like the
Sing - a - pore, Ma - nil - a and Shang - hai. I brush by the
deep and dark that I could bare - ly breathe. I've had to

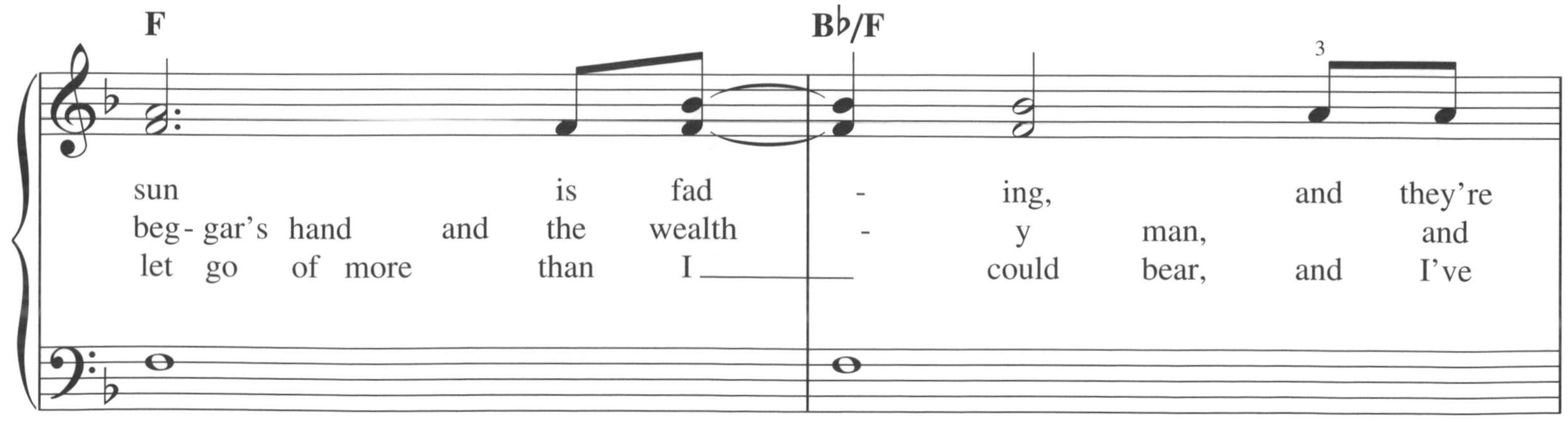
F
B♭/F
sun is fad - ing, and they're
beg- gar's hand and the wealth - y man, and
let go of more than I could bear, and I've

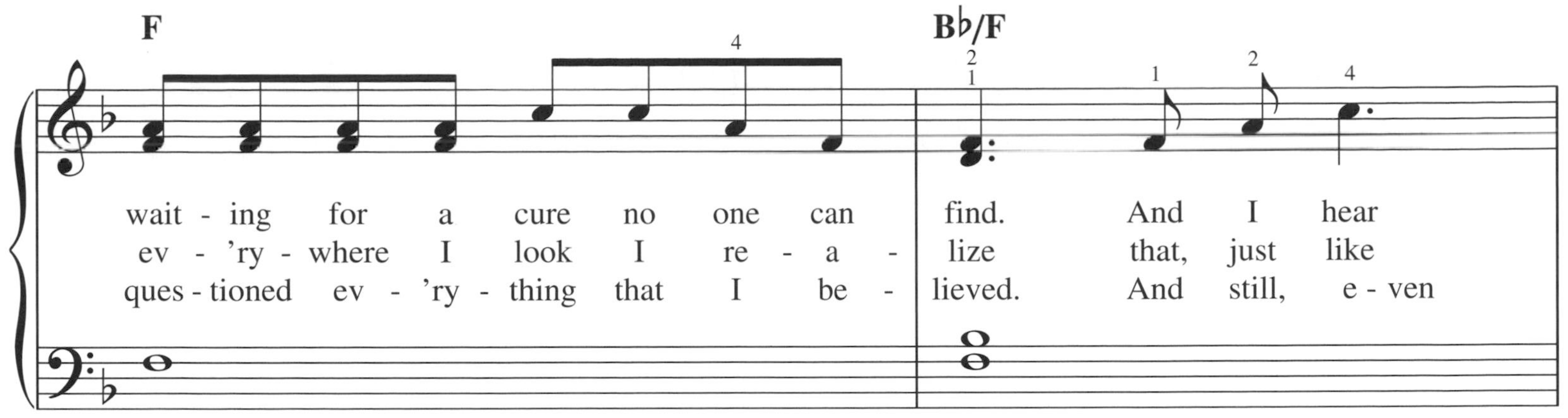
F
Bb/F
wait - ing for a cure no one can find. And I hear
ev - 'ry - where I look I re - a - lize that, just like
ques - tioned ev - 'ry - thing that I be - lieved. And still, e - ven

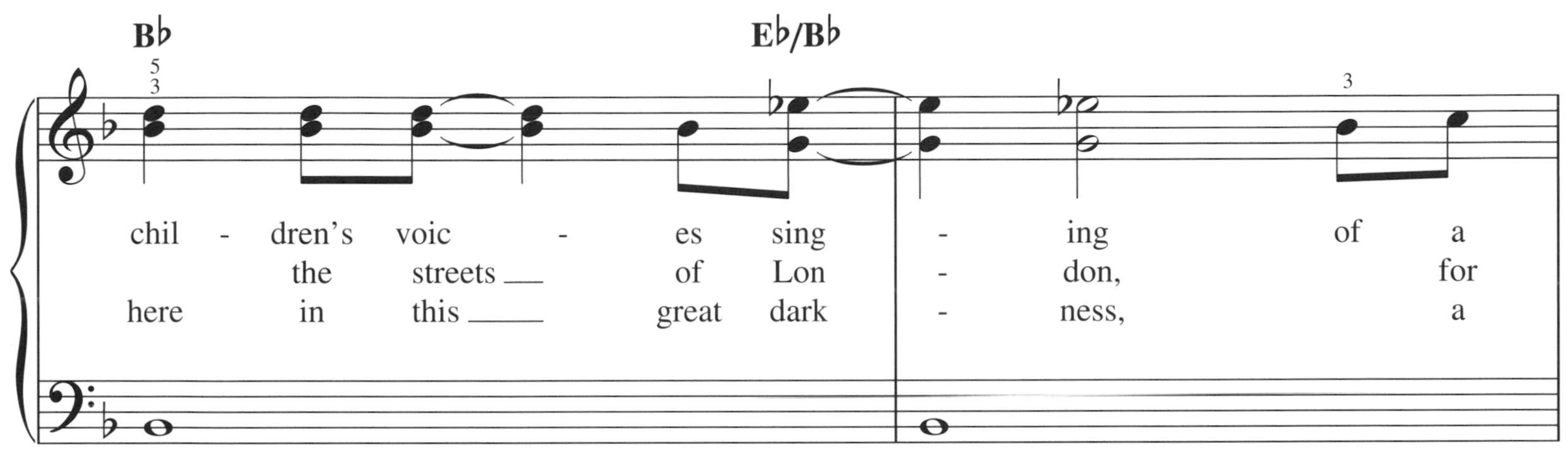
Bb
Eb/Bb
chil - dren's voic - es sing - ing of a
the streets of Lon - don, for
here in this great dark - ness, a

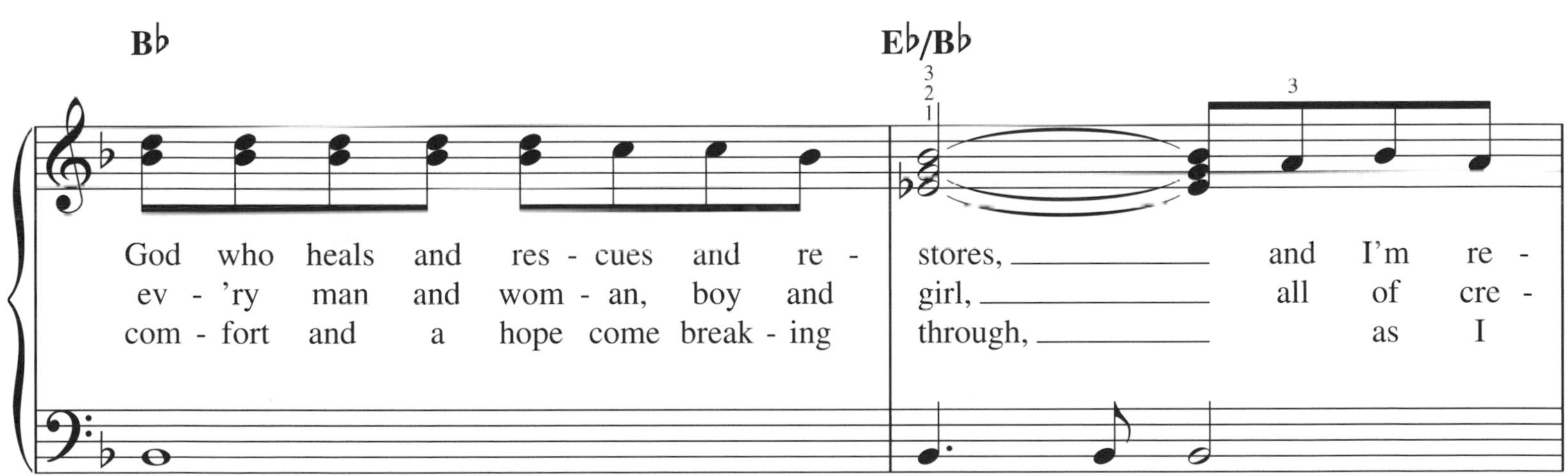
Bb
Eb/Bb
God who heals and res - cues and re - stores, and I'm re -
ev - 'ry man and wom - an, boy and girl, all of cre -
com - fort and a hope come break - ing through, as I

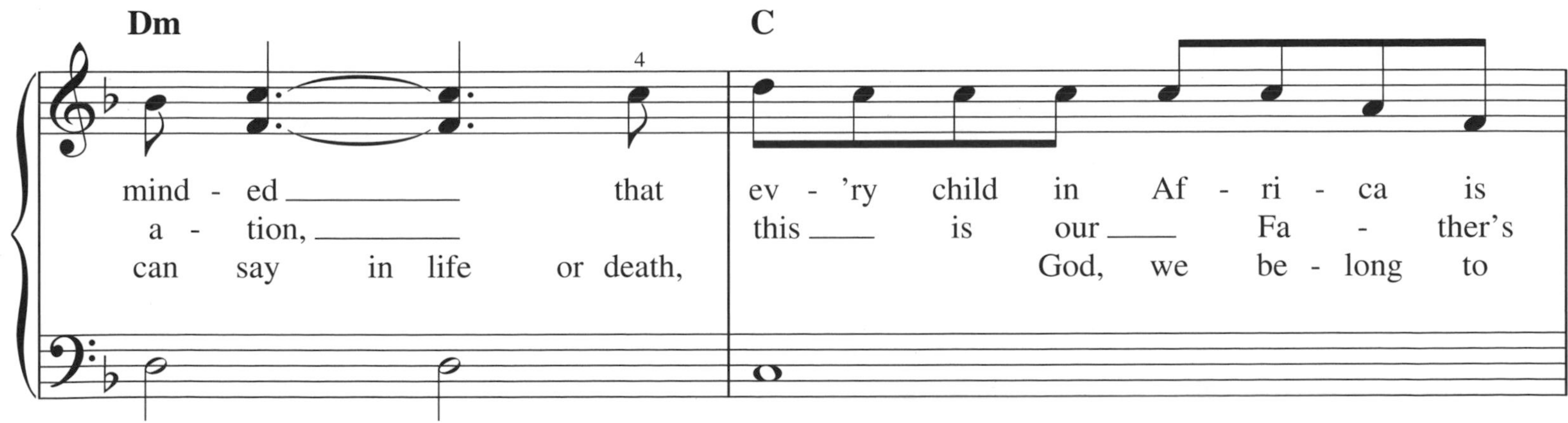
Dm
C
mind - ed that ev - 'ry child in Af - ri - ca is
a - tion, this is our Fa - ther's
can say in life or death, God, we be - long to

F
F/A
B♭
2
Yours.
world.
You.
And it's all
And it's all
And we are
Yours, God,

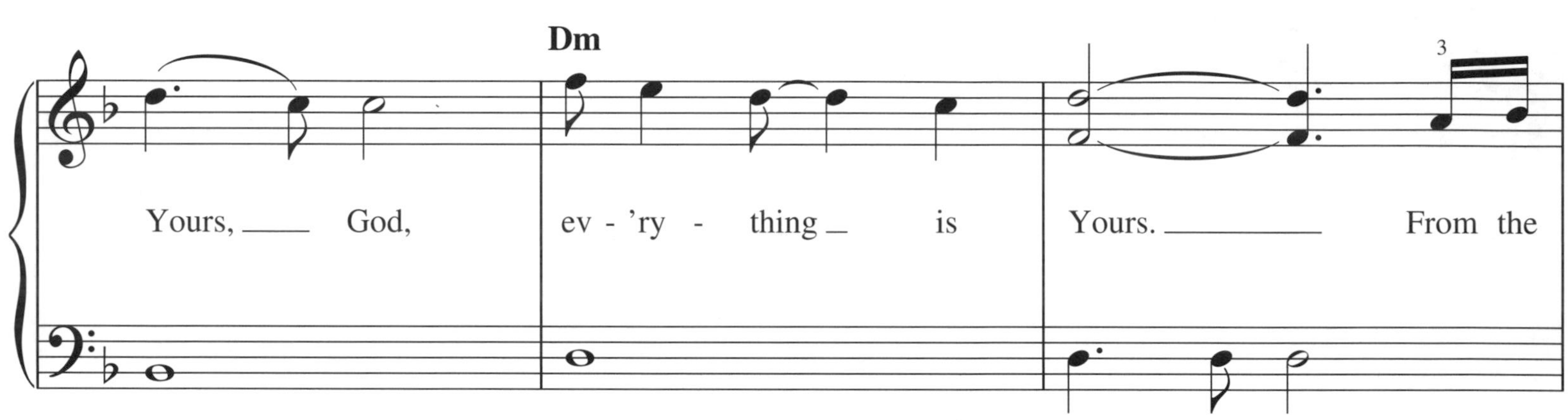
Dm
3
Yours, God,
ev - 'ry - thing is
Yours. From the

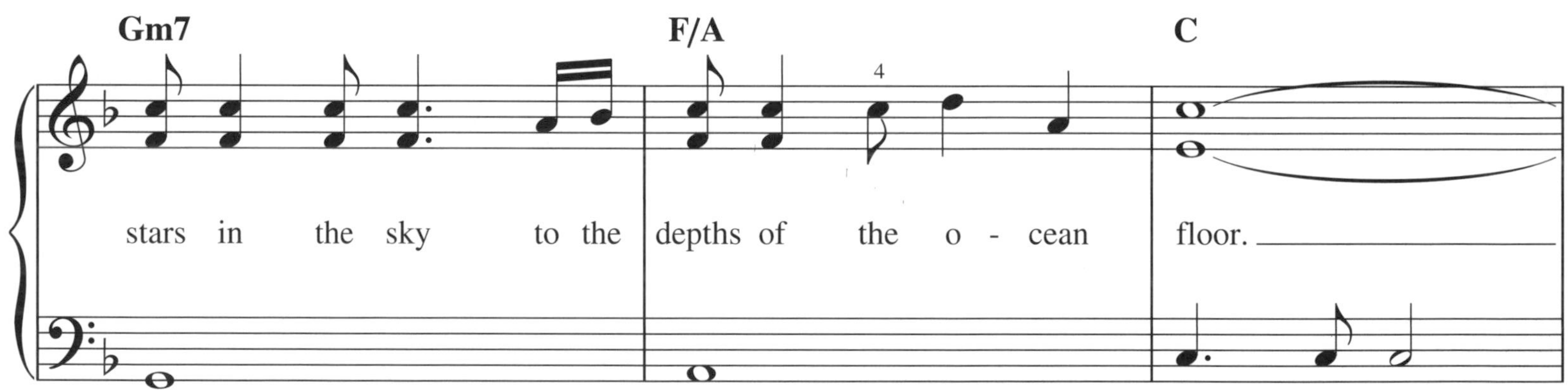
Gm7
F/A
C
4
stars in the sky to the
depths of the o - cean
floor.

F/A
B♭
2
And it's all
Yours, God,
Yours, God,

Dm
Dm
Gm
ev - 'ry - thing is
Yours.
(1.,2.) You're the Mak - er and Keep - er,
(3.) All the great - ness and pow - er and

F/A
B♭
To Coda
Fa - ther and Rul - er of ev - 'ry - thing.
glo - ry, the splen - dor and maj - es - ty,

1.
Csus
2.
F
I walk the
It's all
Yours.

Fsus2
Fsus
Fsus2
D.S. al Coda
And I've walked the

CODA
C
F
ev - 'ry - thing is Yours.

B♭/F
F
Yeah, it's all Yours.

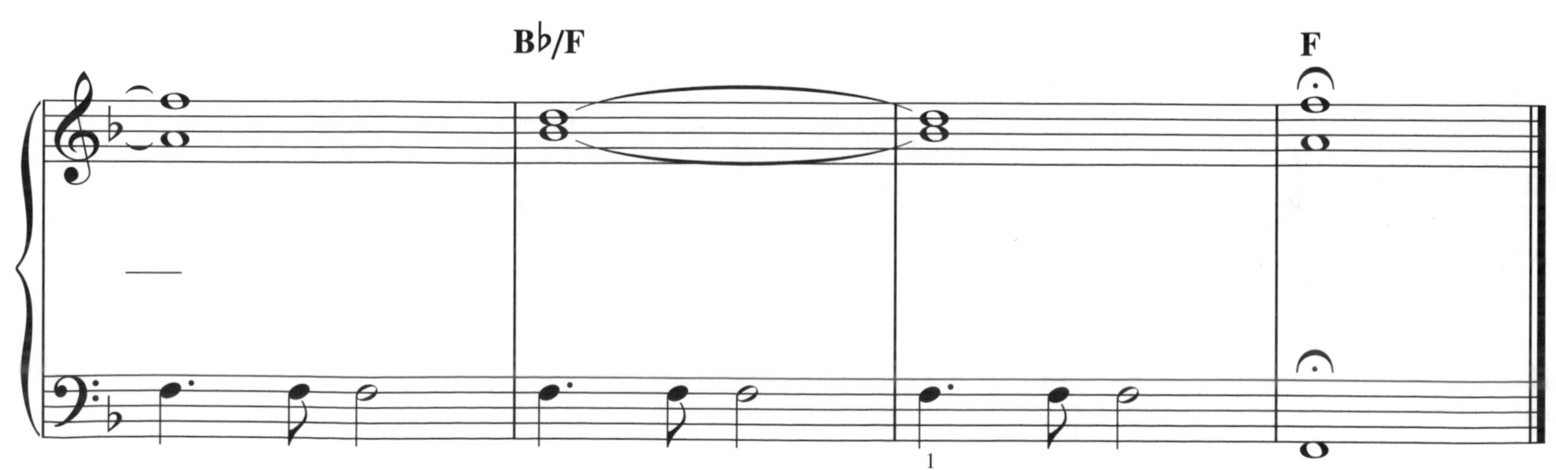
B♭/F
F